Nella Cucina

Nella Cucina

More Italian Cooking from the Host of Ciao Italia

Mary Ann Esposito

Illustrations by Lauren Jarrett

Hearst Books

New York

Library of Congress Cataloging-in-Publication Data

Esposito, Mary Ann.
    Nella cucina : more Italian cooking from the host of *Ciao
Italia* / Mary Ann Esposito.
        p.   cm.
    Includes bibliographical references and index.
    ISBN 0-688-12151-9
    1. Cookery, Italian.   2. Cookery—Italy.   I. Ciao Italia
(Television program)   II. Title.
TX723.E873   1993
641.5945—dc20   92-35623
                                                            CIP

Printed in the United States of America

First Edition

1 2 3 4 5 6 7 8 9 10

BOOK DESIGN BY RICHARD ORIOLO

For Guy, Beth, and Christopher
con molto affetto e ricordate; sempre diritto
and to my father, Roy Saporito,
for the example of his life

Acknowledgments

While writing this book, I have met many new friends, here and in Italy, who have given me greater insight into the inexhaustible subject of Italian food. I am grateful for their enthusiasm and genuine interest in this work.

Once again, I drew on family traditions; my mother and father shared many anecdotes surrounding food customs, some of which I had forgotten but embraced as refreshing surprises.

To my wonderful *amica* Costanza, for whom words are meaningless, for the many roles she plays as my assistant. A debt of thanks to Ruth Moore for helping with the testing of recipes for the *biscotti* chapter; to my editor, Harriet Bell, for her sensitivity, constant encouragement, and professional wisdom; to my copyeditor, Carole Berglie, for her suggestions; to Michael Jones for his guidance; to my agent, Bill Adler, for his faith in this project; to Paul Lally, *un'amico simpatico* and producer of *Ciao Italia,* for never letting the truth slip by; to the talented and dedicated staff of New Hampshire Public Television for their help in the production of the series; to Christina Hoppe of the Department of Italian, University of New Hampshire, for her help in proofreading; to Lauren Jarrett for the delightful illustrations; and last, to Italophiles everywhere: *Vi prego gradire i miei ringraziamenti.*

Special Acknowledgments

Italians have a saying regarding longevity: "Eggs of an hour, bread of a day, wine of a year, and friends of one hundred years." That is how I feel about the underwriters of my Public Television cooking series, *Ciao Italia*. King Arthur Flour of Norwich, Vermont, and Auricchio Cheese of Denmark, Wisconsin, have provided the financial support making it possible for me to share my love of Italian food with you. They will always be "friends of one hundred years."

Contents

Introduction	1
Sapienza nella Cucina / Kitchen Know-how	5
Antipasti / Appetizers	11
Zuppe / Soups	29
Pasta	51
Salse / Sauces	83
Uova / Eggs	103
Carne e Pollame / Meat and Poultry	111
Pesce / Fish	139
Verdure / Vegetables	157
Insalate / Salads	185
Pizza	201
Pane / Bread	221
Biscotti / Cookies	249
Frutte e Salse di Frutte / Fruit and Fruit Sauces	275
I Dolci / Desserts	287
Mail-Order Sources	323
Bibliography	325
Index	327

Introduction

Wherever I travel in Italy I am surrounded by food, from the colorful, boisterous *mercati* ("markets") and small food shops tucked into winding streets to quiet, reflective places like cathedrals and art galleries. In Milan, the *Cenacolo,* or "The Last Supper," depicting a humble meal of bread and wine is spellbinding. Near Siena, at the monastery of Monte Oliveto Maggiore, a beautiful Della Robbia wreath of realistic looking fruits, vines, and flowers welcomes visitors to the serenity of the abbey and surrounding landscape. In soaring cathedrals as well as simple churches, I am bathed in dappled sunlight that streams through stained glass windows like kaleidoscopic clouds, dispersing its luminance into intricate mosaics that dance gracefully across my space, seemingly bringing to life the chubby cherubs who offer bowls of luscious fruits and platters of bread to the Almighty. In another painting, the Virgin lovingly accepts an exotic ruby red pomegranate from her infant son.

Painted flowers and fruits spill over the walls of the Uffizi Art Gallery in Florence, while in the Palazzo Pubblico in Siena, one is reminded of the bounty that the land can provide if tended with care and good management, the ageless message in Lorenzetti's frescoes of "The Effects of Good and Bad Government."

I am as enamored of Italian food as the artists were who depicted it. Like them, I admire its straightforwardness and its symbolism. Whatever I cook has a connecting story between the dish I am preparing and its history. This brings me great satisfaction because to learn about Italian food is to understand its people—their respect for it and the role that food has played in their history. To Italians, food represents more than satisfying hunger. It is the focal point of their traditions. Whether it is *torta pasqualina* (Easter pie) made with thirty-three layers of dough to commemorate the years of Christ's life, or *Ossi dei Morti* (Bones of the Dead, page 264), cookies made in memory of deceased relatives, Italian food preserves history, tradition, and folklore and truly provides "food for thought."

So it seemed natural that I should continue my adventure of cooking, writing, and learning more about Italian food. Even before my first book *Ciao Italia* was on bookstore shelves, I began to think about writing a second work which would bolster the argument that the subject of Italian food is, in a word, inexhaustible, and that it is inherent in almost every facet of Italian life.

Nella Cucina, which means "in the kitchen," contains more of what I like to cook, and more about what I have experienced in my food travels in Italy. It is about food that takes its shape and taste from the seasonal offerings of the year and the sensibility of the cook.

Today, life is changing very quickly in Italy, and so is home cooking. Many of the hallmark recipes that I have come to love, like panforte and panettone, are rarely made at home anymore. They have taken on a commercial look and taste. When I visit Italy, I deliberately go in search of old cooking traditions, but ironically I see people moving away from them. So much of this has to do with economics. The traditional one-income family is rapidly giving way to the two-income family. Women make up a greater part of the work force today, and that means more prepared foods are purchased.

This change in lifestyle has also changed the way many Italians eat, especially in larger cities. I have always felt that closing all business activity in Italy from 1 until 4 P.M. was a wonderful custom. How often I confronted the frustrating word *chiuso* ("closed") in my travels at that time of day. I had only to understand that when Italy shut down in the middle of the day, it was so people could enjoy what was important to them. In those precious and private hours, people stopped thinking about work, children interrupted their schooling, and everyone went home for the main meal of the day. It was at the dinner table that family members concentrated on each other. Today, especially in the larger cities, this wonderful tradition is disappearing as more and more businesses stay open to accommodate an ever-changing lifestyle.

This book is a permanent resting place for traditions that I have grown up with or have discovered. Thousands of viewers of my television series *Ciao Italia* have written to tell me how much they appreciate watching me make some of the traditional recipes. Some of them recall with fondness times when their mothers, grandmothers, aunts, and cousins made many of the dishes that they see on the show but had almost forgotten. In their letters, they search for the return of tradition, when food, diligently prepared, had an honored place on the table. Today, cooking is sometimes viewed as a chore, not a pleasure. The excuse is often that we are just too busy to cook. But we are no busier than our ancestors were, when you consider all the modern conveniences at our disposal.

As a child, I was taught the process of preparing and appreciating good food. Now, I feel gratified when I teach children how to cook—to make bread or tomato sauce, or show them how to roll out pasta—and I am charmed by their acceptance of trying such "mysterious" vegetables as eggplant!

I have always maintained that there is nothing new in food, just its constant rearrangement. The recipes in this book evolved from natural ingredients assembled by the hands of amateur cooks, who intuitively knew what to do with them. Some of the recipes have been given to me by Italian-American cooks who want to keep their heritage alive and pass it on to others. Some are from friends in Italy who are proud to know that Americans love their cuisine; some are from my files, favorites from home and places I have been to in Italy; and others I have developed. Many of the recipes have little smudged notes that indicate how I changed the recipe to suit current thinking on healthy foods—although this current thinking is that a Mediterranean diet, with its emphasis on grains, vegetables, and olive oils, is a very wise choice.

Most of the recipes are not time-consuming, yet they are impressive enough for company. The chapter on cookies was a collaborative effort with Italian and Italian-American women who have been making a variety of Italian cookies for years at church fairs for particular feast days, and each of whom had a story to tell about how the recipes came to be.

If the diversity of Italy's cooking and my enthusiasm for it encourages you to experience it, then *Nella Cucina* becomes our personal celebration of its food.

About the Recipes

Most people think that writing a cookbook is a glamorous task, but let me assure you that it is a labor of love. It takes an inordinate amount of time to write a cookbook—from selecting and cooking the ingredients to measuring and taste testing, to writing about, proofreading, and rewriting the recipe so it is clear. So I am always in the kitchen or at the word processor.

The recipes in my books come from many sources: some are family favorites from home, some are originals of mine, others are from Italian-Americans who have shared their recipes with me, some are from viewers of my television series *Ciao Italia,* and some are adapted from old Italian cooking manuscripts that I have studied.

Not all the recipes in this book make the standard four servings, so I have indicated how many the recipe serves and, in some cases, suggested how you can increase or decrease the recipe if need be.

Since specialty food items are sometimes called for, I have included a list of helpful mail-order sources. I have also included a list of further reading on Italian food and its history because I am a firm believer that you need one to understand the other.

Above all, I want you to have fun in the kitchen, experience Italian food, and enjoy the fruits of your labor.

Sapienza nella Cucina

Kitchen Know-how

What cook doesn't appreciate helpful tips that enhance the flavor and appearance of food, save time and money, and make life easier in the kitchen? Over the years I have learned and adapted the following useful tricks.

- Invest in a small kitchen scale for accurate measuring. This is especially useful when baking.
- Always wash the bowl and lid of your food processor by hand. The bowl will expand in the dishwasher and make the top hard to fit.
- Spray measuring cups and spoons with a vegetable coating before measuring sticky ingredients like molasses, honey, or corn syrup. The ingredients will easily pour out.
- Reuse brown paper shopping bags for draining fried foods. They do not get limp and soggy like paper towels and cost nothing.
- To prevent a crust from forming over cream sauces or pastry cream fillings, place a buttered sheet of waxed paper directly on the surface of the sauce.
- Olive oil purchased in large gallon containers will be easier to use

if the oil is decanted into clean wine bottles, corked, and stored in a cool place.

- Do not add oil to the cooking water for pasta. It will leave a slippery film on the pasta and make it hard for the sauce to adhere.
- When boning chicken breasts, save the breast bones in a plastic bag in the freezer. When you have enough, make broth by placing them in a pot with a whole peeled onion, carrot, and water to cover.
- Defat chicken or beef broth by pouring it over a colander filled with ice cubes. The fat will cling to the ice.
- Rewrap slices of prosciutto individually in plastic wrap to prevent the slices from sticking together.
- To store pancetta, buy ¼-inch-thick slices, wrap each slice individually in freezer paper, and freeze for later use.
- To freeze fresh fish, place it in salted water in a zippered plastic bag.
- Store Parmigiano-Reggiano and Pecorino Romano cheeses in a cool, not cold place, wrapped in damp cheesecloth and then foil.
- In recipes calling for ricotta cheese, drain the cheese for one hour in a colander first to remove the excess water.
- To cook green vegetables, add them to boiling water. Do not bring the vegetables and water to a boil together.
- To keep the color of green vegetables as they cook, add 1 tablespoon olive oil for every four quarts of water. Do not cover the vegetables as they cook.
- Save the cooking water of vegetables and use when making soup.
- Salting and "sweating" sliced vegetables like eggplant and zucchini before cooking will eliminate excess water and require less oil for frying.
- Try roasting cauliflower instead of boiling it. Place the florets in a baking dish and drizzle with olive oil, then sprinkle with minced garlic, salt, and pepper. Mix well. Bake at 350°F. for 25 to 35 minutes, or until the cauliflower is nicely browned and tender.
- Bake beets instead of boiling them to prevent the juices from leaching out. Wrap cleaned, uncooked beets with 2 inches of tops left on in aluminum foil and bake in a 375°F. oven for 40 to 45 minutes, or until tender. Cool, then peel. The skins will slip off easily.
- Limp salad greens can be refreshed by placing them in a bowl of water with a few ice cubes.
- To prevent watery eyes when cutting onions, store the onions in a paper bag in the refrigerator.

- To make garlic paste, peel and dice the cloves, then sprinkle with salt. Let stand 5 minutes, then mash with a fork into a paste.
- For fresh-tasting basil all year, freeze basil leaves in plastic bags. The color will darken, but the flavor will remain. Use for soups, stews, and sauces where visual presentation is unimportant.
- To store parsley and other herbs in the refrigerator, fill a glass with water and place the stem ends in the water. Take out what you need, and keep the rest refrigerated.
- To keep flour fresh, store it in an airtight bag in your freezer. Bring to room temperature before using.
- Pasta dough will be easier to roll if allowed to rest for 10 minutes after kneading. This relaxes the gluten in the flour.
- Store homemade bread in paper, not plastic, bags.
- Use the insert of your slow-cooker for baking panettone or other dome-shaped breads.
- When rolling out pastry dough such as Pasta Frolla (page 299) on a floured surface, place the dough between two sheets of waxed paper and roll over the paper. Peel back the top paper and invert the dough into the tart pan, then peel off the second sheet of waxed paper.
- To keep ground coffee fresh, store it in an airtight jar in your freezer.
- Freeze leftover coffee for flavoring cakes and desserts such as tiramisù.
- To melt chocolate, bring a double boiler of water to the boil, turn off the heat, place the chocolate in the top of the double boiler, and cover with a lid. Let stand until the chocolate is melted.
- For whipped cream, chill the bowl and beaters in your freezer for 15 minutes.
- To color eggs for Easter, wrap them in several damp layers of yellow or red onion skins and boil them. Adding a little white vinegar to the water will help set the color.
- To clean strawberries, stem them and roll them gently over a clean wet sponge.
- Fresh figs can be frozen unpeeled. Wrap them individually in foil and then place them in a plastic bag. Defrost at room temperature.
- To make your own vanilla flavoring, break a vanilla bean into small pieces, place pieces in a jar, and add 1 cup of brandy. Cover the jar and let soak for two or three weeks. Remove the vanilla pieces and discard. Use the liquid as directed in recipes calling for vanilla extract.

Sale e Pepe

Salt and Pepper

The word salt *comes from the name for the Roman god of health, Salus. During the glory days of the Roman Empire and through the Renaissance, salt was a precious and powerful commodity. It was so highly valued that it was even rationed to Roman soldiers; they were sometimes given money with which to buy salt, hence the saying "salt money" and the origin of our word* salary.

As in ancient times, there are three main sources for obtaining salt: sea salt, rock salt, and natural salt springs. Italians use coarse salt, or sale grosso, *and fine salt, or* sale fino. *Coarse salt is used primarily for preserving meats, fish, and herbs and in some cooking. Fine salt is used for all-purpose cooking. I use both of these in my cooking. I prefer the pure, intense flavor of fine sea salt rather than table salt. Table salt has had the trace minerals removed and chemicals added to keep the salt from caking, as required by the Food and Drug Administration. I use coarse salt for preserving basil and other herbs, roasting chicken, and baking fish.*

As mentioned, salt played an important role in Italian history, and there are still many places where it is regarded as precious and used cautiously. During the Renaissance, the popes imposed a heavy salt tax on the Tuscans, who staunchly opposed it and went without salt rather than pay the tax. Some say that is why Tuscan bread is saltless to this day.

Some very old Italian customs involve the use of salt. I first tasted it at my own baptism, when the priest put salt on my tongue. Years later, when I purchased my first car, my mother and grandmother insisted that I drive my car to Mrs. Marino's house, an old family friend, who wanted to impart an ancient Italian blessing on it. I reluctantly arrived at her house on a steamy, hot day. Mrs. Marino, slightly bent and clutching a prayerbook in one hand and a box of salt in the other, appeared in the driveway. Before I could say a word, she was walking around my car, dousing it everywhere with salt and chanting in Italian. Because it was so hot, the salt stuck like glue. My heart sank; salt on the shiny finish of my car was more than I could bear, no matter how much it was going to protect me!

Pepper was also coveted by the Romans, who imported it from Asia and Africa. It was not used as much for cooking or preserving foods as salt was, but rather for medicinal purposes. The saying that something was "as dear as pepper" meant that it was very rare. Even the libri segreti, or secret account books of merchants during the Renaissance, show loans paid off in pounds of pepper! Venetian and Genoan merchants became very wealthy controlling the spice trade from Africa as demand increased not only for pepper but also for ginger, cinnamon, nutmeg, cloves, and saffron.

In cooking, I lean toward freshly ground coarse black pepper for rich ragù meat sauces, some soups, stuffings, and vegetable dishes because I'm used to it and like its flavor and visibility. But in truth, it is used sparingly in some parts of Italy. Both my grandmothers kept big jars of coarse black pepper near the stove. I grind my own as I need it.

As with other spices, it is best to buy peppercorns in small quantities and keep them in a cool place. Storing spices for a long time and near heat sources tends to make them dry up and become flavorless.

In some of the recipes, I have left the amount of salt and pepper up to you, as it really is a matter of personal taste. Where I felt I needed to indicate the amount to use, I have so indicated.

- To make vanilla sugar, place a vanilla bean cut into four pieces in an airtight container with 6 cups of sugar.
- For evenly browned cookies, use shiny cookie sheets and allow about 2 inches space between cookie sheet and sides of oven.
- Use leftover cake and cookie crumbs combined with butter to make a crust for ricotta cheesecake.

Antipasti

Appetizers

Roman cookbook writer and gastronome Apicius was said to be so distraught that he had only ten million *sestertii* left of his life savings to splurge on food that at one banquet he requested and ate poisoned food. So ended the life of a man devoted to promoting the food and cooking of Imperial Rome.

But Apicius's spirit and love of cooking live on in his work *De re Coquinaria ("Concerning Cooking")*. Apicius compiled recipes for hundreds of dishes that have a surprisingly familiar ring, which once again supports my belief that there is nothing new to be discovered in food, just constant rearrangement. Apicius's recipes included chicken wings cooked with honey, cold vegetable relish served with morels, stuffed pumpkin blossom fritters, and stewed and spiced peaches and pears. Book IV, Chapter V, is entitled "Gustum Versatile," or Movable Appetizers, presumably because they were carried from one guest to another. Does this sound like a modern practice?

The serving of antipasti remained popular for centuries after the fall of Rome. During the Renaissance, ostentatious displays of and the serving of antipasti took on new meaning—power. Extravagant dining was a way to court favors from influential and rich friends. Even the clergy got into the act. In 1473 a huge banquet was given by Cardinal Pietro Riario, in honor of Eleanora of Aragon. The guests were seated according to their status. Before the dinner commenced, the Cardinal and Eleanora ate a *collatione* ("snack") of ten sweet dishes decorated with imperial eagles made of crystallized sugar, gilded oranges, and Malvasia wine. This was followed by crabcakes, minced chicken, and goat's liver; small sweetbreads flavored with wine; capon in white sauce with gilded pomegranate seeds; poultry covered with a purple sauce and flavored with Corsican wine; two whole calves; young goats, lamb heads, boiled meat, and sausages; marrow soup; veal; and rabbit and peacocks! Finally came the dinner, which included capon in gelatin decorated with the coat of arms for the Cardinal; gilded white tarts; and gelatins of meat and sweet pears; pounded and silvered eels; fowl pies; three suckling pigs; and geese. The desserts seemed to pale in comparison. Fresh almonds and green walnuts as well as plates of confectionery and marzipan were offered. This whole affair took a mere seventy-two hours to consume between theatrical skits and musical interludes.

Antipasti did not continue to play such an impressive role in the nineteenth and twentieth centuries, and at home it was only part of a special-occasion meal or holiday. As in the days of opulent Roman feasting, numerous kinds of antipasti are found on Italian tables today, whether at home or in a restaurant. Just as in the time of Apicius, antipasti start with something sweet, like figs or melon.

When I invite people to my home for dinner, I often serve antipasti instead of a traditional meal. My guests say that it is hard to differentiate one from the other. This type of entertaining can be a lot of fun, and is a good way for your friends to sample a wide selection of Italian dishes.

I line a large buffet area with both hot and cold antipasti, and make decorative signs that tell my guests what the dishes are. The antipasti are accompanied by huge baskets of *pane casareccio* ("homemade bread") and a selection of Italian wines. Fruit and nuts are served for dessert. In this chapter, I have included a selection of hot and cold antipasti suitable for a party, to start a meal, or to enjoy as a complete meal.

Caponata

Eggplant Salad
Makes about 9½ cups

The word *caponata* has no English translation, but it is usually described as an eggplant appetizer salad with an *agrodolce,* or sweet-and-sour taste.

This traditional family recipe is my favorite. Cocoa, the surprising ingredient here, gives this dish its clean finish. Cocoa was introduced into Sicilian cooking in the seventeenth century by the Spaniards. Other versions of caponata include bits of fried sweet peppers, pear slices, and raw almonds, and cinnamon and cloves are also added. I use small eggplant from my garden. This recipe, makes a lot but keeps well in the refrigerator for several weeks.

8 young eggplant (4 to 5 inches long), cut in 1-inch cubes

Coarse salt

1¼ cups thinly sliced celery (about 2 ribs)

1½ cups boiling water

1½ cups peanut oil

½ cup olive oil

4 onions, thinly sliced (3½ cups)

1 cup tomato paste

1 cup chopped Sicilian olives in brine, drained

½ cup capers in wine vinegar, drained

½ cup sugar

⅔ cup red wine vinegar

2 teaspoons baking cocoa

Freshly ground pepper to taste

Place the eggplant pieces in a colander, salt them, and let them sweat in the sink for 1 hour, then rinse and dry them.

In a small saucepan, add the celery to the boiling water and cook for 3 or 4 minutes. Drain the celery, saving the water, and set aside.

In a large skillet or electric frying pan, heat half the peanut oil. Add half the eggplant pieces and fry until softened and lightly browned, about 12 to 15 minutes. Drain the pieces on brown paper and continue with the remaining eggplant and peanut oil.

In the same skillet, heat the olive oil, add the onions, and sauté until soft and glazed looking, about 10 minutes. Lower the heat and mix in the tomato paste, reserved celery water, olives, capers, sugar, vinegar, and cocoa. Mix well and let the mixture simmer about 5 minutes. Add the eggplant and the celery pieces to the skillet, and mix well to coat the pieces with the sauce. Simmer the mixture uncovered for about 10 minutes. Add salt and pepper to taste.

Place the Caponata on a serving platter, cover, and marinate several hours at room temperature before serving.

Note: Because this recipe makes a lot, I spoon the mixture into jars, cover, and store them in the refrigerator and use as needed. You may want to cut this recipe in half, although this Caponata never lasts long in my house.

Variation: Serve the Caponata in an eggplant that has been cut in half lengthwise and scooped out. Surround the eggplant with slices of Italian bread, lightly fried in olive oil.

Caponata del Marinaio

Sailor-Style Salad
Serves 6 to 8

T his is another Sicilian version of caponata, but this one uses moistened stale bread instead of eggplant. Softening bread in water is said to have originated with seamen who, having to endure a diet of stale ship's biscuit (hardtack) on long journeys, soaked the biscuits in water and then mixed them with anchovies, oil, and olives.

When making this salad, use a firm bread that is moistened just enough to crumble it. This caponata is best made several hours before serving, to allow the bread to absorb all the flavors. It is an ideal antipasto for a hot day and a good example of how bread is never wasted but, rather, used in novel ways.

1 pound loaf firm day-old bread

4 shallots, finely minced

1 4-ounce can anchovies in olive oil, cut in small pieces, oil reserved

2 6½-ounce cans tuna in olive oil

⅔ cup extra-virgin olive oil

1 tablespoon capers in brine, drained and minced

1 tablespoon fresh oregano leaves, or 1 teaspoon dried

Fine sea salt to taste

½ teaspoon coarsely ground black pepper

1 lemon, sliced in thin rounds

1 orange, sliced in thin rounds

Break the bread into 4 chunks. Fill a bowl with water and quickly dip each chunk in water to soften it. Squeeze the bread dry with your hands and crumble it onto a large serving platter.

In a separate bowl, mix the shallots, anchovies with their oil, tuna with its oil, ⅓ cup olive oil, capers, oregano, salt, and pepper. Pour this mixture over the bread and mix well. Drizzle the remaining ⅓ cup olive oil over the top.

Arrange the orange and lemon slices alternately around the edge of a platter with Caponata. Cover tightly with plastic wrap and marinate at room temperature several hours before serving.

Variation: Add ¼ cup finely chopped oil-cured black olives.

Un Po' di Tutto

A Little Bit of Everything
Serves 8

These vegetable-mozzarella sandwiches are a lunch favorite in the late summer and early fall when my garden is bursting with vegetables. If possible use slightly greenish tomatoes for this dish. The amounts are given only as a guide, use more or less as you like.

1 eggplant (1 pound),
    cut into 8 lengthwise
    slices

Coarse salt

6 tablespoons olive oil

3 small zucchini
    (6 inches long), cut
    into ¼-inch-thick
    lengthwise slices

2 large plum tomatoes,
    cut into thin
    lengthwise slices

¼ teaspoon fine sea salt

8 ounces fresh
    mozzarella cheese (*fior
    di latte*), cut into 8
    pieces

2 or 3 fresh basil leaves,
    torn into small pieces

Preheat the oven to 350°F.

Place the eggplant slices in a colander and sprinkle with salt. Fill a large bowl with water and sit it on top of the eggplant for about 1 hour. This will help to rid the eggplant of its bitter juices. Rinse the slices and dry them with paper towels.

Brush a cookie sheet with 2 tablespoons of the olive oil and place the eggplant slices on top in a single layer. Top the eggplant with a few of the zucchini slices.

Place the tomato slices on top of the zucchini, slightly overlapping them. Drizzle ½ tablespoon of olive oil over the top of each slice and sprinkle each with a pinch of sea salt. Top with the cheese slices.

Bake the slices for 25 to 30 minutes, or until the cheese melts and begins to brown. Carefully remove each slice to a serving platter. Sprinkle on the basil and serve immediately.

Variation: Grill the eggplant slices, then top with the remaining ingredients and bake them in the oven. The vegetables and cheese are also good wedged between 2 slices of Italian bread.

Gli Amici Italiani

Italian Friends

Years ago, when my serious interest in Italian food surfaced, I invited two students for dinner who were studying at the university near my home. Ennio, a Florentine, had curly black hair and blue eyes, and wore flashy clothes. Giovanni, who was about ten years older than Ennio, came from Palermo. Of slight stature and soft spoken, he wore thick-rimmed glasses that made him appear very intellectual. He was homesick.

Inviting them both for dinner made my menu selection a bit tricky, since I wanted to serve something typically Florentine and also Sicilian. When they arrived, Ennio presented me with a bottle of extra-virgin olive oil from Florence. His mother was always sending him food packages, including tomato sauce, because he missed her home cooking. Giovanni was holding a brown bag with a tiny basil plant and hoped that I had a good use for it. He said that his mother put basil in everything.

After introducing my family, we all sat down at the table, where several antipasti were waiting. I had prepared caponata, a sweet-and-sour Sicilian eggplant dish; a cold Tuscan-style bean dish with fruity olive oil, and a platter of sweet honeydew melon and prosciutto.

As we ate, we talked of Italy and places where we had all traveled. I was amazed that Giovanni had never been to Rome, and that I could tell him something about the Eternal City! Ennio, a good eater, almost devoured the antipasti; Giovanni was more deliberate and slow. I worried that it did not meet his standards, but was reassured when he said, "È ottimo," or "It's the best." I laughed, telling him how much better the prosciutti and melons were in Italy . . . and Ennio agreed. Ennio was not fond of caponata, a dish he only associated with Sicilian cooking, but Giovanni said it was comfort food, so like his mother's.

For a first course, I brought out a huge platter of penne arrabbiata, or penne in a spicy tomato sauce. Giovanni's eyes lit up when he saw it, as if he had just received good news from home. He loved red hot peppers; they were used a lot in Sicilian cooking. Ennio liked it too, but said his favorite was pasta with olive oil and garlic.

Dinner continued with arista, roast pork perfumed with fresh rosemary. The accompanying eggplant sautéed with tomatoes was a big hit with them, but Chris, my son, gave it two thumbs down.

For salad, I played it safe with insalata mista, or mixed green salad, but for dessert I made the classics of Sicily and Florence: cannoli and zuccotto, a Florentine cake filled with cream and fruit, and shaped like Brunelleschi's famous dome on the cathedral in Florence.

Ennio and Giovanni asked my family if they ate like this every night. Chris said he couldn't remember the last time that "Mom cooked American." This brought a round of laughter from our guests, who retorted that they wouldn't mind trading places with him, and that they did not often eat this much in Italy.

Over espresso, we talked about their impressions of American food. Ennio pressed his hands together, as if praying, and said how much he missed the food of Florence. I was surprised when he told us that many times dinner was just an antipasto of cannellini beans cooked in olive oil and served on crusty bread. He said it was a popular habit these days for three or four antipasti to make up a meal. Giovanni explained that his family was often content with freshly made Pecorino cheese, some oil-cured olives, and bread for supper, or just a plate of pasta or vegetables.

I told them that I liked the idea of beginning a company meal with antipasti, if for no other reason than to show Italian friends how much one loves their food and customs.

When it was time for them to leave, I wrapped up the remains of the desserts and gave them to the young men for their merenda, or snack. Hugs and kisses on both cheeks ended the evening. I felt somewhat satisfied knowing that my Italian friends from two very different parts of Italy had been brought together by sharing a meal reminiscent of their homeland.

Zucca Gialla all'Agrodolce

Sweet and Sour Yellow Pumpkin
Serves 4 to 6

In Italy, pumpkin, or *zucca,* is used as a filling for ravioli, to make gnocchi, baked into bread, and pureed for soup. In Sicily, pumpkin is marinated and served as an antipasto. The beautiful orange color of this dish, mingled with dark green basil leaves and flecks of refreshing mint, reminds one of a beautiful fall day in New England. I use butternut squash because the taste approximates the sweet pumpkins of Sicily. If you use pumpkin, be sure to buy a small sugar pumpkin; a big jack-o-lantern doesn't have any flavor.

1 pound sugar pumpkin or butternut squash

½ cup red wine vinegar

¼ cup sugar

3 fresh basil leaves, torn into pieces

4 fresh mint leaves, minced

⅓ to ½ cup olive oil

1 large clove garlic, cut in half

¼ teaspoon salt

Freshly ground black pepper

Cut the stem off and peel the pumpkin or squash. Cut the pumpkin or squash in half, remove the seeds and stringy pulp, and discard. Cut flesh into strips ⅛ inch thick, 2 inches wide, and about 4 inches long. Set aside.

In a 9- x 12-inch glass dish, mix the vinegar and sugar until the sugar dissolves. Add the basil and mint, mix, and set aside.

In a skillet, heat the olive oil, add the garlic, and press it into the oil with the back of a wooden spoon. Remove the garlic when it starts to turn color and discard it. Fry the pumpkin or squash pieces in batches for about 10 to 12 minutes, or until they soften and start to look glazed and brown.

Remove the strips from the skillet and add them to the vinegar mixture. Add salt and pepper, and stir to mix well. Cover the dish and marinate at room temperature for 3 to 4 hours before serving. Or refrigerate and serve the next day at room temperature.

Cipolline sott'Aceto

Onions in Vinegar
Serves 4

I love the *cipolline,* or onions in a vinegar marinade, that are part of the dazzling antipasti choices available at Trattoria del Pennello on Via Dante Alighieri in Florence. Use small, white onions, no more than 1 inch in diameter. Serve them as an antipasto as an accompaniment to grilled meats or fish. They will keep for several weeks stored in a glass jar in the refrigerator.

1 pound small white onions (unpeeled)	**½ teaspoon salt**
⅔ cup red wine vinegar	**1 tablespoon fresh oregano leaves, or**
2½ tablespoons sugar	**1 teaspoon dried**

Place the onions in a medium saucepan, cover with water, and boil for 1 to 2 minutes. Drain the onions, let cool, then peel off their skins, leaving them whole. Place onions in a glass bowl 3 inches deep and about 6 inches wide.

In a small saucepan, combine the vinegar, sugar, and salt; bring the mixture to a boil. Stir the ingredients with a wooden spoon and boil for 1 minute, or until the sugar is dissolved.

Pour the vinegar mixture over the onions and add the oregano. Coat the onions well with the marinade. Cover the bowl tightly with plastic wrap and let onions marinate at room temperature for several hours. Shake the bowl often to distribute the marinade.

Serve without liquid as an appetizer or as an accompaniment to cold meats such as chicken, turkey, and roast beef.

Funghi Ripieni al Forno

Stuffed Baked Mushrooms
Serves 8

Mushroom gathering in Italy is almost a secretive and elusive venture. Those who know where the best spots are for harvesting keep them to themselves. There are many species available; the most common are *boletus,* or *porcini.* They are cooked very simply with just a touch of seasoning to highlight their woodsy flavor. When porcini are dried, their flavor intensifies and they can be stored for long periods. This recipe substitutes large cultivated mushrooms, since fresh porcini are unavailable, but portobellos or creminis can be used. But using dried porcini as part of the stuffing helps approximate the real thing.

½ cup dried porcini mushrooms	3 salted anchovies, mashed
1 cup cold water	¾ cup toasted bread crumbs
16 large (2 inches wide) mushrooms	⅓ cup grated Pecorino Romano cheese
5 tablespoons olive oil	Salt and pepper to taste
1 teaspoon minced garlic	

Place the porcini in a bowl, cover with cold water, and soak for 30 minutes. Drain the porcini, cut them in small pieces, and set aside. Save the soaking water for a soup or sauce.

Wipe the fresh mushrooms with damp paper towels. Remove the stems by twisting them gently; dice stems and set aside. Arrange the mushroom caps on a sheet of aluminum foil on a baking sheet, and set aside.

In a skillet, heat 3 tablespoons of the olive oil. Add the mushroom stems and garlic, and sauté until stems are soft and liquid has evaporated. Add the anchovies and porcini, and continue to sauté for 1 minute. Remove the mixture to a bowl. Add the bread crumbs, cheese, and salt and pepper. Combine the mixture well and set aside.

Preheat the oven to 350°F.

Fill the mushroom caps with some of the filling, mounding it up slightly. Drizzle the remaining olive oil over the mushrooms.

Place a second sheet of aluminum foil over the mushrooms and seal the edges by folding in on the foil. Bake for 25 minutes. Remove the top sheet of foil and bake an additional 5 minutes. Serve immediately.

Cocktail di Gamberi

Shrimp Cocktail
Serves 4 to 6

One night while attending a cooking school in Sorrento, our chef Lorenzo prepared an antipasto table that consisted of over thirty-five dishes! One of my favorites was this Cocktail di Gamberi. What surprised me about the sauce was so many ingredients I thought were strictly in the American culinary domain.

This is a wonderful and simple presentation for a dinner party. The ingredients can be doubled successfully. The original recipe called for canned pineapple, for which I can find no culinary use. Fresh pineapple is far superior.

1 cup mayonnaise

2 tablespoons ketchup

1 teaspoon Worcestershire sauce

1½ tablespoons brandy

2 tablespoons heavy cream

⅛ teaspoon black pepper

½ cup diced fresh pineapple

1½ pounds large shrimp (30 per pound), cooked

1 head romaine lettuce

1 small head radicchio

1 large orange, sliced in thin wedges

1 large lemon, sliced in thin wedges

Mix the mayonnaise, ketchup, Worcestershire sauce, and brandy. Add the cream, pepper, and pineapple and fold in. Reserve and refrigerate half the sauce. Mix the remaining sauce with the shrimp, folding in carefully. Cover the shrimp and marinate in the refrigerator until ready to serve.

Cut the romaine lettuce into thin shreds. Tear the radicchio into bite-size pieces.

Half-fill 4 to 6 fruit-cup glasses or wide-mouth goblets with some of the romaine and radicchio. With a spoon, divide the shrimp among the glasses and garnish each with a wedge of lemon and orange. Serve as a first course; pass the reserved sauce on the side.

Note: When using frozen shrimp, put them in a colander and run cold water over them. The shells will easily pop away from the body. To cook; place peeled shrimp in boiling water to which the juice of ½ lemon has been added. The shrimp will cook in 2 to 3 minutes.

Panini Arrostiti

Broiled Sandwiches
Serves 6

The success of this quick but appealing sandwich depends upon the ingredients being cut almost paper thin and uniform in size. These are a snap to put together, wonderful for a luncheon accompanied by a green salad and fresh fruit. Or team them with Zuppa di Fagioli (page 40) for a fall or winter supper. These sandwiches can also be made cocktail size for a more formal affair.

6 slices Italian bread, cut ¾ inch thick from a 9-inch round	¼ pound prosciutto, thinly sliced
6 tablespoons extra-virgin olive oil	2 plum tomatoes, cut in thin rounds
2 small zucchini cut lengthwise in thin strips	½ pound sliced mozzarella or Fontina cheese
	Black pepper to taste

Place the bread in a single layer in a broiling pan and drizzle each slice with 1 tablespoon olive oil. Top each slice with the remaining ingredients in the order given. Sprinkle with a little black pepper.

Broil the sandwiches about 6 inches from the heat until the cheese has bubbled and is nicely browned. Serve the sandwiches immediately.

Note: Use fresh mozzarella (*fior di latte*) if available. Its mild and delicate taste are unbeatable. A combination of mozzarella and Fontina works well, too.

Rotolo al Prosciutto

Prosciutto Roll
Serves 8

A *rotolo di pasta* is a sheet of pasta dough, spread with a filling like spinach and then, rolled up like a jelly roll. It is boiled, baked, and then served as an appetizer. In this antipasto version, the rotolo resembles an airy omelet. Cut into slices, it is an elegant start to any meal.

Parchment paper, available in housewares stores, makes it easy to roll up the dough.

8 tablespoons (1 stick) butter

2 tablespoons unbleached all-purpose flour

1⅓ cups milk

4 large eggs, separated and at room temperature

1 tablespoon minced fresh parsley

½ teaspoon grated nutmeg

½ teaspoon salt

½ pound prosciutto, thinly sliced

Grease a 17- x 11-inch jelly-roll pan with 1 tablespoon of the butter. Use 2 tablespoons of the butter to grease 2 sheets of parchment paper, cut to fit the pan. Place one sheet in the pan. Set the other aside.

In a small bowl, beat together the remaining butter with the flour to form a uniform paste.

In a saucepan, scald the milk, add the butter mixture, and whisk it into the milk; whisk continually over medium heat for about 5 minutes, or until the mixture is thick and smooth. Remove the saucepan from the heat and add the egg yolks, one at a time, whisking each completely before adding another. Whisk in the parsley, nutmeg, and salt. Place the saucepan in a bowl of ice cubes and stir the mixture until it is cold. Transfer the mixture to a large bowl and set aside.

Preheat the oven to 350°F.

In a bowl, beat the egg whites until stiff, then gently fold them into the egg mixture with a spatula. Carefully spread the batter evenly in the jelly-roll pan. Bake for about 25 minutes, or until a cake tester inserted in the center comes out clean.

Remove the pan from the oven and carefully turn it upside down onto the remaining sheet of buttered parchment paper, placed over a clean towel. Carefully remove the top piece of parchment paper and discard. Arrange the prosciutto slices evenly over the top of the dough. Starting at the shortest end, roll the dough up like a jelly roll, using the parchment paper as a guide for rolling. Let the rotolo rest for about 15 minutes, wrapped in the parchment paper.

Unwrap the rotolo and cut into ½-inch slices. Arrange the slices on an attractive serving dish. Serve immediately.

Bigne con Formaggio e Prosciutto

Little Puffs of Cheese and Ham
Makes about 4½ dozen

Cream puffs called *bigne* are a popular sweet in Italy. They are usually filled with a pastry cream and are light and delicate. Fontina cheese and prosciutto are added in this savory appetizer version. These bite-size morsels are best served warm. A pastry bag without a tip makes them easier to assemble.

3 large eggs	⅓ cup diced Fontina cheese
1 cup water	
2 tablespoons (¼ stick) butter	¼ cup grated Parmigiano-Reggiano cheese
1 cup unbleached all-purpose flour	¼ pound diced prosciutto

Preheat the oven to 400°F. Lightly grease 2 baking sheets.

Crack the eggs into a bowl and set aside. In a saucepan, bring the water to a boil, add the butter, and melt. Add the flour, mixing vigorously with a wooden spoon until the mixture is thick and all the flour is incorporated, then remove the pan from the heat and add the eggs one at a time, stirring vigorously after each addition. Add the cheeses and prosciutto, and mix well.

Spoon some of the mixture into a pastry bag with a ½-inch plain nozzle. Squeeze 1-inch balls onto the baking sheets, spacing them evenly. These will not rise, so do not worry that they are too close. Bake for 20 minutes, or until the tops are nicely browned. Serve warm.

Note: These can be frozen in plastic bags after they have cooled. Defrost and warm in the oven to serve.

Zuppe

Soups

*Z*uppa. *Minestra.* What's the difference? Both these words mean "soup," but *minestra* refers to a thick soup, with a medley of colorful fresh vegetables and some rice, beans, or pasta, or a combination of all three. *Minestrone,* which means a "big soup," is probably the best known of this type, but there are many regional variations. In Genoa, a spoonful of pesto is stirred into the minestrone. In Naples, the vegetables are diced into very small pieces, cooked in a rich vegetable broth, and the soup is served at room temperature in the summer. In Milan, the soup is sprinkled with Parmigiano-Reggiano just before serving. In Tuscany, thick vegetable soup is called *ribollita* because it is made the day before serving and then reboiled. Pasta e Fagioli (page 38), one of my favorite "comfort" foods, is a thick, southern Italian soup made with borlotti beans and a short, tubular pasta called ditalini.

Vegetables, beans, rice, bread, potatoes, and pasta are the basics in many soups, but there are also fish soups of every description to be found in Italy. Some of the best I have eaten are in Venice. One of the oldest, *broeto* is more a fish stew than a soup. It is still prepared using one type of fish and very little broth. But many fish soups utilize a mixture of the local catch: mullet, eels, cuttlefish, and octopus.

Elsewhere in Italy, there are soups made with marble-size meatballs and escarole; soup made from cornmeal, called *polentina;* and soup made richer with the addition of thin ribbons of *frittata,* an egg omelet.

Grandma Galasso liked to poach eggs in Zuppa Povera (page 34), a nourishing vegetable soup. Grandma Saporito sautéed vegetables for her soups in the fatty marrow of beef bones and used fresh herbs instead of an excessive amount of salt. All vegetable trimmings, including celery tops and the leaves and stems of broccoli, fennel, and Swiss chard flavored their soups, as well as the neck bones from beef and chicken. Even lettuce was added. Still done in Italy today, this comes as a refreshing surprise to those who think of lettuce only as the canvas for raw salads. My grandmothers collected rainwater in old barrels and used it for cooking the vegetables, believing that rainwater was purer than city water, and therefore made better soup.

Brodo di Pollo

Chicken Broth
Makes 3½ to 4 quarts

I prefer to use homemade chicken broth instead of canned. There is much less salt, and the broth tastes light and fresh. My grandmothers always used the oldest hen the chicken man had because its long, slow cooking produced the most flavorful broth. I always make plenty and freeze what I don't use.

4 pounds chicken wings, necks, or parts

1½ teaspoons coarse salt

1 clove garlic, peeled

1 large white onion, peeled and quartered

2 large plum tomatoes, fresh or canned, quartered

1 bay leaf

2 sprigs each parsley and basil, tied together with string

Juice of 1 lemon

1 rib celery with leaves, cut into 4 pieces

2 medium carrots, peeled and cut in half

5 black peppercorns

Put the chicken pieces in a 7- or 8-quart stockpot and add the salt and cold water to cover. Cover the pot and bring to a boil. Skim off the foam that collects with a slotted spoon. Add all the remaining ingredients, reduce the heat, and simmer, covered, for 45 minutes to 1 hour. Skim off any additional foam that collects as the soup cooks.

Remove the chicken pieces with a slotted spoon and reserve the meat for another use. Pour the soup and vegetables through a large strainer lined with cheesecloth into another pot or a large bowl. With the back of a spoon, press on the vegetables to release all of the juices. Discard the solids left in the strainer. Cover the soup and refrigerate overnight.

With a spoon, remove the congealed fat from the top of the soup. The broth is ready to use or can be frozen for up to 3 months.

Brodo di Manzo

Beef Broth
Makes 3½ to 4 quarts

Good homemade beef broth is a must for hearty soups like Onion Soup (page 45) and for adding flavor to meat sauces. Ask your butcher for meaty beef shin bones. While this recipe makes a clear broth, you can also pick off the meat from the shin and chicken, cut up the vegetables, throw in a handful of pasta or rice, and have a hearty and healthful soup.

1 pound meaty boneless beef shin	1 rib celery with leaves, cut into quarters
1 pound beef brisket	2 large tomatoes, coarsely chopped
2 or 3 beef neck bones	
1½ pounds chicken parts	5 black peppercorns
1 tablespoon coarse salt	4 or 5 sprigs parsley, tied together with string
1 large white onion, peeled and cut in half	
2 medium carrots, peeled and cut in half	

Put all the meats and chicken in a large stockpot and add the salt and cold water to cover, bring to a boil, and boil for 5 minutes. Skim off the froth that accumulates with a slotted spoon. Lower the heat to medium and add all the remaining ingredients. Stir well with a wooden spoon and let the mixture simmer for 2½ to 3 hours. (The chicken will cook faster than the beef; remove it when tender, after about 1 hour. Let cool, remove the chicken meat from the bones, and reserve for another dish.)

As the soup cooks, skim off the foam that collects on the top with a slotted spoon. When the meats are tender, remove them along with the bones; reserve the meat for another use. Pour the broth and vegetables through a colander lined with cheesecloth into another pot or a large bowl. Press on the solids with the back of a spoon to release the juices; discard the solids in the colander. The broth is ready to use or can be frozen for up to 3 months.

Zuppa di Frittata

Egg Omelet Soup
Serves 4

At our house, we ate lots of eggs. They were cheap, fresh, and filling. Grandma Galasso went overboard with eggs. She packed omelet sandwiches for my school lunch. When she made too many omelets, or *frittate,* the leftovers were cut up and put into boiling chicken broth. This was served with chunks of peasant bread for a simple supper. This frittata is very thin and light, making it easy to roll up.

2 large eggs

4 tablespoons water

1 tablespoon unbleached all-purpose flour

¼ teaspoon salt

1 teaspoon minced fresh rosemary, or 1 tablespoon minced fresh parsley

2 tablespoons grated Pecorino Romano cheese

½ teaspoon grated lemon zest

2 tablespoon olive oil

1½ quarts Chicken Broth (page 31)

In a bowl, whisk together the eggs, water, flour, salt, rosemary or parsley, cheese, and lemon zest. Set aside.

In a skillet, heat the olive oil, pour in the egg batter, and fry over medium-high heat until the frittata is set. Use a wooden spatula to lift the edge of the frittata to allow the uncooked portion to run underneath it.

Carefully turn the frittata out onto a dish, and with your fingers, gently roll it up into a jelly roll. Let it cool 5 minutes, then cut it into thin strips.

In a pot, bring the broth to a boil. Carefully add the egg strips and boil gently for 1 minute. Ladle the soup into individual bowls and serve immediately.

Variation: Skip the soup and serve the frittata between pieces of crusty bread or with a salad for a light luncheon.

Zuppa Povera

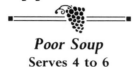

Poor Soup
Serves 4 to 6

Not only was my grandmother Galasso a good cook, but she was also a shrewd businesswoman. The house I grew up in belonged to her. To make ends meet for her large family of eight children, she rented out the bathtub, the only one in the neighborhood, on Saturday nights for five cents a person. She also rented rooms and provided simple meals for factory workers. This soup, which is inexpensive to make and very nourishing, was served to many a boarder in my grandmother's kitchen.

½ cup long-grain rice

1½ cups water

2 tablespoons beef
   marrow or olive oil

2 ribs celery,
   sliced thin

½ cup minced onion

2½ cups (4 ounces) fresh
   spinach, washed and
   torn into pieces

1 pound very ripe plum
   tomatoes, peeled,
   seeded, and diced

2 cups hot Chicken
   Broth (page 31)

2 cups hot water

2 tablespoons tomato
   paste

1 teaspoon salt

¼ teaspoon coarsely
   ground black pepper

4 to 6 large eggs

1 tablespoon minced
   fresh parsley

In a medium pot, boil the rice in the water until rice is cooked, about 10 minutes. Set aside.

In a medium soup pot, heat the beef marrow or olive oil until hot. Add the celery and onion, and sauté the vegetables until soft. Add the spinach and cook until wilted. Add the tomatoes, stirring the mixture for a few minutes, then add the hot broth, hot water, and tomato paste. Stir to dissolve the paste, then add the salt, pepper, and rice. Cover the pot and let the soup cook gently for about 5 minutes.

Raise the heat and bring the soup to a boil. Gently crack each egg into the soup, spacing them so they do not touch. Gently boil the soup until the eggs are set. Sprinkle on the parsley. Serve the soup immediately, allowing 1 egg per person.

Note: I sprinkle grated Pecorino Romano cheese on top.

Zuppa di Lenticchie

Lentil Soup
Serves 6 to 8

My dad remembers his mother's (Nonna Saporito) endless use of lentils; lentil soup and lentils with sausage were two familiar dishes when he was growing up. I presoak lentils the night before making this soup; this step can be eliminated, but the cooking time will be longer. At the end of the cooking time, I add a tiny soup pasta called acini di pepe for added texture and taste. This is a thick, hearty soup, which keeps well and may need to be thinned the next day with a little water or broth.

1½ cups lentils	1 28-ounce can plum tomatoes, with liquid
2 quarts water	
¼ cup olive oil	Salt and pepper to taste
1 medium onion, peeled and chopped	½ cup acini di pepe or pastina
2 ribs celery, sliced	Freshly grated Pecorino Romano cheese

Place the lentils in a bowl, add water to cover, and soak overnight.

Drain and discard the soaking water. Wash the lentils well in warm water, place in a soup pot, cover with the 2 quarts water, and bring to a boil. Add the oil, onion, celery, and tomatoes. Lower the heat and simmer the mixture, covered, for about 35 minutes, or until the lentils are tender. (The cooking time will be about 1½ hours if the lentils were not presoaked.)

Add salt, pepper, and the pasta. Cook for about 15 minutes longer, or until pasta is *al dente*. Ladle the soup into bowls and serve immediately, sprinkled with a little Pecorino Romano.

Variation: Add pieces of cooked chicken or sausage to the soup along with the pasta.

Minestrone alla Moda Genovese

Minestrone, Genoa Style
Serves 8 to 10

In Genoa as well as in Sorrento, this soup is often eaten at room temperature, although in Sorrento pesto is not added. The soup is often eaten on Sunday night, after the big meal on Sunday afternoon; and in many small villages, it is still made with rainwater collected in barrels. Be sure to soak the beans a day before you make the soup.

¼ pound cannellini or borlotti (cranberry) beans, soaked overnight

3 tablespoons olive oil

½ cup chopped onion

2 leeks, washed and chopped, white part only

1 medium eggplant (1 pound), peeled and diced

2 medium carrots, peeled and sliced

2 ribs celery, sliced

2 medium potatoes, peeled and diced

2 medium tomatoes, diced

2 cups hot Chicken Broth (page 31)

4 cups hot water

1 cup chopped raw spinach

1 cup diced zucchini

1 cup shredded green cabbage

¼ pound vermicelli or stelline

3 tablespoons Pesto (page 92)

Salt and pepper to taste

Drain the beans from the soaking water, place them in a pot, cover with water, and cook about 30 minutes, or until still quite *al dente*, and set aside.

In a large pot, heat the oil. Add the onion, leeks, eggplant, carrots, celery, and potatoes and sauté for about 8 minutes, or until the vegetables just begin to exude their juices.

Add the tomatoes, hot broth, hot water, beans, and additional hot water to just cover the mixture. Bring to a boil, lower the heat to a simmer, and cook covered for about 30 minutes.

Add the spinach, zucchini, cabbage, and pasta and cook another 20 minutes or until the pasta is *al dente.* Stir in the Pesto. Add salt and pepper to taste and serve immediately.

Note: There is a saying in Genoa that *chi mangia pesto, non lascia mai Genova*—"He who eats pesto never leaves Genoa."

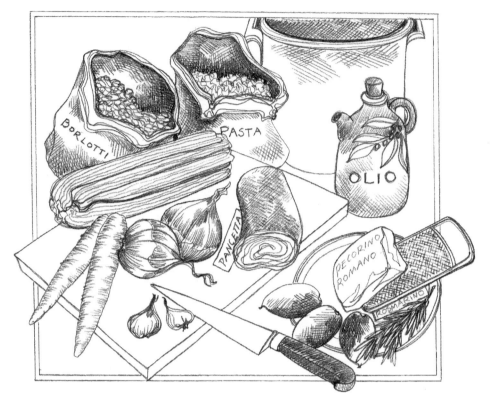

Pasta e Fagioli

Pasta and Beans
Serves 8

Almost every southern Italian family has a version of pasta and beans, called *pasta e fasola, pasta fazool,* or *pasta e fagioli.* In my version I use the speckled red borlotti, or cranberry bean, although this is a matter of preference since kidney or cannellini beans can also be used. Italians make this hearty soup with fresh beans when in season. In the winter, dried beans are first soaked and then cooked. The pasta used is a small tubular macaroni called ditalini. Substituting elbow macaroni is acceptable.

1½ cups dried borlotti
   (cranberry) beans

8 cups cold water

2 cups (8 ounces)
   ditalini

2 medium carrots,
   peeled and cut into
   quarters

1 rib celery, cut into
   quarters

2 medium onions,
   peeled and cut into
   quarters

1 large clove garlic,
   peeled

2 ounces pancetta or
   bacon

Leaves from 2 sprigs fresh
   rosemary

½ cup olive oil

3 plum tomatoes, peeled,
   seeded, and diced

Salt and pepper to taste

Freshly grated Pecorino
   Romano cheese

Place the beans in a large bowl, cover with cold water, and let sit overnight.

The next day, drain the beans, place them in a large soup pot, and cover with cold water. Bring the beans to a boil and cook for 20 to 25 minutes, or until they are still *al dente.* Add the pasta and boil the mixture for about 15 minutes more, or until the pasta is *al dente.*

While the beans are cooking, make a *battuto,* or minced mixture, of the carrots, celery, onions, garlic, pancetta, and rosemary. In a skillet, heat 2 tablespoons of the olive oil, add the minced mixture, and sauté for about 5 minutes, or until the vegetables begin to soften. Add the tomatoes, cover the skillet, and simmer for about 12 minutes.

When the pasta is cooked, add the vegetable mixture, stirring well. Add salt and pepper and serve the soup immediately in individual soup bowls. Drizzle a little of the remaining olive oil over the soup and pass the cheese to sprinkle over the top.

Note: Crusty Italian bread and a simple green salad of romaine and radicchio round out this meal.

Zuppa di Fagioli

Bean Soup
Serves 4 to 6

Beans are an ancient food. During the rise of the Roman Empire, beans were used as ballots for voting: white beans for yes, black beans an emphatic no.

Today beans make up a good part of my cooking. My pantry is lined with dried beans of every description from brown-speckled borlotti to grayish white cannellini. In this recipe, a meal in itself, bread is added to thicken the soup; other times I puree some of the beans to thicken it.

1½ cups dried cannellini or small white beans	1 28-ounce can whole plum tomatoes, chopped
¼ pound pancetta or bacon	3 cups Chicken Broth (page 31)
1 medium onion, peeled and diced	1 teaspoon coarse salt
1 large carrot	1 teaspoon coarsely ground black pepper
2 ribs celery	¼ to ½ cup extra-virgin olive oil
1 clove garlic, peeled	
2 tablespoons olive oil	4 to 6 slices stale Italian bread, cut into chunks
2 sprigs fresh rosemary	

Place the beans in a bowl, cover with water, and soak overnight. Next day, drain off the water, place the beans in a large pot, cover with fresh water, and bring to a boil. Cook the beans for 15 minutes. Drain off the water and set the beans aside.

Mince together the pancetta, onion, carrot, celery, and garlic. Set aside.

In a soup pot, heat the olive oil, add the minced ingredients and rosemary, and sauté the mixture over medium heat until the vegetables are soft and the pancetta begins to brown, about 5 minutes.

Add the beans and coat well with the vegetables. Add the tomatoes, broth, salt, and pepper. Stir the mixture well, cover the pot, and cook on medium-low heat for about 35 minutes, or until the beans are tender but not mushy. Keep the soup on warm.

In a skillet, heat ¼ cup of the olive oil, add the bread chunks, and sauté until nicely browned. Add more oil as needed. Drain the chunks on brown paper.

To serve, place a few of the bread chunks in each soup bowl and ladle some of the soup over the bread. Serve immediately.

Minestra di Riso e Zucchini

Rice and Zucchini Soup
Serves 6

This light soup can be put together very quickly if you have some chicken broth in the freezer. I use Maratelli rice, an Italian semifine variety, but domestic short-grain rice works just as well.

½ cup short-grain rice

1½ cups water

2 tablespoons olive oil

1 tablespoon butter

2 medium leeks, white part only, washed and thinly sliced (1¼ cups)

1 medium zucchini, sliced paper thin (2¼ cups)

1 large plum tomato, peeled, seeded, and diced (⅔ cup)

6 cups hot Chicken Broth (page 31)

1 teaspoon fine sea salt

¼ teaspoon freshly ground black pepper

Freshly grated Parmigiano-Reggiano cheese

In a saucepan, cook the rice in the water until it is *al dente,* firm but not hard, 8 to 10 minutes. Drain the rice well in a strainer and set aside.

In a 2-quart soup pot, heat the olive oil and butter over medium-high heat. Add the leeks, stir with a wooden spoon, and let them wilt, about 2 minutes. Do not let them brown. Add the zucchini and cook until soft but not mushy, about 5 minutes. Add the tomato and carefully stir to blend the vegetables. Cook about 1 minute.

Reduce the heat to low and carefully add the hot broth. Stir the vegetables once or twice, add the salt and pepper, and simmer the soup, covered, for 5 minutes. Add the rice and simmer 5 minutes more. Serve the soup immediately with the grated cheese.

Zuppa di Zucca e Spinaci

Squash and Spinach Soup
Serves 6 to 8

Now, this soup uses real ingenuity. A vibrant green, the soup is beautiful to look at as well as eat. I call this a kitchen-sink soup because it uses vegetables, milk, and pasta, and was created just by having the ingredients on hand.

1 10-ounce bag fresh spinach, washed, drained, and stemmed	3 cups water
	1 cup milk
4 tablespoons (½ stick) butter	1½ teaspoons fine sea salt, or more to taste
1 medium onion, peeled and diced	Freshly ground black pepper
1 pound yellow summer squash (about 3 small), cubed	1 cup ditalini or other soup pasta
	Grated Parmigiano-Reggiano cheese, for serving
1 pound potatoes, peeled and cubed	

Place the spinach in a 3-quart soup pot, cover, and cook without any additional water until limp, about 3 minutes. Drain the spinach in a colander and let cool. Press out the excess water with a wooden spoon, then coarsely chop the spinach. Set aside.

Wipe out the soup pot, return it to the heat, and melt 2 tablespoons of the butter. Add the onion and sauté over medium heat until soft. Add the squash and potatoes, and cook the vegetables together, stirring often, for about 5 minutes. Add the water, milk, salt, and pepper. Stir, combining ingredients well, cover the pot, and boil gently for 20 minutes, or until the potatoes are tender. Turn off the heat.

In a skillet, heat the remaining butter. Add the spinach and cook for 3 or 4 minutes. Add the spinach to the soup and stir well to blend.

In a food processor, puree the soup in batches until smooth. Return the soup to the soup pot and set aside.

In a medium saucepan, boil the pasta in salted water until *al dente*. Drain and add to the soup.

To serve, reheat the soup and serve in individual bowls. Pass the cheese for sprinkling on top.

Variation: Use thin slices of uncooked yellow squash as a garnish.

Zuppa di Cipolla

Onion Soup
Serves 4

This rich soup is great for a Friday-night supper. It can be ready in less than an hour, assuming you have some beef broth in the freezer. I make it with a combination of beef and veal broth for extra richness.

½ cup olive oil

¼ pound pancetta or salt pork, diced

5 large onions, thinly sliced

5 to 6 cups Beef Broth (page 32)

2 tablespoons grated Parmigiano-Reggiano cheese

Salt and pepper to taste

4 slices Italian bread

2 teaspoons dry sherry

8 slices Swiss, Gruyère, or Provolone cheese, plus additional grated, if desired

In a large soup pot, heat 2 tablespoons of olive oil over medium-high heat, add the pancetta or salt pork, and sauté for about 2 minutes. Add the onions, cover the pot, and cook slowly for about 15 minutes, stirring often, until limp. Add the broth and grated cheese, stir well, re-cover the pot, and simmer the soup for about 30 minutes.

In a skillet, heat ¼ cup of the olive oil and fry the bread slices on each side until golden brown. Add additional oil as needed. Drain the bread on brown paper and set aside.

To serve, ladle the soup into individual ovenproof soup bowls. Add ½ teaspoon sherry to each bowl. Place a slice of cheese on top of each bowl, then a slice of bread and another slice of cheese. Sprinkle with additional grated cheese, if desired. Place the soup bowls under the broiler and broil until the cheese is melted and golden brown. Serve immediately.

Zuppa di Asparagi

Asparagus Soup
Serves 4

In the spring, I seek out asparagus. I look for solid, stately bundles wrapped with string, sitting in neat rows, perched atop crushed ice. I buy the very thin asparagus because they remind me so much of the slender ones of Umbria. When I get my bundle home, I make this quick and creamy soup, using the cooking water from the asparagus.

1¼ pounds asparagus	3 large shallots, diced
2 cups water	¼ cup light cream
2 tablespoons (¼ stick) butter	½ teaspoon fine sea salt

Cut off the tough ends of the asparagus and discard. Place the asparagus in a sauté pan with the water. Cover the pot, bring the asparagus to a gentle boil, and cook for 3 or 4 minutes (depending on size), just until a knife easily pierces the stem end.

Drain the asparagus in a colander over a bowl, reserving the cooking water. When cool, cut the asparagus into 1-inch pieces. Dice some of the pieces to equal ½ cup and set aside.

In a saucepan, melt the butter over medium-high heat. Add the shallots and cook slowly until they begin to soften. Add all the asparagus except the ½ cup, and continue to cook for about 4 minutes, or until the asparagus is very soft.

Transfer the mixture to a food processor or blender and puree until smooth. Return the mixture to the saucepan, add 1½ cups of the reserved cooking water, cream, and salt. Cook slowly, stirring with a wooden spoon to blend the ingredients. Add the reserved diced asparagus. If the mixture appears too thick, add a bit more of the cooking water. Serve immediately.

Note: Sometimes I add diced prosciutto, sautéed in butter until crisp, as a garnish.

Zuppa di Lattuga
e Fagiolini

Lettuce and Green Bean Soup
Serves 8

My grandmothers looked upon green leafy vegetables as good candidates for soup. But I thought they went too far when I watched them making soup from lettuce! They used bitter lettuce, but I have changed their recipe and use romaine. This is a refreshing soup in the summer, but since the ingredients are available year-round, you can enjoy it any time.

2 heads (2 pounds total) romaine lettuce	½ cup unbleached all-purpose flour
6 ounces fresh green beans, cut into thirds (about 2 cups)	6 cups hot Beef Broth (page 32)
1½ teaspoons fine sea salt	2 large egg yolks
1½ cups cubed bread slices	½ cup heavy cream
6 tablespoons (¾ stick) butter	⅔ cup grated Asiago or Parmigiano-Reggiano cheese
1 shallot, diced	¼ teaspoon freshly grated nutmeg

Remove the cores from the lettuce, tear into pieces, and place in a colander. Rinse the lettuce well and let drain.

Cook the beans in boiling salted water until tender, but not mushy, about 7 minutes. Drain the beans well and set aside.

Preheat the oven to 350°F.

Place the bread cubes on a baking sheet and toast until nicely browned, about 10 minutes. Place in a bowl and set aside.

In a soup pot, melt the butter over medium-high heat. Add the shallot and sauté until limp but not brown. Sprinkle on the flour and mix with a wooden spoon until incorporated. Mixture will appear pasty but will smooth

out. Add the hot broth and continue to stir with a whisk until the mixture begins to boil. Add the lettuce, stir the mixture well, lower the heat, cover the pot, and cook for 35 minutes, stirring occasionally.

Place the soup in a food processor or blender in batches and process until smooth. Return the soup to the pot and keep warm over low heat.

In a bowl, whisk together the egg yolks and cream. Add 1 cup of the soup to the egg mixture and whisk to blend. Add the egg mixture to the soup pot and whisk for about 4 or 5 minutes. Add the beans, cheese, nutmeg, and remaining salt to the soup and stir well.

To serve, ladle the hot soup into individual bowls, sprinkle a few toasted bread cubes on top of each, and serve at once.

Pasta

Last Christmas I received a very concerned call from my mother and father, who wanted assurances that I would be home the next day to receive a "very special package from the Federal Express man." They were so excited about sending this package and reassured me that only I, not my brothers and sister, was to receive something truly unique. The next day I waited in curious excitement for the doorbell to ring. Sure enough, a large Styrofoam box arrived right in the middle of an interview I was having with a radio reporter. The reporter had just finished asking me how important food really was when I was a young girl. The timing could not have been better because the answer was in that package. I lumbered into the kitchen with it, and within minutes had removed an Arctic-size piece of dry ice that lay smoldering on top of the contents. My guest stood by for the unveiling. Out came six large bags of frozen, superjumbo stuffed macaroni shells, with a note from my mother that said, "Just pour tomato sauce over these and put them in the oven to bake. Merry Christmas."

Those jumbo shells reminded me of just how big a part pasta played in our humble home cooking, as well as in the cuisine of Italy.

Pasta is an ancient food. We will really never know who invented it, but it was eaten by the Etruscans and the Romans; it was written about in thirteenth-century cooking manuscripts, and fantasized about in Boc-caccio's *Decameron.*

During the Renaissance, pasta—especially lasagne, ravioli, and tor-tellini, was found, but only on the tables of the wealthy. In the nineteenth century, pasta came to be viewed as poor food, especially in Naples. In this century, Mussolini went so far as to consider banning it from the Italian diet because he thought it made the army lethargic! Hardly the way to win the war!

At home, as well as in southern Italy, people were known as *mangia-maccheroni,* or macaroni eaters, because it was consumed daily. To this day, I prefer a plate of well-prepared macaroni to almost anything else. I fre-quently use my grandmother Saporito's chitarra for making Maccheroni alla Chitarra (page 56). The chitarra is a small wooden rectangular instru-ment with taut strings pulled across it. A sheet of flattened pasta is placed on top of the chitarra and rolled with a rolling pin, the strings cutting the dough. What falls beneath is perfectly shaped golden spaghetti. The strings also produce a melodious sound, much like that of a guitar. Whoever came up with this simple invention was a genius. In mythology, the credit went to Vulcan, the inventor-god of gadgets, who is said to have first constructed a wooden instrument with wire that transformed a lump of dough into the smooth, golden strings of pasta. Modern-day Vulcans have given us the simple hand-crank pasta machine, which also produces silky strands of pasta.

My imagination runs wild when I think of what can be done with pasta. In my grandmothers' day, imagination and leftovers, not written recipes, determined what we ate. Without question, the dough was always made from fresh eggs and white flour.

Many, but not all these pasta dishes can be made with homemade pasta or with any good-quality imported dried pasta. My favorite is the Del Verde brand.

Pasta

Basic Egg Pasta
Makes about 1½ pounds, enough for 4 to 6
servings

I've received hundreds of letters from readers and viewers telling me how much they've enjoyed learning how to make homemade pasta. For those of you who haven't tried it, I urge you to do so. Even the best imported pasta doesn't hold a candle to pasta made by hand.

For easy reference, I repeat my basic pasta recipe from my first book, *Ciao Italia*.

4 large eggs	**½ cup semolina flour**
About 2½ cups unbleached all-purpose flour	**⅛ teaspoon salt**

To make the dough in a food processor, put the eggs in the bowl of the processor and process until smooth. In a bowl, mix 2½ cups all-purpose flour, the semolina flour, and salt. Add the flour mixture to the eggs 1 cup at a time and process just until a ball of dough starts to form. Add a little water if the dough seems dry, a little more flour if it seems wet. The dough should not be so sticky that it clings to your fingers. Turn the dough out onto a floured surface and knead it, adding additional flour as necessary, for about 5 minutes or until smooth. Cover and let rest for 10 minutes before rolling out and cutting into the desired shape.

To make the dough the traditional way, combine 2½ cups all-purpose flour, the semolina flour, and salt in a mound on a work surface. Make a well in the center of the flour and break the eggs into the well. Beat the eggs with a fork. Then, using the fork, gradually incorporate the flour from the inside walls of the well. When the dough becomes too firm to mix with the fork, knead it with your hands, incorporating just enough of the flour to make a soft but sticky dough. You may not need all the flour. Brush the excess flour aside and knead the dough, adding additional flour as necessary, for about 10 minutes or until smooth. Cover and let rest for 10 minutes before rolling out and cutting into the desired shape.

continued

Cut the dough into 4 pieces. Work with 1 piece at a time, keeping the remaining dough covered. Roll the dough out on a floured surface as thin as possible, or use a pasta machine to roll the dough out to the thinnest setting. Drape the sheets of pasta over dowel rods suspended between 2 chairs to dry slightly, about 5 minutes.

If cutting the pasta by hand, roll up each sheet loosely like a jelly roll, then cut it into fettucine, vermicelli, or lasagne strips with a sharp knife. Or cut the pasta into the desired width with the attachment on the pasta machine. Hang the pasta strips over dowel rods as you cut them, or spread on floured towels, then cook immediately or dry for storage.

Cook the pasta in a large pot of boiling water until *al dente,* 2 to 3 minutes. Drain, sauce, and serve immediately. Or dry and store the pasta: Hang the strips over dowel rods suspended between two chairs until very dry. (I usually leave it on the rods for a day.) When the ends of the pasta begin to curl, it is dry enough. Wrap it loosely in aluminum foil and store for up to 3 months.

Pezze e Piselli

Patches and Peas
Serves 4

When my mother made pasta the scraps that were too dry to put through her pasta machine were cut by hand into squares that resembled little patches. They were combined with sweet peas, bits of bacon or ham, and onions. I like this dish so much that I make extra pasta dough to satisfy my craving. While this dish is my comfort food, it can also serve as a first course for a dinner party.

1½ to 1¾ cups unbleached all-purpose flour

⅛ teaspoon salt

2 large eggs

¼ cup extra-virgin olive oil

1 medium onion, thinly sliced

4 ounces prosciutto or pancetta, chopped

1½ cups fresh or frozen and thawed peas

½ cup hot Chicken Broth (page 31)

Salt and pepper to taste

4 tablespoons (½ stick) butter, at room temperature

½ cup grated Parmigiano-Reggiano cheese, plus additional for serving

Mound the flour on a work surface and sprinkle on the salt. Make a well in the center of the mound and crack the eggs into it. Gently mix the eggs with a fork and start working in the flour from the inside of the well. When the mixture is no longer easy to move with a fork, use your hands to work the ingredients into a smooth ball of dough. You may not need all the flour. Cover the dough with a bowl and let it rest for 10 minutes.

Divide the dough in half and work with 1 piece at a time. Flatten the dough with a rolling pin and run it through a pasta machine set to the thinnest setting. Cut the dough in half lengthwise with a pastry wheel or knife. Then cut 2-inch squares or "patches" from each piece. Repeat with the remaining dough. Place the "squares" on a lightly floured cloth in a single layer.

In a skillet over medium-high heat, heat the olive oil and sauté the onion slices until soft. Add the prosciutto or pancetta, and sauté for 3 or 4 minutes, or until it begins to brown. Add the broth and peas. Simmer the mixture for about 3 minutes, or until the peas are tender but not mushy. Add salt and pepper and keep the mixture warm but uncovered.

In a large pot, bring 4 quarts of water to a boil. Add the patches and cook them until *al dente*. Drain the patches in a colander, place them in a serving bowl with the butter and the cheese, and mix gently. Add the pea mixture, combining the ingredients well. Serve at once and pass additional cheese.

Note: Instead of cutting square patches by hand, place each sheet of dough over the teeth of a ravioli form and roll over it with a rolling pin to form the pieces.

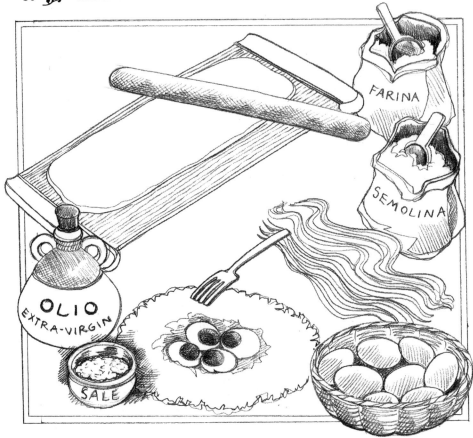

Maccheroni alla Chitarra

Macaroni on the Guitar
Makes about 1 pound of dough, serves 4

This pasta, and the technique for making it, is said to have originated in the Abruzzi, but my Sicilian *nonna,* Grandma Saporito, made this macaroni all the time. Sometimes the pasta goes by the name *tonnarelli,* but to me it was just Maccheroni alla Chitarra. It is a little thicker than fettucine. If you do not have a chitarra, roll and cut the dough as you would for linguine, or buy a commercial brand. Be sure to lightly spoon the flour into your measuring cup. This macaroni can be served with a basic tomato sauce or with Ragù d'Agnello (page 96).

2½ to 3 cups unbleached all-purpose flour

½ cup semolina flour

⅛ teaspoon salt

4 large eggs

2 tablespoons extra-virgin olive oil

In a bowl, mix 2½ cups of all-purpose flour, the semolina flour, and the salt. Pour the flour onto a work surface and make a well in the center. Crack the eggs into the center of the well and add the olive oil. Beat the eggs and oil carefully with a fork. Begin to incorporate the flour from the inside wall of the well into the flour mixture until you cannot move the fork; then mix with your hands until a ball of dough is formed. Add additional flour if the dough is sticky. Brush aside the unused flour and knead the dough until smooth. Cover the dough with a bowl, and let rest for 10 minutes.

Cut the dough into 4 pieces. Work with 1 piece at a time and keep the rest covered on a floured surface.

If you have a chitarra, roll out the dough so that it is one third shorter than the length of the chitarra. Place the piece of dough on top of the chitarra and roll over it forcefully with a rolling pin. The macaroni will fall beneath the chitarra. Place the macaroni on clean towels and continue with the rest of the dough.

In a large pot of boiling water, cook the macaroni until *al dente*. This will only take 3 or 4 minutes. Drain the macaroni, place a thin layer of sauce in a serving bowl, and top with the macaroni. Toss it well, then add additional sauce to just coat the macaroni. Serve immediately.

Pasta di Castagne

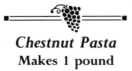

Chestnut Pasta
Makes 1 pound

I ate chestnut pasta for the first time in Perugia, at the Hotel La Rosetta, about eight years ago. It had an unexpected taste for pasta—somewhat sweet—but the accompanying cream sauce was the perfect foil for the sweetness.

Chestnut flour, made from dried chestnuts, can be found in Italian markets. It has a very fine texture, and I find that it absorbs a lot of liquid. The dough is soft when rolled, so you may need to add additional flour. I make my chestnut pasta on my Grandmother Saporito's chitarra, but a pasta machine or rolling by hand, works fine too.

2½ cups unbleached all-purpose flour	⅛ teaspoon salt
1 cup chestnut flour	4 large eggs

Mix the flours and salt on a wooden surface, shape into a mound, and form a well in the mound. Add the eggs to the well and begin beating them with a fork. Start to incorporate some of the flour into the well, and when you can no longer move your fork with ease, work the mixture with your hands until a ball of dough is formed. Sprinkle the work surface with some of the reserved flour and knead the pasta until it is a smooth, nonsticky ball. Add additional flour as needed. Let the dough rest for 10 minutes on a floured surface under a cloth.

Divide the dough into 4 pieces and roll and cut 1 piece at a time with a pasta machine into fettucine, linguine, or spaghetti. Spread the pasta on floured towels and either let dry totally for later use or cook immediately in 6 quarts of boiling water until *al dente,* about 2 to 3 minutes. Drain and toss with Porcini Mushroom Sauce (page 101).

Broccoli e Spaghetti alla Mamma

Mom's Broccoli and Spaghetti
Serves 4 to 6

My mother often had prepared dinner before most people in the house had read the morning newspaper. When she was busy all day this was one of her quick standby meals.

Fresh, ripe tomatoes make the difference here. Peel them by placing them in boiling water for 1 or 2 minutes, then drain and let cool. The skins will easily peel off.

¼ cup plus 1 tablespoon olive oil

2 cloves garlic, peeled and thinly sliced

2 pounds plum tomatoes, peeled, seeded, and pureed

3 or 4 fresh basil leaves, minced

½ teaspoon salt

¼ teaspoon freshly ground black pepper

1 pound broccoli, trimmed and broken into small florets

1 cup fresh or frozen peas

1 pound spaghetti or rigatoni

Grated Pecorino Romano cheese, for serving

In a saucepan, heat ¼ cup of the olive oil, add the garlic, and let soften, but not brown. Lower the heat, then add the tomatoes, basil, salt, and pepper. Stir the sauce well, cover, and simmer for 15 minutes.

In a pot, cook the broccoli, uncovered, in boiling water until the stems are just tender about 5 to 7 minutes. Add the peas and continue to cook for 3 minutes. Drain the vegetables well, add them to the tomato sauce, and keep warm.

Brush a serving bowl with the remaining olive oil and set aside.

In a large pot, bring 4 to 6 quarts of water to a boil and cook the spaghetti until *al dente*. Drain well. Place the spaghetti in the bowl, pour over the sauce, and mix well. Pass the cheese separately.

Bucatini con le Sarde

Spaghetti with Sardines
Serves 4

Sardines never seem to get their day in the culinary sun. Most of us have only had them packed in oil because fresh sardines deteriorate very quickly and do not ship well. If you are ever fortunate enough to eat delicate fresh sardines, you'll sing their praises thereafter. Sardines, or *sarde,* are caught in the waters around Sicily and Sardinia, and are used a great deal in the cuisines of these two islands. A specialty of Palermo is a hollow spaghetti called *perciatelli,* or bucatini served with fresh sardines. Fresh, young herring may be substituted for the sardines. In this recipe I have used canned sardines, and people still lick their fingers after eating.

¼ cup golden raisins	½ cup Calamata olives, pitted and chopped
2 3.55-ounce cans sardines in oil, cut in pieces, oil reserved	3 tablespoons pine nuts
1 rib celery, minced	4 fennel tops
1 medium onion, peeled and minced	1 pound bucatini or perciatelli
1 16-ounce can plum tomatoes, chopped	Salt and pepper to taste

In a bowl, soak the raisins for 30 minutes until plumped. Drain.

In a skillet, heat 4 tablespoons of the reserved sardine oil (add additional olive oil, if necessary), add the celery and onion, and sauté the mixture over medium-high heat until soft. Lower the heat, add the sardines, and cook for 3 or 4 minutes. Add the tomatoes, olives, and pine nuts, then the raisins. Cover the skillet and cook the sauce over low heat for 15 minutes.

Bring 6 quarts of water to a boil in a large pot. Add the fennel tops and blanch for about 4 minutes. Remove the fennel, drain, chop fine, and add to the sauce. Add the bucatini to the same water, and cook until *al dente,* not mushy. Drain the bucatini, place it in a large serving bowl, and pour the sauce over it. Mix well and serve immediately.

Note: It is not customary to use grated cheese over pasta and fish dishes, but here I like a good grating of Pecorino Romano.

Variation: Try fusilli instead of the bucatini for the pasta. It is a long, curly spaghetti that goes very nicely with this sauce.

Bucatini all'Amatriciana

Pasta in the Style of Amatrice
Serves 4

Amatrice, a town in the region of Lazio, is the inspiration for this dish made with bucatini, a chunky, tubular pasta. It is accompanied by a spicy tomato sauce that can be made *pochi minuti* ("in a few minutes"). Use pancetta, which is unsmoked pork belly, available in Italian food markets, or substitute Canadian or slab bacon.

2 tablespoons extra-virgin olive oil	4 cups diced fresh or canned plum tomatoes
½ cup diced pancetta	Salt and pepper to taste
1 medium white onion, peeled and diced	1 pound bucatini or spaghetti
½ teaspoon dried hot red pepper flakes	½ cup grated Pecorino Romano cheese

In a skillet, heat the olive oil, add the pancetta, and sauté until the pancetta starts to shrivel. Add the onion and continue to sauté until the onion is soft. Add the red pepper flakes and sauté for several minutes. Then add the tomatoes, salt, and pepper and simmer the mixture, covered, for 10 minutes. Keep the sauce warm.

In a large pot of boiling water, cook the bucatini until *al dente*. Drain the bucatini well, place it in a serving bowl, and toss with half the sauce. Sprinkle on the cheese and serve at once, passing additional sauce on the side.

Vermicelli alla Siracusana

Vermicelli, Syracusan Style
Serves 4

Vermicelli means "little worms"—not a very appealing name for thin strands of spaghetti. But forget the translation; there is no pasta dish to my mind that has more zing and personality than this Syracusan dish. It has all the right attributes of spiciness, flavor, color, and drama. Easy on the budget and quick to prepare, this recipe is in my winner's circle.

½ cup olive oil

2 cloves garlic, peeled

3 salted anchovy fillets

4 cups cubed eggplant (about 1 pound)

1½ cups (about 3) seeded and chopped ripe plum tomatoes

1 small yellow bell pepper, seeded and cut into thin strips

¼ cup (about 14) pitted and chopped oil-cured black olives

¼ cup salted capers, rinsed

5 fresh basil leaves, torn into shreds

Fine sea salt to taste

¼ teaspoon coarsely ground black pepper

1 pound vermicelli

Freshly grated Pecorino Romano cheese, for serving

In a large skillet, heat the olive oil and sauté the garlic until soft, then discard. Add the anchovies, stirring to dissolve them in the oil. Add the eggplant and sauté the pieces until they become soft and golden, about 10 minutes.

Add the tomatoes to the skillet and let the mixture cook, covered, over medium heat for 5 to 6 minutes. Stir in the pepper strips, olives, capers, basil, and salt and pepper. Mix well, cover the pan, and continue cooking for about 20 minutes.

Fill a large pot with water, bring to a boil, then add the vermicelli and cook until *al dente*. Drain the pasta in a colander and quickly add to the vegetables. Heat the mixture and serve. Pass the grated cheese on the side.

Penne con Cinque Formaggi

Penne with Five Cheeses
Serves 4

This is high-class macaroni and cheese, as prepared in Italy by my friend and cooking teacher, Lorenzo Fluss. Ziti may be used in place of penne.

1 pound penne or ziti	**¼ teaspoon freshly grated nutmeg**
4 tablespoons (½ stick) butter	**¼ cup grated Parmigiano-Reggiano cheese**
1⅔ cups cubed cheese— a combination of mozzarella, Bel Paese, Swiss, and Provolone	**¼ cup heavy cream**
¼ teaspoon coarsely ground black pepper	**1½ tablespoons minced fresh parsley**
	Salt to taste

In a large pot, boil the pasta in 4 quarts boiling water until *al dente*. Drain the pasta in a colander and return to the pot over low heat. Add the butter and mix well with a wooden spoon to coat the pasta well.

Sprinkle the cubed cheese on top of the penne and let it remain on top for 1 or 2 minutes to warm. Then stir vigorously with a wooden spoon to melt the cheeses. Add the pepper and nutmeg, and stir in the Parmigiano-Reggiano cheese. Add the cream and parsley, and continue stirring until well mixed. Add salt to taste and serve immediately.

Pennette in Padella

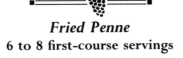

Fried Penne
6 to 8 first-course servings

Pennette is a type of macaroni that resembles small quill pens. They are either ridged (pennette rigate) or smooth, and vary in length. For this dish, a specialty of Tre Vaselle, a charming hotel and cooking school nestled among the Lungarotti vineyards of Torgiano, the pennette are no more than ¼ inch long. The method of browning the pasta first makes an unusual, but hearty dish.

½ ounce dried porcini
mushrooms

5½ tablespoons extra-
virgin olive oil

1 pound pennette
rigate

6 tablespoons brandy

4 ounces shiitake
mushrooms, chopped

¼ cup chopped fresh
parsley

3½ cups hot Chicken
Broth (page 31)

6 tablespoons heavy
cream

½ cup grated
Parmigiano-Reggiano
cheese

Fine sea salt to taste

½ teaspoon coarsely
ground black pepper

Place the porcini mushrooms in a small bowl, cover with cold water, and
soak for about 30 minutes or until they are soft. Drain the porcini, dice
them, and set aside. Reserve the liquid.

In a skillet at least 14 inches wide and 2 inches deep, heat 3½
tablespoons olive oil until hot. Add the pennette and brown quickly, about
7 or 8 minutes, constantly stirring with a wooden spoon. Be careful not
to burn them. They should look *unevenly* toasted. Add the brandy, continue
to stir, and let the alcohol evaporate. Remove the skillet from the heat and
set aside.

In a separate skillet, heat the remaining 2 tablespoons olive oil, add
the porcini and shiitake mushrooms, and sauté for about 3 minutes. Add
the parsley, sauté 1 minute more, and set aside.

Return the skillet with the pennette to the heat. Add enough broth
to almost cover them, plus ½ cup reserved soaking liquid. Stir the mixture
well, bring to a boil, cover the pan, lower the heat, and cook for 6 or 7
minutes, stirring often. The pennette should be cooked only until very *al
dente,* almost crunchy.

Uncover the pan, raise the heat, and let the remaining liquid almost
totally evaporate. Add the mushroom and parsley mixture, combining well,
then add the cream and cheese, and continue to stir and cook for 1 minute.
Add the salt and pepper, mix well, and serve immediately.

Lasagne con Melanzane alla Marianna

Mary Ann's Eggplant Lasagne
Serves 8 to 10

Lasagne is an ancient food. The Romans were dishing it out during the heyday of the Roman Empire. A fourteenth-century cooking manuscript directs the cook to boil the lasagne noodles (made without eggs) in capon broth and then layer the noodles with grated cheese. In my version, freshly made noodles are layered with thin, lengthwise slices of eggplant and topped with tomato sauce.

Sauce

- 2 tablespoons extra-virgin olive oil
- 1 large clove garlic, peeled and minced
- 1 large white onion, peeled and minced
- 2 28-ounce cans plum tomatoes, crushed
- ½ cup water
- ½ cup dry red wine
- 3 or 4 fresh basil leaves
- 1 tablespoon sugar
- Salt and pepper to taste
- 1 firm medium eggplant, about 8 to 9 inches long
- Peanut oil, for frying
- ½ recipe Basic Egg Pasta (page 53), or ½ pound store-bought lasagne noodles
- 1 pound mozzarella cheese, sliced

In a large saucepan, heat the olive oil, add the garlic and onion, and sauté until soft. Lower the heat; add the tomatoes, water, wine, basil, sugar, salt, and pepper. Simmer the mixture for 20 minutes. Set aside.

Wash and dry the eggplant. Cut into ⅛-inch lengthwise slices and place in layers in a colander. Sprinkle salt between the layers and let sit for 1 hour. Rinse and dry the eggplant slices with a towel.

In a skillet, heat enough peanut oil to coat the bottom. Add a few eggplant slices at a time and sauté quickly, about 2 minutes on each side or until soft. Drain the pieces on brown paper. Set aside.

If using homemade pasta, cut the dough into 3 pieces. Work with 1 piece at a time and roll the dough ⅛ inch thick. Cut 2 sheets from each piece to fit a 9- x 13-inch lasagne pan. Set aside on a floured towel in a single layer.

In a large pot, bring about 8 quarts of water to the boil. Add a few homemade lasagne strips at a time and parboil for 1 to 2 minutes. Remove the noodles to a waiting pan of ice water. This will cool the noodles and allow you to handle them. Continue cooking the remaining noodles in small batches. Drain the noodles on dry towels. (If using store-bought noodles, skip the parboiling step and layer the noodles *uncooked.*)

Preheat the oven to 350°F.

Spread 1 cup of the sauce in the bottom of the lasagne pan. Add a layer of lasagne strips. Cover the strips with ½ cup sauce. Add a layer of eggplant. Sprinkle with salt and pepper and add a layer of cheese. Spread ½ cup of sauce over the cheese. Make 2 more layers of lasagne strips, sauce, eggplant, salt and pepper, and cheese. Spread the top layer with 1 cup sauce. Cover the dish with foil and bake for 35 to 40 minutes. Let stand 5 minutes before cutting.

Note: Make a day ahead of serving. After baking, remove the foil and cover the pan with a sheet of waxed paper, then replace the foil. This prevents the acid in the tomato sauce from eating through the foil and leaving little bits of foil on the top of the sauce.

Cannelloni ai Funghi

Cannelloni with Mushrooms
Serves 6

Cannelloni are neat rolled cylinders of pasta filled with anything from vegetables and meat to cheese and seafood. Baked under a blanket of sauce, they make a prized first or second course. For this version, dried porcini and button mushrooms are combined with cheese and prosciutto and topped with a white sauce. This whole dish takes about two hours to make, although you can make the filling and sauce a day ahead. If so, the sauce will need to be thinned with additional milk, and warmed over low heat.

½ cup dried porcini
  mushrooms

1 cup cold water

1 12-ounce package
  fresh button
  mushrooms

3 tablespoons olive oil

1 clove garlic, peeled
  and minced

½ teaspoon salt

¼ teaspoon black
  pepper

2 cups ricotta cheese,
  well drained

¼ cup grated Asiago
  cheese

¼ teaspoon grated
  nutmeg

5 ounces Emmentaler
  cheese, thinly sliced

¼ pound prosciutto,
  thinly sliced

Sauce

7 tablespoons butter

4 tablespoons
  unbleached all-
  purpose flour

2½ cups milk

1 teaspoon salt

½ teaspoon grated
  nutmeg

¼ cup grated Asiago
  cheese

Dough

Approximately 1½ cups
  unbleached all-
  purpose flour

⅛ teaspoon salt

2 large eggs

1 tablespoon olive oil

To make the filling, place the porcini in a bowl, cover with cold water, and soak for 30 minutes. Drain and dice the porcini; reserve the liquid for another use.

Clean the button mushrooms with damp paper towels, then thinly slice them.

In a skillet, heat the olive oil, add the mushrooms and garlic, and sauté the mixture for about 4 minutes. Add the porcini and continue to sauté until the mushrooms are soft and the liquid has evaporated, about 5 to 7 minutes more. Add salt and pepper, mix well, then transfer to a bowl.

In a bowl, mix the ricotta and ¼ cup Asiago cheese and the nutmeg. Add the mushroom mixture and blend well. Cover the bowl and refrigerate until ready to use.

Cut the Emmentaler slices and prosciutto in half. You should have 12 slices of each. Cover and set aside.

To make the sauce, melt 4 tablespoons of the butter in a saucepan, over medium-high heat. Add the flour and whisk the mixture for 1 minute or until a smooth paste is formed. Lower the heat, and gradually add the milk, continually whisking until the sauce starts to thicken. Remove the sauce from the heat, add the salt and ¼ teaspoon of the nutmeg, and stir to blend. Keep the sauce covered and warm. (If you make the sauce a day ahead, cover and refrigerate. When ready to put the cannelloni together, reheat the sauce and thin it with a little milk.)

If making the dough by hand, mix 1¼ cups of the flour and the salt on a work surface. Make a well in the center of the flour, add the eggs and olive oil, and mix with a fork or your fingers until a ball of dough is formed. Use additional flour as needed. Knead the dough until smooth and elastic. Let rest, covered, for 10 minutes.

If using a food processor, pulse the flour and salt together, then add the eggs and oil through the feed tube. Remove the dough and knead on a floured surface until smooth and elastic.

On a floured surface, cut the dough into 2 pieces. Use a pasta machine set to the thinnest setting or roll by hand into two 36- x 5-inch sheets. Cut each sheet into six 6- x 5-inch rectangles and place them on a clean towel.

In a large pot, bring 4 quarts of water to the boil. Add 6 rectangles at a time and boil 1 minute. Scoop from the water and place rectangles in a baking pan full of ice water. When cool enough to handle, dry the rectangles on clean towels.

Preheat the oven to 375°F. Lightly grease a 14- x 9-inch or larger baking pan with butter. Set aside.

To fill the cannelloni, place a piece of Emmentaler cheese on each rectangle. Top with a piece of prosciutto and about 3 tablespoons of the filling, carefully spreading it evenly. Roll up the rectangles from the short side like a jelly roll.

continued

Place the cannelloni in a single layer in the baking pan. Reheat the sauce, thinning it with a little milk if necessary, and spread it over the top. Dice the remaining 3 tablespoons butter and scatter it over the top. Sprinkle on the remaining ¼ cup Asiago cheese and grate the remaining nutmeg over the top.

Bake for 30 to 35 minutes or until heated through, then run under the broiler for about 2 minutes to brown the top. Serve immediately.

Note: Parmigiano-Reggiano cheese can be substituted for the Asiago.

Il Teatro dell'Opera

The Opera House

My introduction to Italian opera took place at the Teatro Communale in Florence. As my husband and I hopped off the bus, with tickets in hand, we were engulfed in a sea of enthusiastic Italians, all politely pushing their way into the opera house. They came dressed for the occasion: women in bright brocades and dangling earrings; men in smart silk suits and bow ties.

The evening's offering was Claudio Monteverdi's L'incoronazione di Poppea ("The Coronation of Poppea")—the tragic story of the Roman empress who was both mistress and wife of Nero. Expecting a long evening, we made our way to the foyer of the theater to get an aqua minerale. I knew the Italians took opera very seriously, but I did not realize that they also took their refreshments seriously. No candy bars and pretzels here; instead, the smells of semolina gnocchi swimming in melted butter, neatly layered lasagne, and ribollita, the classic twice-boiled soup of Tuscany. The glitterati stood around holding china plates, silver utensils, and cloth napkins; they were lapping up their native cuisine and sipping fine Chianti, all the while keeping an eye on the dessert table, where a tantalizing array of ricotta cheesecake and macedonia ("fruit salad"), as well as tiramisù, a ladyfinger and espresso combination, and zuccotto, a cake laced with liqueur and shaped like a cap, played havoc with decision making.

We finished our drinks just as the lights began to flicker and we returned to our seats. I leaned over to my husband Guy, pressing in his hand the few pieces of Baci candy I had brought along in case we got hungry, and whispered, "Is there anything the Italians don't do with style?" He whispered back: "Okay, so we ate before we got here! How were we supposed to know? I just hope this opera has subtitles."

Timballo di Maccarun

Molded Macaroni Casserole
Serves 8 to 10

Pasta means "paste," something made from flour and water. It has become a generic term when referring to all types of pasta, whether made from just flour and water or with eggs as well. In southern Italy, pasta is called *macaroni* or *maccarun,* as was said at home. The many shapes and sizes that macaroni come in are created by bronze die-plates that extrude the mixture of semolina flour and water, and give its artistic, final shape. In this recipe the familiar elbow shape is used to make an impressive molded casserole called a *timballo*.

¾ **pound ground beef sirloin**	4 **cups cooked elbow macaroni (2 cups dry)**
½ **pound ground veal**	1½ **cups diced mozzarella cheese**
2 **slices stale bread**	
2 **large eggs, slightly beaten**	½ **cup diced Provolone cheese**
3 **tablespoons minced fresh parsley**	2½ **cups tomato sauce, plus extra as needed**
2 **tablespoons minced fresh basil**	**Olive oil, for greasing pan**
Salt and pepper to taste	7 **lean slices prosciutto, or** ¼ **pound pancetta**
⅔ **cup grated Parmigiano-Reggiano cheese**	

In a bowl, gently combine the ground meats. In a separate bowl of water, dip the bread slices just until softened, then squeeze out the water, crumble the bread, and add to the meats along with the eggs, herbs, salt, pepper, and Parmigiano-Reggiano cheese. Mix just to combine the ingredients. Set aside.

In a separate bowl, combine the cooked macaroni with the remaining cheeses and 1 cup of tomato sauce. Set aside.

Grease the bottom and sides of a 9-inch springform pan with olive oil. Cut a piece of parchment paper to fit the bottom of the pan. Place

the slices of prosciutto or pancetta in the bottom of the pan in a spokelike or circle fashion. Cover the slices and sides of the pan with about two thirds of the meat mixture. Make sure there are no gaps. Gently fill the center of the pan with the macaroni mixture, patting it down firmly.

With a rolling pin, roll the remaining meat mixture between 2 sheets of waxed paper to fit the top of the pan. Remove 1 sheet of the waxed paper and invert the meat over the top of the pan. Carefully pull back the remaining sheet of waxed paper. Neatly press the edges of the meat all the way around the pan, making sure that there are no gaps.

Preheat the oven to 350°F.

Cover the top of the pan tightly with a piece of aluminum foil. Place the pan on a baking sheet and bake for 30 minutes, covered. Remove the foil and bake 15 minutes longer, or until the meat is browned on top.

Remove the pan from the oven. Run a knife around the edges of the pan. Place a serving platter over the pan and invert onto the platter. With a pot holder, carefully release the spring and lift off the sides of the pan. Remove the bottom of the pan and the parchment paper. Let the timballo cool for 5 to 10 minutes.

Serve the timballo cut into wedges and pass extra tomato sauce on the side.

Gnocchi di Patate
con Salsa di Gorgonzola

Potato Gnocchi with Gorgonzola Sauce
Serves 8

There are many variations on *gnocchi,* or dumplings. Some are made with potatoes, others with a combination of spinach and potatoes, and still others like those of Sardinia use saffron in the dough. There are also gnocchi made from semolina flour, which is light and delicate. This recipe comes from my Italian friend Maria Castaldo, a southern Italian who doesn't top these potato gnocchi with the traditional tomato sauce; rather, she uses a Gorgonzola cheese sauce, something more common in the north of Italy. The trick to making potato gnocchi is to add just the minimum amount of flour to the potatoes—otherwise the gnocchi will be too heavy. I always weigh my flour when making these dumplings. Two cups of lightly spooned flour, or 8 ounces, seems to work well.

2 pounds potatoes	1 teaspoon salt
2 cups unbleached all-purpose flour	½ cup grated Parmigiano-Reggiano cheese
1 large egg, slightly beaten	½ pound Gorgonzola cheese
2 tablespoons minced fresh Italian parsley	1 cup heavy cream
1 teaspoon freshly grated nutmeg	2 tablespoons Fresh Tomato and Basil Sauce (page 85)

Boil, bake, or microwave the potatoes until tender. Cool and peel them, then place in a large bowl. Mash the potatoes with a hand masher. You should have about 4 cups of mashed potatoes. Add the flour, egg, parsley, nutmeg, salt, and ¼ cup grated cheese. Mix well with your hands. If the mixture seems too sticky, add up to ½ cup more flour. To test for the right amount of flour, make a few gnocchi and drop them into a pot of boiling water. If they rise to the surface and hold their shape without disintegrating, the proportion of flour to potato is correct.

Divide the dough into 6 pieces. Work with 1 piece at a time on a floured surface and roll it into a rope about 30 inches long and the width of your middle finger. Cut the rope with a knife into 1-inch pieces. Roll each piece on the tines of a fork and place the gnocchi on a floured baking sheet in a single layer. Continue until all the dough is used.

For the sauce, cut the Gorgonzola in chunks and place in a saucepan with the cream and tomato sauce. Heat the mixture over medium-high heat until the cheese is melted. Keep warm.

In a large pot, bring 6 quarts of water to a boil. Gently add the gnocchi and cook just until they bob to the surface. Drain them with a slotted spoon, place in a serving dish, and toss with half the sauce. Add the remaining sauce, sprinkle on the remaining ¼ cup of grated cheese, and serve hot.

Gnocchi di Ricotta

Ricotta Dumplings
Serves 6

These are gnocchi as made in the Marches. Unlike potato gnocchi, which are shaped on the tines of a fork and boiled, these are shaped into ovals or eggs using two soup spoons and then baked. They are light and delicious. Chill the mixture first for easier forming.

1⅓ cups ricotta cheese,
   well drained

1 cup packed cooked
   spinach, well
   squeezed and
   chopped

¼ cup diced Fontina
   cheese

¼ cup diced Swiss
   cheese

¼ cup grated
   Parmigiano-Reggiano
   cheese

¼ cup plus
   2 tablespoons toasted
   fresh bread crumbs

2 tablespoons
   (¼ stick) butter,
   softened

2 large egg yolks,
   beaten

Salt to taste

1 teaspoon freshly
   grated nutmeg

1½ cups tomato sauce

In a large bowl, mix all the ingredients except the tomato sauce.

Preheat the oven to 350°F.

Using 2 soup spoons, form gnocchi into oval or egg shapes using a little less than ¼ cup of the mixture for each. There should be about twenty 2½-inch-long gnocchi. Place them close together, but not touching, in a buttered 13½- x 8-inch baking dish. Cover the gnocchi with the tomato sauce and bake for 20 to 25 minutes or until hot. Serve immediately.

Note: Sometimes a white sauce (Salsa di Besciamella, page 102) is used in addition to the tomato sauce. Spread the baking dish with the white sauce before adding the gnocchi.

Gnocchi al Zafferano

Saffron Gnocchi
Serves 10 to 12

Saffron, once more precious than gold, was one of the most exotic spices of Renaissance Italy. It was used mainly as a coloring agent, rather than for taste, to give many dishes eye appeal. It is still expensive. Most of it now comes from Spain, but Sardinia also exports it. What makes saffron so expensive is the fact that the stigmas of the crocus flower, from which saffron is obtained, must be extracted by hand and it takes over a hundred thousand dried stigmas to make one pound of saffron!

I use saffron sparingly in soups and some chicken and fish dishes, and to tint frosting. A traditional dish in Sardinia made with saffron is Saffron Gnocchi. My adaptation makes about 12 dozen, if you cut the pieces ½ inch in length; however, you can make them 1 inch long if you wish. Cook what you like and freeze the rest.

⅛ teaspoon powdered saffron	⅔ cup semolina flour
1 cup very warm water	1 tablespoon plus ⅛ teaspoon salt
1 large egg	2½ cups tomato sauce, heated
2¼ to 2½ cups unbleached all-purpose flour	

In a large bowl, dissolve the saffron in the water. Add the egg and beat well with a fork.

In a separate bowl, combine 2¼ cups of the all-purpose flour with the semolina and ⅛ teaspoon salt. Add the flour mixture to the saffron and water, and mix with your hands until a ball of dough begins to form. Gradually add enough of the remaining flour to form a soft, but not sticky ball of dough. Turn the dough out onto a floured surface and knead it until smooth. Let the dough rest, covered for 10 minutes.

Knead the dough again on a floured surface until smooth and elastic. Cut the dough into 6 pieces and cover. Roll 1 piece at a time into a 21- or 22-inch-long rope, ¾ inch wide. Cut the rope into ½-inch pieces and press each piece against the tines of a fork or clean comb to create lines. Place the gnocchi on lightly floured trays or clean towels.

In a large pot, bring 7 to 8 quarts of water to a boil. Add 1 tablespoon of salt and the gnocchi. Cook until the gnocchi are *al dente.* They will bob to the top of the cooking water. Drain the gnocchi well using a handled strainer, and place in a serving dish that has been lined with a thin layer of tomato sauce. Add the gnocchi, top with additional tomato sauce, toss gently, and serve.

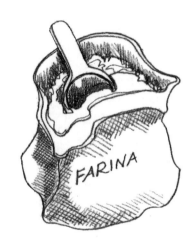

Gnocchi di Zucca alla Moda Mia

Pumpkin Gnocchi, My Way
Serves 16, makes about 160 gnocchi

The Gastronomical Guide of Italy lists over a dozen ways to prepare gnocchi, which does not surprise me. I have experimented with many ways to make these delicate dumplings, including this one for Pumpkin Gnocchi, a northern Italian specialty. Italian pumpkins tend to be sweeter than ours, so I have substituted butternut squash. These make a delightful first course for a fall dinner.

The dough is rather soft, but produces a very light *gnocco*. Be careful not to add more flour than needed. How much to add will depend on the wetness of the squash, the size of your egg, the flour used, and the humidity in the air. The recipe was tested in my kitchen on a wintry Saturday morning and used the amount of flour listed, but it is only a guide. Like potato gnocchi, these can be rolled off the tines of a fork at lightning speed, or fashioned delicately between the palms of your hands. They have a slightly sweet flavor that complements the rosemary sauce.

1½ pounds butternut squash

1 large egg

¼ cup grated Parmigiano-Reggiano cheese

⅓ cup finely crushed amaretti cookies (about 6 cookies)

¼ teaspoon freshly grated nutmeg

2 to 2½ cups unbleached all-purpose flour

Sauce

12 tablespoons (1½ sticks) butter

3 large fresh rosemary sprigs

Preheat the oven to 375°F.

Cut the squash in half lengthwise, scoop out the seeds and stringy membrane, and discard. Place the squash cut side down in a baking dish and add about ½ cup water. Cover the dish with aluminum foil and bake until the squash is tender, about 30 to 35 minutes.

Remove the squash from the oven and let cool completely. Scoop the flesh from the squash halves and place in a small sieve over a bowl. Press on the squash with a spoon to remove as much water as possible. There should be about 1¼ cups well-drained squash. Place the squash in a bowl and add the egg, cheese, amaretti, and nutmeg. Mix well to combine.

On a work surface, place 2 cups of flour in a mound and make a well or hole in the center. Scoop the squash mixture into the well and gradually begin adding the flour into the squash until you have a ball of dough. If you need more flour, add it a little at a time. This is a soft dough and too much flour will yield a heavy dumpling. To test for the right amount of flour, form a dumpling by pinching off a 1-inch piece, rolling it gently into an oblong shape, and placing it in a small pot of boiling water. If it holds together and does not disintegrate in the water, the flour-egg ratio is fine. If it falls apart, add more flour.

On a well-floured surface and with well-floured hands, knead the dough gently until it is smooth. Roll it into an 8-inch log. Cut the log into 4 equal pieces. Working with 1 piece at a time, roll each piece into a 20-inch-long rope about 1 inch wide. Cut each rope into forty ½-inch pieces and press each piece gently against the tines of a fork, or roll between the palms of your hand into a 1-inch oblong. Place the pieces on a floured towel. Let the gnocchi rest 15 minutes.

In a skillet, melt the butter, add the rosemary sprigs, and swirl them in the butter for several minutes to infuse the butter with their flavor. Remove the sprigs and discard. Keep the sauce covered and warm.

In 6 quarts of boiling water, cook the gnocchi until they rise to the surface, about 2 to 3 minutes. Drain carefully using a serrated spoon. Place the gnocchi in a serving platter and pour the butter sauce over them. Serve immediately.

Salse

Sauces

$\mathscr{W}$hile many antiquarian cooking manuscripts do exist, their focus is on the eating habits of well-to-do Italians. Although we do know that the peasants ate a type of gruel, there really is no written record of what the average person's diet consisted of.

According to Apicius, the Roman gourmet and food writer, fish, wine, and honey sauces were popular on Roman tables. *Garum,* a fish sauce, was made from sardines pounded into a pulp with spices such as oregano, fennel, and mint. Salt and vinegar were added and the sauce was served with meat, fish, or bread. The modern-day garum sauce is familiar to us as made with anchovies.

During the Renaissance, and especially during Lent and all other fast days, sauces made from dairy products, meat, or fowl were forbidden. Nuts, particularly almonds, were pounded into a pulp, mixed with water and bread, and used as a sauce. Today, Italians create their own regional flavorings using them sparingly, especially on pasta, to complement other ingredients.

Making a sauce can take many forms. There are long simmering ragù-type sauces, a combination of sautéed aromatic vegetables like carrots, celery, onions, and garlic with meat, either lamb, veal, pork, or beef, and some type of liquid. Most people think of tomatoes as an essential ingredient for a ragù, but there are ragù sauces that contain no tomatoes.

Battuto e Soffritto

The terms **battuto** *and* **soffritto** *are important to Italian cooking.* **Battuto** *comes from* **battere,** *which means "to beat," or in this case, to mince very fine.* **Soffritto** *derives from* **soffriggere,** *which means "to sauté, or fry in a small amount of fat."*

These two culinary techniques are usually employed together when making sauces, stews, and soups. To make a battuto, raw aromatic vegetables like celery, carrots, and onions, fresh herbs such as basil, rosemary, and thyme, garlic; and some pancetta are chopped with the aid of a mezzaluna ("rocking knife") until very fine, almost the consistency of a paste. A little olive oil is heated in a skillet, and the **battuto** *is added and becomes a* **soffritto,** *which means that the ingredients are sautéed gently until they are soft. At this point, the remaining ingredients for the dish are added and cooked.*

There are also quick sauces and uncooked sauces. Quick sauces include the combination of cream and cheese, or butter and cheese heated together to dress delicate strands of fettucine or rich, filled pasta such as tortellini.

Uncooked sauces include fresh tomatoes and oil served over hot spaghetti; pesto served over trenette, and even a bread-crumb sauce served over vegetables.

Above all, do not look for uniformity in Italian sauce making. As with all Italian cooking, creativity is left to the cook.

Salsa Fresca di Pomodori e Basilico

Fresh Tomato and Basil Sauce
Makes about 9 cups

When my grandmothers and mother made tomato sauce, sometimes a *battuto* of minced celery, carrot, and onion was used to flavor the sauce; or red wine was used to enrich it. Sometimes just fresh, ripe tomatoes simply flavored with basil and oil were the only ingredients. This sauce is versatile and can be used on everything from pizza and pasta to eggplant and calzoni.

5 pounds ripe plum tomatoes, or 3 28-ounce cans crushed plum tomatoes

½ cup extra-virgin olive oil

½ cup diced onion

3 cloves garlic, peeled and minced

1½ cups dry red wine

Coarse salt and black pepper to taste

4 or 5 sprigs fresh basil

If using fresh tomatoes, core them, cut them into coarse chunks, and puree in a food processor until smooth. Strain the fresh or canned tomatoes through a fine sieve to remove the seeds. Set aside.

In a deep heavy pot, heat the olive oil. Add the onion and sauté until soft. Add the garlic and sauté until soft. Add the fresh or canned tomatoes and stir to blend. Add the wine, salt and pepper, and basil and stir well. Bring to a boil, lower the heat, and simmer for 25 minutes. The sauce is ready to use, or it can be refrigerated for up to 1 week or frozen for up to 3 months.

Salsa di Pomodori Crudi

Uncooked Tomato Sauce
Makes 2 cups

On a recent trip to Italy, I had dinner at Benvenuto, a restaurant in Florence that the locals would rather tourists not know about. Before the restaurant opens regular customers line up in front of the place. Finally the owner unlocks the door and everyone files in, first to greet Cesare, the talking myna bird who bids each a *Buon Giorno,* and then to stake out a spot at long communal tables, where friends and strangers break bread together. The menu is typical Tuscan fare, but one of the best dishes is a simple plate of spaghetti topped with an uncooked tomato sauce and a knob of butter. This is the perfect quick-and-easy sauce to make when tomatoes, basil, and parsley are in season. The sauce can be prepared two days ahead and stored in the refrigerator.

½ cup extra-virgin
  olive oil

2 cloves garlic, peeled

7 large basil leaves,
  stemmed

¼ cup tightly packed
  parsley leaves,
  stemmed

½ teaspoon fine sea salt

Freshly ground black
  pepper to taste

1 pound (about 3 or 4)
  large meaty plum
  tomatoes

4 tablespoons (½ stick)
  butter

Pour the olive oil into a glass bowl and set aside. On a cutting board, place the garlic, basil, and parsley in a mound, mince the ingredients together with a knife, and add to the olive oil.

Core and cut the tomatoes in half and squeeze out the seeds. Dice the tomatoes and add them with the salt and pepper to the olive oil. Blend the sauce well with a spoon, cover the dish with plastic wrap, and refrigerate for 2 days before using; or cover the dish and marinate at room temperature for several hours for use the same day.

To serve, divide cooked spaghetti among individual serving bowls, then divide the sauce among the dishes, placing it on top of the spaghetti in the center. Add a tablespoon of butter to each bowl, and serve.

Salsa di Pomodori Secchi

Sun-Dried Tomato Sauce
Makes 1 cup

I demonstrated this sauce for guests at a dinner at the Four Seasons Hotel in Boston. From the looks on peoples' faces, it was a winner. This dense sauce can be made in minutes. Be sure to toss and coat the spaghetti or rigatoni well with the sauce.

¼ cup olive oil

1 large clove garlic, peeled and minced

4 anchovies in olive oil, drained and chopped

1 tablespoon salted capers, rinsed

1 cup oil-packed sun-dried tomatoes

4 tablespoons dry red wine

Coarsely ground black pepper to taste

Grated Parmigiano-Reggiano cheese, for serving

In a skillet, heat the olive oil, add the garlic and anchovies, and stir with a wooden spoon until the anchovies dissolve into the oil. Add the capers, tomatoes, and wine and cook 2 minutes, stirring often. Transfer the mixture to a food processor and pulse until the tomatoes are in small bits. Return the sauce to the skillet and reheat just before serving.

Salsa Pompeiana

Pompeii Sauce
Makes about 6 cups

If you like a slightly hot sauce, this is for you. It calls for fresh hot chili pepper, known as *peperoncino,* a common ingredient in southern Italian cooking. This sauce is put together very quickly and is good over spaghetti, for eggplant dishes, and as a topping for pizza. The sauce freezes very well.

½ cup olive oil

3 cloves garlic, peeled and chopped

1 fresh hot red pepper, finely chopped

6 cups chopped fresh or canned plum tomatoes

1 teaspoon coarse salt

5 or 6 basil leaves, chopped

In a saucepan, heat the olive oil, add the garlic and red pepper, and sauté until soft. Add the tomatoes and salt, mix well, and simmer the mixture for 15 minutes. Stir in the basil and cook 2 minutes more. The sauce is ready to use.

Variation: Add 1 cup (4 ounces) diced mozzarella cheese to 2 cups of Salsa Pompeiana. Heat until the cheese begins to melt.

Salsa di Acciugata
e Pomodori alla Maria

Maria's Anchovy and Tomato Sauce
Makes about 2 cups

For some time, I've been corresponding with a viewer from New Jersey, a young woman named Maria, whose family comes from Naples. We write in Italian, reminiscing about Italy and, of course, food. Maria loves to cook; she sends me her recipes and I reciprocate with some of mine. Her recipe for a quick tomato sauce is made memorable with the addition of anchovies and olives. The only change I made in her recipe was decreasing the number of *peperoncini,* or chili peppers.

1 2-ounce can flat anchovies in olive oil

1 clove garlic, peeled and minced

3 small red chili peppers

4 fresh basil leaves

⅔ cup pitted and chopped oil-cured black olives or ⅔ cup drained, pitted, and chopped green olives in brine

3 tablespoons minced fresh parsley

1 16-ounce can whole peeled plum tomatoes, chopped and juice reserved

Salt and pepper to taste

Drain the anchovies of their oil and place the oil in a frying pan over medium heat. Chop the anchovies fine. Add the anchovies, garlic, and chili peppers to the oil and sauté until the anchovies begin to dissolve, about 2 to 3 minutes. Add the basil, olives, and 1 teaspoon of the parsley and continue to cook a few minutes longer. Add the tomatoes with their juice and salt and pepper. Mix well, cover the pan, and let the sauce simmer for about 20 minutes. Add the remaining parsley to the sauce and serve immediately over spaghetti.

Note: I use very small dried chili peppers the size of my fingernail. If you do not like very hot sauces, reduce the number of peppers.

Salsa di Oliva Nera

Black Olive Sauce
Makes 1¼ cups

Prepare this pungent sauce early in the day and let it sit at room temperature so the flavors develop. I serve it over *farfalle,* or butterfly-shaped macaroni, but any short macaroni will do.

7 tablespoons olive oil

1 medium onion, peeled and diced

½ cup pitted and chopped black oil-cured olives (about 27 olives)

3 plum tomatoes, peeled, seeded, and diced

Salt to taste

Black pepper to taste

1 tablespoon chopped fresh parsley

In a saucepan, heat the olive oil, add the onion, and sauté over medium heat until the onion softens. Add the olives, tomatoes, salt, and pepper. Stir the mixture and let simmer, covered, for 10 minutes. Turn off the heat, add the parsley, and stir to blend. Let the sauce sit at room temperature several hours. When ready to use, reheat the sauce and pour it over pasta.

Pesto

Pesto
Makes 2 cups

Pesto, a regional specialty of Liguria, and in particular, the city of Genoa, is made from basil, a tender herb with a pungent flavor. Pesto is traditionally served over trenette, long strands of pasta, similar to tagliatelle. It is also wonderful on salmon steaks and as a final touch to Minestrone alla Moda Genovese (page 36).

1½ cups tightly packed fresh basil leaves	½ cup extra-virgin olive oil, plus extra for sealing
3 cloves garlic, peeled	¼ cup pine nuts
3 tablespoons grated Parmigiano-Reggiano or Pecorino Romano cheese	Salt and freshly ground black pepper, optional

In a food processor, combine the basil and garlic and process to a coarse puree. Add the cheese and process to blend. With the motor running, add the olive oil in a thin stream through the feed tube. Add the pine nuts and blend the mixture until smooth. Season with salt and pepper if you wish.

To store, transfer the pesto to a jar and pour a thin layer of olive oil over the top to preserve. Refrigerate up to 1 week.

Note: You can also make this the traditional way using a marble mortar and a wooden pestle. Grind the basil and garlic together to a coarse puree. Add the nuts and grind to a smooth puree. Blend in the cheese. Blend in the oil a little at a time. Season to taste.

Marinata di Gaetano

Guy's Marinade
Makes ⅔ cup

This *marinata* ("marinade") is my husband, Guy's creation, and we use it for marinating and grilling chicken breasts or large shrimp. The tangy lemon flavor nicely complements the fresh pesto. This recipe makes enough to marinate 2 pounds of boneless chicken breasts or shrimp.

⅓ cup extra-virgin olive oil	Juice of 1 lemon
2 tablespoons red wine vinegar	1 teaspoon grated lemon zest
3 tablespoons Pesto (page 92)	½ teaspoon salt
	¼ teaspoon black pepper

In a jar with a screw cap, combine all the ingredients and shake until well blended.

To use the marinade, place chicken pieces in a glass dish large enough to hold in 1 layer. Pour the marinade over the chicken, cover the dish, and refrigerate several hours before grilling. Turn the chicken pieces occasionally in the marinade. If using shrimp, peel them first before marinating.

Preheat the grill, place the chicken or shrimp on the grill, and cook, basting frequently with the marinade.

Ragù Casalinga

Homestyle Ragù
Makes 7 cups

 One frantic Saturday morning, when I was home between stops for my book tour, I looked in the refrigerator to see what my husband Guy had left while I was away. I spotted a handful of beans, a few carrots, and some dried-out prosciutto. I added some meat, a little bit of this and that, and I had a respectable ragù perfect for serving over rigatoni.

1¼ pounds top round
   steak, cut ¼ inch
   thick

1 medium onion,
   peeled and quartered

1 celery stalk,
   quartered

1 medium carrot,
   quartered

1 clove garlic, peeled

Leaves of 1 sprig fresh
   rosemary

2 ounces proscuitto,
   diced

¼ cup olive oil

1 teaspoon fine
   sea salt

1 teaspoon coarsely
   ground black pepper,
   or more

1 28-ounce can crushed
   plum tomatoes

½ cup sweet
   Marsala wine

1 cup fresh green beans,
   quartered

Wipe the meat with paper towels and cut into 1-inch pieces.

Make a battuto by mincing together the onion, celery, carrot, garlic, rosemary, and prosciutto. In a large skillet, heat the oil, add the battuto, and sauté slowly over low heat until the vegetables are soft but not brown. Transfer the vegetables to a dish.

Add the meat pieces to the skillet; do not crowd them. Brown the meat slowly on both sides, then sprinkle with the salt and pepper, and return the battuto to the pan.

In a bowl, mix the tomatoes with the wine and pour over the meat mixture. Mix with a wooden spoon. Cover the pan, reduce the heat to a simmer, and let the mixture cook 45 minutes. Add the beans, cover the pan, and continue to cook for 10 minutes or until the meat and beans are tender. Serve.

Ragù d'Agnello

Lamb Sauce
Makes 4 cups

This ragù, from the Abruzzi, is made with sweet as well as hot peppers. Serve over Maccheroni alla Chitarra (page 56).

3 cloves garlic, peeled and cut in half	1 bay leaf
2 tablespoons fresh rosemary leaves	1 pound ground lamb
2 tablespoons fresh thyme leaves	⅔ cup dry red wine
⅓ cup olive oil	1 1-pound can plum tomatoes, seeded, chopped, juice reserved
1 small hot red pepper, chopped	½ teaspoon salt or more to taste
2 medium red bell peppers, seeded and cut into thin strips	Freshly ground black pepper

With a knife, mince the garlic, rosemary, and thyme together to make battuto. Set aside.

In a medium skillet, sauté the minced battuto ingredients in the olive oil over medium heat until they begin to soften. Add the red pepper, sweet peppers, and bay leaf, and continue to sauté about 1 minute. Add the lamb and brown it slowly. Raise the heat to medium-high, add the wine, stir with a wooden spoon, and cook until most of the wine has evaporated.

Add the tomatoes, reserved tomato juice, salt, and pepper; stir well. Cover the skillet, lower the heat, and simmer for 30 minutes. Discard the bay leaf before serving.

Salsa di Cavolfiore
alla Signora Vallone

Mrs. Vallone's Cauliflower Sauce
Serves 4 to 6

This recipe comes from Mrs. Vallone, a friend of my parents. She called it Cauliflower Sauce, even though the cauliflower remains as florets when cooked. It is really spaghetti and cauliflower in tomato sauce.

1 head cauliflower, cut into 1-inch florets	1 28-ounce can crushed plum tomatoes
4 quarts boiling water	Freshly ground black pepper
1½ teaspoons salt	
⅓ cup olive oil	5 basil leaves, minced
3 medium cloves garlic, peeled and chopped	3 tablespoons grated Pecorino Romano cheese
1 large onion, finely chopped	1 pound spaghetti, broken into thirds
1 1-pound can whole plum tomatoes, chopped, juice reserved	

Cook the cauliflower in boiling water with 1 teaspoon salt until just tender, about 6 minutes. Drain the cauliflower, reserving the cooking water.

In a large skillet, sauté the garlic and onion in the olive oil until onion is soft. Add the chopped tomatoes and cook, covered, for about 6 minutes. Uncover the skillet, add the crushed tomatoes, remaining salt, and pepper, and continue to cook over medium-low heat for 15 minutes. Add the cauliflower, basil, and cheese. Stir, then cover and keep warm.

Bring the reserved cauliflower water to a boil, add the spaghetti, and cook until *al dente,* tender but not mushy. Drain the spaghetti well, then add it to the sauce, mixing well to distribute the ingredients. Serve immediately.

Variation: Add ½ cup pitted and chopped oil-cured olives to the sauce.

Salsa di Finocchio
e Panna

Fennel Cream Sauce
Makes 2½ cups

Crunchy, thin slices of fennel were a frequent part of the fresh salads served at home after the main meal. I also serve fennel as a baked or fried vegetable, and as a delicate and versatile sauce served over baked chicken, grilled fish, and fettucine. The sauce is enough to dress 1 pound of fettucine or linguine.

1 pound fennel	¾ teaspoon fine sea salt
1 teaspoon salt	1 cup heavy cream
3 tablespoons butter	½ teaspoon grated nutmeg
3 tablespoons minced shallots	¼ teaspoon coarsely ground black pepper
1 teaspoon fennel seeds	

Wash the fennel and trim any brown spots. Cut off the stalks and feathery leaves, and reserve. Cut the bulb in half lengthwise.

In a large pot, place the bulb, stalks, half the leaves, and salt. Fill the pot with water just to cover the ingredients, cover the pot, and bring to a boil. Boil the fennel about 15 minutes or until very soft. Remove the fennel, stalks, and leaves; reserve the cooking water. Discard the cooked leaves and stalks.

Cut the fennel halves into quarters and puree in a food processor or blender until smooth, adding ¼ cup of the cooking liquid through the feed tube. Set the fennel puree aside.

In a saucepan, heat the butter, add the shallots and fennel seeds, and sauté until the shallots are very soft but not brown. Add the fennel puree and sea salt, and cook, stirring with a wooden spoon, for about 3 minutes. Slowly add the cream, blending well.

Return the mixture to the food processor or blender and process until smooth. Transfer the sauce to a saucepan over low heat and add the

nutmeg, pepper, and 1 teaspoon of minced reserved fennel leaves. Stir to blend. The sauce is ready to serve.

Note: Boil the fettucine in the fennel cooking water for added flavor.

Salsa di Limone Arucola e Capperi

Lemon, Arugula, and Caper Sauce
Makes about ¾ cup

I like this green-flecked sauce served over grilled or baked salmon. The lemon and peppery arugula flavors are distinctive, so a little goes a long way. This sauce is also good on cold poached fish.

2 tablespoons (¼ stick) butter

1 clove garlic, peeled and minced

1 tablespoon unbleached all-purpose flour

2 tablespoons fresh lemon juice

½ cup dry white wine

1 cup chopped arugula leaves

1 tablespoon salted capers

⅛ teaspoon black pepper

In a small saucepan, heat the butter, add the garlic, and sauté until the garlic softens. Sprinkle on the flour, blend it in with a small whisk, and cook for about 2 minutes.

Mix the lemon juice and wine, stir into the mixture, and cook until it starts to thicken. Do not let the mixture get too thick. Add the arugula and cook about 1 minute. Add the capers and blend.

Pour the sauce into a food processor or blender and process until smooth. Return the sauce to the saucepan. Reheat and serve immediately over fish.

Note: If your sauce is too thick, thin it with a little water or white wine.

Salsa di Porcini

Porcini Mushroom Sauce
Makes about 2½ cups

Dried porcini mushrooms give this sauce its woodsy taste. The sauce can be made ahead and the cream added just before reheating. It can also be pureed in a food processor for a smoother texture, but I like the bits of porcini. Use it on a beef tenderloin or pork tenderloin roast.

1½ cups dried porcini
   mushrooms

1½ cups cold water

4 tablespoons
   (½ stick) butter

½ cup thinly sliced
   shallots

1 small clove garlic,
   peeled and minced

2 tablespoons
   unbleached all-purpose
   flour

½ cup dry red wine

Salt and pepper to taste

3 tablespoons heavy
   cream

Place the porcini in a bowl and cover with cold water. Soak until mushrooms are soft, about 30 to 35 minutes, then drain the porcini in a colander set over a bowl. Strain and reserve the liquid. Chop the porcini into small pieces and set aside.

In a skillet over medium heat, melt the butter and add the shallots. Sauté until the shallots begin to brown, then add the garlic and sauté until soft. Add the porcini and sauté about 5 minutes.

Sprinkle the flour over the mixture in the skillet and stir to blend. Lower the heat, add the wine, and simmer mixture for 2 to 3 minutes. Add 1 cup of the reserved mushroom liquid and stir until mixture begins to thicken slightly. Add salt, pepper, and cream, stirring constantly.

Note: If the mixture is too thick, thin it with a little of the reserved porcini liquid.

Salsa di Porcini

Porcini Mushroom Sauce
Makes 1½ cups

I use this porcini sauce for Chestnut Pasta (page 58). It is enough to dress about ½ pound of pasta. You can double the recipe if you wish.

½ cup dried porcini
    mushrooms

1½ cups cold water

2 tablespoons
    (¼ stick) butter

⅔ cup fresh button
    mushrooms, sliced

1½ tablespoons
    unbleached all-
    purpose flour

4 tablespoons heavy
    cream

Salt and pepper to taste

Place the porcini in a small bowl, cover with cold water, and let stand about 30 minutes or until soft. Drain the porcini, and strain and reserve the soaking water. Cut the porcini into small pieces and set aside.

In a skillet, melt the butter over medium heat, add the porcini and button mushrooms, and sauté until the button mushrooms begin to exude some of their juice. Sprinkle the mushrooms with the flour and sauté for 2 minutes more. Add 1¼ cups of the reserved soaking liquid and continue to stir until the mixture begins to thicken slightly. Lower the heat to medium-low, add the heavy cream, and blend well. Let it reduce about 5 minutes. Season with salt and pepper. Sauce is ready to serve.

Salsa di Besciamella

White Sauce
Makes 4 cups

This bechamel, or white sauce, can be used to make lasagne, cannelloni, and Gnocchi di Ricotta (page 76).

4 cups milk

8 tablespoons (1 stick) butter

½ cup unbleached all-purpose flour

1 teaspoon salt

½ teaspoon grated nutmeg

In a medium saucepan, scald the milk (bring to just under a boil), remove from the heat, and set aside.

In another saucepan, melt the butter over medium-high heat. Add the flour and stir with a wooden spoon until smooth, cooking the paste about 1 minute. Slowly stir in the milk, salt, and nutmeg; cook, stirring, until the mixture comes to a boil. Continue stirring until the sauce thickens, about 5 minutes. Remove the sauce from the heat. The sauce is ready to use.

*U*ova

Eggs

My grandmother Galasso kept a refrigerator shelf full of fresh eggs, which she collected on her weekly visits to the "chicken man." Eggs were used to enrich pasta and breads; made into *frittate* for lunch and dinner, boiled for breakfast, scrambled with vegetables such as zucchini for Saturday lunch, and stirred into pots of boiling soups. Ask for a fried egg and it came with a topping of tomato sauce.

I use large and extra-large eggs in all my recipes. But these terms are relative when comparing eggs in various grocery stores. I try to buy my eggs from people who raise laying hens, but I realize that this is not practical for most people. So how do you know how fresh an egg is? As Harold McGee explains in his book *On Food and Cooking,* the smaller the air cell in the egg, the better the egg. Eggs lose carbon dioxide and moisture if stored over long periods of time; their mass shrinks and the empty space at the widest end of the shell becomes larger. To test the freshness of an egg, put it in a pan of cold water; if it floats, it's an old egg; if it sinks to the bottom, it is fresh.

Are brown eggs better than white eggs? According to McGee: "Despite beliefs to the contrary, neither shell color nor the fertilization of the ovum has any nutritional significance." In today's health-conscious world, the advice is to be wary of consuming too many eggs because of the high cholesterol in egg yolks. In my grandmother's day, this was an unknown concern. We consumed eggs every day; my eighty-year-old father ate a boiled egg every morning for breakfast up until a few years ago; now he has one every other day, and is the picture of good health!

As with everything, moderation is the key.

Cassateddi ca Ricotta

Ricotta Cheese Pancakes
Serves 4

Ricotta cheese is really not cheese at all, but the recooked whey, or leftovers, from cheese making. The word *ricotta* means "recooked." True ricotta is made from sheep's milk. Most of what we buy in grocery stores is made from cow's milk, which bears little resemblance in flavor or texture to the real thing. My grandmothers also used a pressed and salted type of ricotta called ricotta salata, which can be grated and used with pasta, in fillings for vegetables, or in this savory thin pancake. Ricotta salata is available in grocery cheese sections. If unavailable, use Pecorino Romano cheese.

5 large eggs, beaten	Salt and pepper to taste
1 cup grated ricotta salata	⅓ cup olive oil
2 tablespoons toasted bread crumbs	2 roasted red bell peppers (page 174), cut in julienne strips
1 tablespoon minced fresh parsley	

In a bowl, beat the eggs with a whisk until light; add the cheese, bread crumbs, parsley, salt, and pepper to taste. Mix well, cover the bowl, and refrigerate for 2 hours to help thicken the batter.

In a 10- or 12-inch skillet, heat the oil until very hot. Using a ⅓-cup measure, pour out the mixture, spacing it as if making a small pancake. When the edges of the pancake start to brown and the top is not runny, carefully turn the pancake over using 2 spatulas and cook the other side until golden brown. Repeat with remaining batter.

Arrange pancakes on a serving plate and garnish with the strips of red pepper. Serve immediately.

Note: This is a delicious luncheon dish or can be served as part of an antipasto buffet. I use a warming tray.

Frittata con Ricotta

Ricotta Cheese Omelet
Serves 6

Many times I watched my grandmother Galasso take a scoop of fresh ricotta and fry it in olive oil and butter. When it was a light golden brown, she sprinkled black pepper and a little salt over it, and it became lunch with a piece of homemade bread. I make a frittata with eggs and cheese.

6 large eggs	½ teaspoon salt
1 tablespoon grated Parmigiano-Reggiano cheese	Freshly ground black pepper to taste
1⅓ cups ricotta cheese	2 tablespoons olive oil
2 tablespoons finely minced fresh parsley	1 teaspoon butter

In a bowl and with a wire whisk, beat the eggs and grated cheese until fluffy. Add the ricotta, parsley, salt, and pepper and whisk until the mixture is smooth. Set aside.

In a 12-inch skillet, heat 1 tablespoon of the olive oil and the butter until hot. Pour in the egg mixture and cook over medium heat until the bottom of the frittata starts to set.

Lift the edges of the frittata with a spatula and let the uncooked top mixture run underneath. Continue cooking until the top is not runny.

Place a flat dish or round pizza pan larger than the skillet over the top and invert the frittata onto it. Add the remaining olive oil to the skillet. Slide the frittata back into the skillet and cook the remaining side until set. Turn it out onto a serving dish and serve immediately, cut into wedges.

Frittata di Borragine

Borage Omelet
Serves 4 to 6

My grandmother Galasso used lots of greens in her cooking. Cardoons, dandelions, spinach, and escarole found their way into frittate of one sort or another. In Italy she used borage leaves, a plant that defies all boundaries and grows where it will among the crags, rocks, and roadsides of Italy. The young, tender leaves, with the taste of bitter cucumber, were used in salads. Larger leaves were cooked like spinach and used in omelets. If you can't find borage, use endive, Swiss chard, or spinach.

½ **pound borage,
stemmed, leaves
washed and drained**

6 **large eggs**

½ **cup grated
Parmigiano-Reggiano
cheese**

Salt and pepper to taste

1 **tablespoon olive oil**

1 **teaspoon butter**

Place the borage in a large frying pan. Add just enough water to cover the bottom of the pan. Cover the pan and cook the borage until wilted and tender, about 10 minutes. Drain the leaves in a colander, pressing on them with the back of a spoon to extrude as much water as possible. Cut the borage into pieces and set aside.

In a large bowl, whisk the eggs. Add the cheese and whisk to blend well. Add the borage, salt, and pepper and mix well.

In a frying pan, heat the olive oil and butter until hot. Add the egg mixture and cook until the eggs begin to set. Lift the edges of the frittata and let the uncooked egg run underneath. When the eggs are set, turn the frittata out onto a serving dish. Cut into wedges and serve.

Variation: Serve tomato sauce on the side, or place the wedge between 2 slices of peasant bread for a hearty sandwich.

Frocia d'Ova ca Pastetta

Fried Egg Sandwiches
Makes 18 sandwiches

Making sandwiches for my school lunchbox was Grandma Galasso's domain, but peanut butter sandwiches were very rare. Instead I could look forward to this elaborate egg sandwich, flecked with pieces of Swiss chard and salty cheese. It began as a frittata made with eggs and ricotta salata. After the frittata was cooked and cooled, it was cut into pieces and placed in a yeast dough. If eaten at home, it was topped with fresh tomato sauce. For school lunches, pieces were sandwiched between bread slices. If you can't find ricotta salata, substitute Pecorino Romano cheese.

Dough

1¾ cups very warm
    water (110° to
    115°F.)

1½ tablespoons active
    dry yeast

2 tablespoons sugar

1½ tablespoons olive oil

4 to 4½ cups unbleached
    all-purpose flour

1 teaspoon salt

6 to 8 cups vegetable
    oil, for frying

Filling

½ pound Swiss chard

6 large eggs

1 cup grated ricotta
    salata or Pecorino
    Romano cheese

¼ teaspoon freshly
    ground black pepper

1 tablespoon butter

1 tablespoon olive oil

2 cups tomato sauce

To make the dough, place the warm water in a large bowl and add the yeast. Mix well and let rest, covered, for 10 minutes. Add the sugar and olive oil and mix again.

In a separate bowl, mix 4 cups of the flour with the salt and add it gradually to the yeast mixture. Mix well with your hands until you have a ball of dough. Add additional flour if the dough seems sticky. Turn the dough out onto a floured board and knead it until smooth.

Lightly grease a bowl with a little oil and add the dough. Cover the bowl with plastic wrap and let rise until doubled, about 1½ hours.

Preheat the broiler.

Wash and stem the Swiss chard. Place it in a skillet with about 1½ cups water. Cover the skillet and cook until the chard is limp, about 6 minutes. Drain the chard well in a colander. Let cool 5 to 10 minutes, then squeeze dry with your hands and cut it into thin strips and set aside.

In a separate bowl, mix the eggs gently with a whisk. Add the chard, ricotta, and pepper; blend gently.

In a 12-inch ovenproof frying pan, heat the butter and olive oil until hot. Pour in the egg mixture and cook the frittata until it has set on the underside. Place the frying pan under the broiler and broil until the eggs set on top. Remove the pan from the broiler and invert frittata onto a wood board; let frittata cool. Cut into ¼-inch-wide strips about 2 inches long and set aside.

Punch the dough and knead for a few minutes on a lightly floured surface. Divide the dough into 18 pieces and roll each out with a rolling pin into a 5-inch circle. Lay a few strips of the frittata in the center and fold the dough over to make a turnover. Press the edges closed with a fork. Place them on a clean towel.

In an deep-fryer, heat the oil to 375°F. Add a few of the turnovers at a time and fry until golden brown. Drain on brown paper.

Serve the turnovers with a dollup of tomato sauce over the top.

Variation: Eliminate making the dough and place wedges of frittata between slices of good bread.

Uova Strapazzate alle Erbe

Scrambled Eggs with Herbs
Serves 4

Every morning before going to school I could count on having a soft-boiled or scrambled egg. On Sundays, eggs were dressed up a bit with the addition of fresh herbs.

6 large eggs	1 tablespoon minced fresh marjoram
3 tablespoons milk	½ teaspoon salt
1 tablespoon minced fresh parsley	Black pepper to taste
2 tablespoons minced scallion tops	3 tablespoons butter

In a bowl, beat the eggs and milk with a whisk. Add the herbs, salt, and pepper; blend well, then set aside.

In a skillet, heat the butter but do not let it brown. Add the egg mixture and scramble the eggs with a fork until set. Serve at once.

Carne e Pollame

Meat and Poultry

Cooking and teaching in the kitchens of Italy is a sharing and learning process for me as well as my students. I have cooked in everything from well-equipped professional kitchens to some very primitive ones. No matter where I cook I come away each time with a greater appreciation for the foods of Italy and the ways in which the cook respects and prepares them. I have also come to realize that the right attitude is important when cooking in Italy. In other words, "When in Italy, do as the Italians do."

Not long ago I went to Italy to give cooking classes to Americans in Montalcino, a quiet Tuscan town famous for its Brunello wine. For one particular class, I was focusing on meat and planned to prepare a country rabbit dish with wine and juniper berries and then two simple veal dishes. The students were to meet me early in the morning in the town's community center kitchen used occasionally, I was told, for special functions.

Bright and early and eager to get cooking, I walked the mile and a half from my hotel. Along the way were breathtaking views of deep valleys and neat stone houses with peach and flower trees and vegetable gardens. Finally arriving at the center, I made my way through the old stone building to the kitchen. My heart sank when I saw it. An old beat-up stove, a refrigerator the size of my high school locker, and a stone sink that the ancient Romans would have recognized were at my disposal in a narrow room that I doubted would comfortably hold the ten students who were waiting for me. I took a deep breath and greeted everyone with a high-pitched "*Buon Giorno,*" not having time to check to see what kinds of pots, pans, and utensils were available.

I spent more time improvising than cooking. First was the rabbit lesson. When I asked for two rabbits, I assumed I would get cut-up rabbits all ready for the next step. Instead awaiting me were two whole, freshly skinned but otherwise uncleaned rabbits. I knew no one in the class would ever deal with rabbit this way, so I quickly motioned to my husband to help me perform a private disjointing of the rabbit as well as removal of the entrails. That done, I could now present the recipe to the students. They were to brown the rabbit first in oil and pancetta, make a sauce with the drippings, and then finish baking the dish.

Alas, we had only one frying pan, two forks, and a battered baking dish. That was only the beginning. We also had a gas oven with a fickle pilot light. When we did get it started, the oven only heated to lukewarm. We looked like a team of oven assembly-line workers, all trying our best to get the oven going.

My husband could see my frustration and was determined to keep what little equipment we had in the kitchen at the ready. He would wash the pot or utensil I had used and have it ready for the next step. That's where I ran into trouble. Distracted by the almost useless oven, I decided to get the browning of the rabbit pieces done. I directed the students' attention to the top of the stove where I was working, all the while explaining that from the drippings in the pan we would make our sauce, and how this dish would be better than what we could have prepared stateside, because the rabbit was freshly killed and Italians buy their meat fresh daily at the market. I explained that meat is not eaten as often as vegetables, pasta, rice, and beans, and that Italians love to stuff meat with all kinds of savory fillings perfumed with herbs.

As the pieces browned, I removed them to the one dish we had. When I was finished, I prepared to make the sauce. Unfortunately, my well-meaning and organized husband was one step ahead of me, having rid the pan of all the drippings while I was talking, and cleaned and returned it to the burner ready for the next recipe. You can imagine my despair when I discovered that the drippings had been thrown out! And so we improvised once again, using a bit of pancetta, olive oil, and wine to reproduce our drippings. We forgot about the oven and finished the dish atop the stove. Somehow it all turned out. And it taught a lesson more important than the one I had planned: Whether in the kitchens of Italy or at home, ingenuity and adaptability are the secrets of good cooking.

Granatini

Little Meat Bundles
Serves 6

Meats stuffed and rolled with vegetables, bread crumbs, cheese, and cured meats are an Italian specialty. The word *involtini* on an Italian menu means either a little bundle of meat stuffed with a savory filling, or a stuffed and rolled vegetable such as eggplant or sweet peppers. In Sicily, they are called *granatini*.

2 pounds veal or pork cutlets, sliced into 12 4- x 2-inch slices and pounded thin	1 cup dry white wine
⅔ pound freshly ground pork sausage	3½ cups Fresh Tomato and Basil Sauce (page 85)
Flour, for dredging	3 or 4 fresh basil leaves, torn into small pieces
3 tablespoons olive oil	1 teaspoon salt
3 tablespoons butter	¼ teaspoon coarsely ground black pepper
1 large onion, peeled and thinly sliced	2 cups shelled peas

Divide the sausage meat among the meat slices and roll each piece up like a jelly roll. Hold the rolls closed with toothpicks or tie with string. Roll the pieces in flour, shaking off the excess. Set aside.

In a large skillet, heat the olive oil and brown the rolls on all sides. Remove the rolls to a dish.

Add the butter to the skillet and sauté the onion until soft and glazed. Add the wine, tomato sauce, basil, salt, and pepper. Stir with a wooden spoon to blend well.

Return the meat rolls to the skillet, cover the pan, and gently cook for 15 to 20 minutes, or until a fork easily pierces the meat.

Add the peas and cook 2 to 3 minutes longer. Serve the rolls with some of the sauce poured over them.

Note: I often serve this dish with a side of penne, a slant cut of macaroni. It is also very good with rice or wedges of polenta.

Involtini della Nonna

Grandma's Meat Bundles
Serves 4

Imagination was always the key to home cooking. Such was the case when my grandmother and mother wanted to make rolled veal bundles (*involtini*) without the veal! They substituted boneless pork. The results can fool company!

6 tablespoons extra-
virgin olive oil

2 ounces prosciutto,
diced

¼ cup diced onion

6 tablespoons toasted
bread crumbs

¼ cup chopped walnuts

½ cup raisins, minced

2 tablespoons grated
Pecorino Romano
cheese

1 tablespoon minced sage
leaves

1 large egg

Salt and pepper to taste

8 small boned pork chops

Flour, for dredging

1 cup sweet Marsala wine

2 tablespoons water

2 tablespoons (¼ stick)
butter

In a skillet, heat 3 tablespoons olive oil, add the prosciutto and onion, and sauté until the onion is soft and the prosciutto begins to brown. Add the bread crumbs and continue sautéing until the crumbs pick up the excess oil. Add the walnuts and raisins, and blend, cooking about 1 minute.

Transfer the mixture to a bowl, add the cheese, sage leaves, and egg, and mix well. Season to taste with salt and pepper, and set aside.

Trim the pork pieces of any visible fat, then pound with a meat hammer until no more than ⅛ inch thick, at least 4 inches wide, and 5 inches long. Divide the filling among the pork pieces, spreading it evenly. Roll up each piece like a jelly roll and tie with string or hold in place with toothpicks.

Place some flour on a plate and roll the meat bundles in it, shaking off the excess. Set the bundles aside.

Wipe out the skillet, heat the remaining 3 tablespoons olive oil and brown the meat bundles well on all sides. Transfer the rolls to a warm platter. Turn the heat to high, scrape up any of the meat bits that have clung to the pan, and add the wine and water. Cook, stirring until it boils, then remove from the heat, add the butter, and beat with a whisk until the sauce has thickened a little. Pour the sauce over the rolls and serve immediately.

Stracotto alla Lombarda

Beef Stew, Lombardy Style
Serves 6

The success of this classic beef stew from Lombardy depends on several things: the marinating time (overnight is best), the use of a good red wine, and the flavoring of the onions with pancetta, or Italian bacon. Once cooked, the stew is even better the next day, served with slices of golden polenta.

3 pounds boneless rump
  or eye round roast

2½ cups dry red wine
  such as Barolo

1 cup diced onion

1 large clove garlic,
  peeled and minced

1 rib celery, diced

¼ teaspoon freshly
  grated nutmeg

2 bay leaves

2 whole cloves

4 tablespoons
  (½ stick) butter

½ cup diced pancetta

2 tablespoons all-
  purpose flour

Coarse salt and pepper to
  taste

Place the meat in a deep heatproof, noncorrosive casserole just large enough to hold it. Add the wine, half the onion, and the garlic, celery, nutmeg, bay leaves, and cloves. Cover the meat and refrigerate several hours or overnight, turning the meat occasionally.

When ready to cook, drain the meat from the marinade and wipe dry. Drain the vegetables and reserve. Save the marinade.

Wipe the casserole dry and melt the butter. Add the pancetta and the remaining onion. Sauté for 3 or 4 minutes or until the pancetta just begins to crisp and the onion is soft. Transfer the mixture to a plate and reserve.

Rub the meat with the flour and add to the drippings in the casserole. Brown the meat slowly on all sides. Return the pancetta mixture to the casserole along with the reserved vegetables. Cook slowly about 5 to 10 minutes. Add salt and pepper to taste, and pour in the reserved marinade. Bring the mixture to the boil, then lower the heat to a simmer, cover the pot, and cook about 2 hours or until the meat is tender.

Remove the meat to a platter. Remove the bay leaves and cloves and discard. Place the remaining liquid and vegetables in a food processor or blender and pulse until smooth. Slice the meat and top with the sauce.

Spezzatino alla Birra Scura

Beef Stew in Dark Beer
Serves 4

The Egyptians are credited with inventing beer. Papyri from around 1300 B.C. called for the regulation of beer shops to prevent the excesses of beer drinking. Since that time, beer has been an ingredient in cooking as well. One of the dishes that I recall from my childhood is a beef stew long simmered in beer, then served over polenta, potatoes, rice, or pasta. It was even better served the next day. I have reduced the original recipe considerably, but you can successfully double the ingredients.

¾ teaspoon coarsely
ground black pepper

1½ teaspoons fine
sea salt

1½ pounds boneless beef
chuck, cut into
1-inch pieces

5 tablespoons olive oil
or lard

1 large onion, peeled and
cut into thin slices

1 bay leaf

3 tablespoons tomato
paste

1 12-ounce can dark beer

On a plate, mix the salt and pepper. Add the meat pieces and toss to coat well. Set aside.

In a heavy skillet or Dutch oven, heat the olive oil over medium-low heat. Add the onion and bay leaf, and cook until the onion is wilted and very soft, but not brown.

Raise the heat to medium-high, add the beef pieces, and brown well.

In a small bowl, mix the tomato paste with the beer. Let the foam subside, then add the mixture to the beef. Stir well, bring to a boil, then lower the heat to simmer, cover the skillet, and cook until beef is tender, about 45 minutes.

Serve immediately.

Ossobuchi in Vino

Veal Shanks in Red Wine
Serves 4

*O*ssobuco literally means "a bone with a hole in it," but it has become synonymous with the veal shank and marrow. The Milanese way to prepare it is to braise it slowly and then serve it with gremolada, a mixture of fresh lemon zest, garlic, and parsley. I deviate from the classic here, incorporating the sauce ingredients in a different way, and then slow-simmer the veal in red wine with onions and shallots. Make sure to use a heavy Dutch oven large enough to hold the ossobuchi in one layer. Serve this with oven-roasted potatoes and fresh asparagus.

3 to 4 tablespoons
olive oil

2 medium onions, peeled
and sliced

2 shallots, peeled and
sliced

2 cloves garlic, peeled
and sliced

4 veal shanks, 1½ to
2 inches thick (about
2½ pounds)

½ teaspoon salt

Freshly ground pepper

⅔ cup or more dry red
wine

1 tablespoon fresh lemon
juice

2 tablespoons minced
fresh parsley

In a heavy pot, heat the olive oil, add the onions and shallots, and sauté slowly until they begin to soften. Add the garlic and continue to sauté until the garlic softens.

Add the veal shanks and brown slowly on both sides. Sprinkle with salt and pepper, then slowly add the wine, lemon juice, and parsley. Stir to blend, cover the pot, lower the heat, and simmer for 45 minutes to 1 hour, or until fork-tender. Add more wine as needed to keep the meat from drying out. Serve the veal shanks immediately, with some pan juices.

Tournedos allo Speck

Fillet of Beef with Speck
Serves 4

Speck is aged, smoked pork thigh, made in the Alto-Adige region of Italy. It lends a wonderful flavor to stews and stuffings. To recreate this elegant *secondo piatto,* or second course, of fillet of beef or tournedos, substitute smoked bacon for the speck. This is an expensive but quick dinner party choice.

4 tablespoons olive oil	Salt and pepper to taste
2 large shallots, peeled and minced	1 tablespoon Dijon mustard
4 ounces lean smoked bacon, cut into thin strips	4 tablespoons cognac
	½ cup heavy cream
1 bay leaf	1 tablespoon minced fresh parsley
4 beef fillets (6 ounces each)	

In a skillet, heat the olive oil, add the shallots, bacon, and bay leaf, and sauté the mixture until the bacon begins to brown. Add the fillets and brown for about 4 minutes on each side. Salt and pepper the fillets to taste, remove from the skillet to an ovenproof plate, and keep warm. Discard the bay leaf.

Add the mustard and cognac to the drippings in the skillet, mix well, then add the cream and parsley. Bring the mixture to a boil, stirring constantly. Return the fillets to the skillet along with their juices and cook for about 2 to 3 minutes.

Place the fillets on a serving platter, pour over the sauce, and serve immediately.

Note: This dish is also good with pancetta, or Italian unsmoked bacon.

Portafogli di Lonza

Stuffed Pork Chops
Serves 6

In this company dish, which I serve often, center-cut pork chops with pockets (*portafogli*), house a savory stuffing of ham and cheese. I team this dish with individual rice timbale and sautéed spinach with pine nuts and raisins.

6 center-cut pork chops ¾-inch (about 2½ pounds), with pockets cut in	1 tablespoon chopped fresh Italian parsley
¼ pound ham, diced (about 1 cup)	½ teaspoon salt
2 ounces mozzarella cheese, diced (½ cup)	¼ teaspoon coarsely ground black pepper
1 large egg, beaten	2 tablespoons (¼ stick) butter
2 tablespoons grated Parmigiano-Reggiano cheese	3 fresh sage leaves
2 tablespoons fresh bread crumbs	3 tablespoons dry Marsala wine
	½ cup water

Wipe the chops dry with a paper towel and set aside.

In a bowl, mix the ham, mozzarella, egg, Parmigiano-Reggiano, bread crumbs, parsley, salt, and pepper. There should be about 1½ cups stuffing. Open each pocket in the chops and fill with 2 tablespoons stuffing. Close with toothpicks or sew shut with string. Set aside.

Preheat the oven to 350°F.

In a large ovenproof skillet, melt the butter, add the sage and pork chops, and brown the meat over medium-high heat for about 2 minutes on each side. Add the wine and water.

Place the skillet in the oven and bake for 8 minutes. Cover the pan with a lid or tightly with foil and continue to bake for 25 to 30 minutes more, or until the meat is fork-tender. Serve at once with some pan juices poured over the top.

Costolette di Maiale
con Salsa di Porcini

Pork Chops with Porcini Mushroom Sauce
Serves 4

These pork chops are made memorable by the addition of porcini and button mushrooms blended together. Although porcini are expensive, you need only a few to release their distinctive, earthy flavor.

½ cup (1 ounce) dried porcini

1 cup cold water

Flour, for dredging

8 center-cut pork chops, ½ inch thick (1¾ pounds)

¾ cup toasted bread crumbs

½ teaspoon salt

¼ teaspoon black pepper

1 tablespoon minced fresh parsley

2 large eggs, lightly beaten

¼ cup plus 2 tablespoons olive oil

2 tablespoons (¼ stick) butter

1 teaspoon minced garlic

2 cups sliced fresh button mushrooms

Place the porcini in a bowl, add the cold water, and soak for about 30 minutes. Cut the porcini into small pieces and set aside. Drain the soaking liquid through a strainer lined with cheesecloth, then reserve the liquid.

Place some flour on a plate and lightly coat the chops on both sides, shaking off the excess.

On another plate, spread the bread crumbs and season with the salt, pepper, and parsley. Dip the pork chops in the beaten egg and then in the bread crumbs, coating both sides. Place the chops on a plate and let them "dry" for about 10 minutes.

In a skillet large enough to hold all the pork chops, heat ¼ cup of oil and 1 tablespoon of butter. Fry the chops over medium-high heat for 6 to 7 minutes on each side, until nicely browned. Remove the chops to a serving dish and keep warm.

Put the remaining oil and butter in the skillet. Add the garlic, porcini, and button mushrooms and sauté until mushrooms are soft but not watery. Sprinkle in 1 tablespoon of flour and stir quickly to blend with the mushrooms. Slowly add the reserved porcini liquid and stir until the sauce has thickened slightly, about 1 minute. Pour the sauce over the pork chops and serve immediately.

Salsiccia Fresca

Fresh Sausage
Makes 5 pounds

One of the culinary triumphs in Italian regional cooking is the ability of the *macellaio* ("sausage maker") to flavor his product unique from his fellow sausage makers. But flavor has a lot to do with what the pigs are fed— anything from acorns and grain to the whey left over from cheese making. The parts of the pig used to make sausage are important, too. The butt is popular, but in some areas pork shoulder is used.

The right balance of fat to meat is important otherwise the sausage will be too dry. I use 70 percent meat to 30 percent fat. Seasonings are the whim of the cook, but coarse salt, butcher's pepper, and fennel seeds are commonplace. Sometimes sage and hot red pepper are also added. Once ground, the seasoned meat is pushed into hog casings and tied at the end. Sausage can be grilled, fried, or baked. It also freezes well, uncooked, for up to 3 months.

5 pounds boneless pork butt with some fat, ground once on coarse grind and once on medium grind

2 tablespoons coarse salt, or more to taste

2 tablespoons coarsely ground black pepper, or more to taste

3 tablespoons fennel seeds

1 tablespoon crushed dried red pepper flakes, or more to taste

1 1-pound package natural hog casings (available in meat section of your grocery store or in butcher shops)

In a large bowl, combine the pork and seasonings; mix well. Test for seasoning by frying a small patty; add seasoning, if necessary.

In another bowl, soak 3 casings in several changes of cold water to remove the salt. Cut the casings into 12- to 14-inch lengths, if necessary. (Keep the remaining casings still packed in salt in the refrigerator for future use.)

Slip one end of a casing onto the throat of a sausage funnel. Place the funnel under the kitchen faucet and run cold water through casing. With the water running, slide the casing further up onto the funnel, leaving about 3 inches at the end. Turn off the water and tie a knot in the end of the casing.

Push the sausage meat, a little at a time, through the funnel with your thumb. Fill the casing, leaving about 2 inches free at the end to knot; do not pack too tightly. Tie the end and poke holes with a toothpick in the casing to release any air bubbles. Repeat with the remaining sausage meat and casings. Cook immediately, or refrigerate for up to 2 days.

To bake the sausages, preheat the oven to 350°F. Place the sausages in a baking dish and add just enough water to cover the bottom of the pan. Bake, uncovered, for 25 to 30 minutes, or until nicely browned; as excess water and fat accumulate in the pan, drain off. Drain sausages on paper towels and serve.

To fry, place the sausages in a large skillet and add just enough water to cover the bottom of the pan. Cook over medium heat, turning occasionally, for 25 to 30 minutes, or until browned; as excess water and fat accumulate in the pan, drain off. Drain sausages on paper towels and serve.

Pollo al Sale

Chicken Roasted in Salt
Serves 4

Italians use two types of salt in their cooking, fine and coarse. I prefer the flavor of fine sea salt. Sea salt is not chemically treated like table salt. I use coarse salt for sprinkling over roasts and for preserving herbs like basil. I also like it literally smothering this roasted chicken. The heavy salt layer acts like a cooking vessel and seals in the juices of the chicken.

2 cloves garlic, peeled
and chopped

1 roasting chicken (about
3½ pounds), washed
and dried

Leaves from 1 large sprig
rosemary

3 or 4 fresh sage leaves

Juice of 1 lemon

2 pounds coarse salt

Place the garlic in the cavity of the chicken. Lift up the breast skin with your hand, and randomly place the rosemary and sage between the skin and meat. Close the chicken cavity with string, tying the tail, drumsticks, and wings together. Rub the outside of the chicken all over with the lemon juice.

Preheat the oven to 375°F.

In a roasting pan just large enough to hold the chicken, spread 3 cups of the salt. Place the chicken directly on the salt and pat the remaining salt over the chicken to cover it.

Roast the chicken for 1 to 1½ hours, or until a drumstick can easily be pulled away from the body. Remove the chicken to a cutting board and pry off and discard the salt layer. Cut the chicken into pieces and serve immediately.

Note: For a little *alta cucina,* or improvised cooking, serve this with a sauce of fresh cranberries, pears, and dried prunes (page 286).

Petti di Pollo con Arucola

Chicken Breasts with Arugula
Serves 4

Peppery arugula and ricotta salata are the perfect stuffing for this chicken dish. Arugula is a salad green with a definite taste of radish, usually served in a salad, mixed with other greens. Cooked, it is used as a filling for ravioli. Ricotta salata is a salted sheep's milk cheese that is delicious grated over pasta and in stuffings. A good substitute is Pecorino Romano cheese.

¼ **pound arugula**

¼ **cup water**

4 **tablespoons olive oil**

2 **ounces (3 slices)
prosciutto, diced**

1 **clove garlic, peeled
and minced**

½ **cup (2 ounces) grated
ricotta salata**

½ **cup toasted bread
crumbs**

1 **tablespoon minced
rosemary leaves**

½ **teaspoon fine
sea salt**

**Freshly ground black
pepper**

1¼ **pounds boned
chicken breasts**

Wash and stem the arugula and place the leaves in a small saucepan. Add the water, cover the pan, and cook until the arugula wilts, about 3 minutes. Drain in a colander, pressing on the arugula with the back of a spoon. Chop fine and place in a bowl. There should be ½ cup.

In the same saucepan, heat 1 tablespoon of the olive oil, add the prosciutto, and sauté until it begins to brown. Add the garlic and sauté until soft.

Add the prosciutto, garlic, cheese, and pepper to the arugula. Mix and set aside.

Preheat the oven to 350°F.

In a dish, mix the bread crumbs, rosemary, salt, and pepper. Set aside.

Remove any visible skin or fat from the chicken breasts. With a small, sharp knife, make a 3-inch-long and 1-inch-deep slit along one side of each breast. Stuff some of the arugula filling in each breast and close with a toothpick.

Brush each breast on both sides with 2 tablespoons of the remaining oil, then lightly press some of the bread crumb mixture all over to coat breasts.

Brush a 9-inch baking dish with the remaining tablespoon of oil. Arrange the breasts in a single layer and bake for about 35 minutes, or until fork-tender and nicely browned. Serve immediately.

Pollo e Patate con Vino

Chicken and Potatoes with Wine
Serves 6 to 8

This medley of vegetables, fresh herbs, and chicken is best when prepared a day in advance.

8 or 9 small potatoes (about 11 ounces)	2 tablespoons (¼ stick) butter
1 teaspoon salt	3 tablespoons olive oil
1 medium onion, peeled and quartered	½ cup dry white wine
1 rib celery, cleaned and quartered	4 tablespoons tomato paste
1 medium carrot, peeled and quartered	2½ cups hot Beef or Chicken Broth (page 32 or 31)
1 small clove garlic, peeled	2 ounces prosciutto, cut into strips
2 fresh sage leaves	Fine sea salt to taste
Leaves from 1 large sprig fresh rosemary	Coarsely ground black pepper to taste
3½ pounds chicken drumsticks	2 tablespoons minced fresh Italian parsley
Flour, for dredging	

Wash the potatoes well and set aside. Bring a medium saucepan two-thirds full of water to a boil. Add the salt and the potatoes, and boil for 7 to 8 minutes, or until semicooked. Drain the potatoes in a colander and set aside.

Place the onion, celery, and carrot on a cutting board along with the garlic, sage, and rosemary leaves. With a knife, finely dice the vegetables and seasonings together. Set aside.

Wash and dry the chicken pieces. Dredge in flour, shake off the excess, and set aside.

In a large heatproof casserole or frying pan, heat the butter and olive oil. Add the minced vegetables and cook slowly over low heat for 5 to 8 minutes, or until the vegetables are soft but not browned.

Add the chicken pieces and continue to cook over low heat, turning the pieces to brown evenly. Raise the heat to medium-high, add the wine, and cook until it evaporates, about 5 minutes.

Dissolve the tomato paste in the hot broth. Add half the broth to the chicken, stir, cover the pot, and let cook over medium heat for 20 minutes.

Peel the potatoes and cut in half. Add along with the remaining broth to the chicken and cook, covered, for 20 minutes longer, or until the chicken is tender. Five minutes before the chicken is cooked, add the prosciutto, sea salt, and pepper.

To serve, place the chicken on a dish with the sauce. Sprinkle on the parsley.

Note: I cook this in the same dish that I plan to serve in.

Variation: Use turkey instead of chicken.

Pollo Rustico

Rustic Chicken
Serves 4

My husband loves this rustic chicken dish, which is even better eaten the day after it is prepared. The pancetta and onions add the right balance of flavor. Team this dish with polenta, pasta, rice, or potatoes.

1½ cups cubed eggplant	2 whole chicken breasts
Salt	(about 2 pounds)
¼ to ½ cup peanut oil	½ teaspoon fine sea salt
2 ounces pancetta, diced	¼ teaspoon coarsely ground black pepper
1 medium white onion, peeled and thinly sliced	¾ cup dry white wine
1 large clove garlic, peeled and minced	2 ripe large plum tomatoes, diced
2 tablespoons olive oil	3 or 4 fresh basil leaves, chopped

Place the eggplant in a colander. Sprinkle with salt and let stand for 1 hour. Rinse and dry well.

In a skillet, heat ¼ cup peanut oil. Add the eggplant and sauté until soft, about 6 to 7 minutes. Add more oil as needed. Set the eggplant aside.

In a heavy, heatproof 9-inch deep casserole, sauté the pancetta over medium-high heat until it begins to brown. Add the onion and sauté until soft. Add the garlic and continue cooking until garlic is soft. Remove the ingredients to a dish and set aside.

Heat the olive oil in the casserole, add the chicken breasts, and brown slowly on each side. Sprinkle with salt and pepper. Add the reserved pancetta mixture along with the wine, tomatoes, and basil and stir to blend well.

Cover the casserole and cook the chicken slowly for 45 minutes. Add the eggplant and cook 5 minutes more. Remove the chicken breasts to a cutting board and cut in half. Serve the chicken with the vegetable mixture spooned over the top.

Fegatini di Pollo con Cipolle

Chicken Livers and Onions
Serves 4

Our refrigerator at home had geographic boundaries—some shelves devoted to Italian food, others to "American" food. But there were no half-eaten bowls of shimmering gelatin, processed cheese spread, or canned luncheon meat. Instead, there was tripe waiting to be washed and cooked in tomato sauce, a huge zucchini salad took up most of one refrigerator shelf, and chicken feet, heads, and necks waited to be turned into broth. Chicken livers were there too, the standard fare for Saturday-night dinner. How I hated them! My parents and grandmother always scolded us about rebelling against eating chicken livers. My mother not only relishes that I actually cook them now, but also can't get over that I would include them in my cookbook. Be sure not to overcook the livers or they will be tough.

1½ **pounds chicken livers**

5 **tablespoons olive oil**

3 **tablespoons butter**

2 **medium white onions, thinly sliced**

2 **tablespoons chopped fresh Italian parsley**

¼ **cup dry red wine**

Fine sea salt to taste

½ **teaspoon coarsely ground black pepper**

Wash the livers well under cold water and pat dry. Set aside.

Heat the oil and butter in a skillet. Add the onions and sauté slowly until almost caramelized; add more butter and oil if necessary. Remove the onions to a dish.

Raise the heat to medium-high, add the livers, and cook about 2 minutes, turning frequently. Return the onions to the skillet, sprinkle on the parsley, add the wine, and stir well. Cover the skillet and cook about 4 minutes more.

Remove the livers to a serving dish and season with salt and pepper. Serve immediately.

Coniglio alla Moda Mia

Rabbit, My Way
Serves 4

Wild game dishes are very popular in Italy. In this recipe wild rabbit is marinated overnight in lemon juice and water to take away some of the "gamey" taste. If you like a stronger flavor or are using domestic rabbit, eliminate the marinating.

3 pounds wild or domestic rabbit, cut up	3 tablespoons red wine vinegar
Juice of 1 lemon	2½ cups peeled, seeded, and crushed plum tomatoes
¼ cup olive oil	
⅔ cup diced pancetta or prosciutto	½ cup dry white wine
1 medium white onion, peeled and thinly sliced	2 tablespoons minced fresh sage
	1 teaspoon coarse salt
2 cloves garlic, peeled and minced	1 teaspoon coarsely ground black pepper

Place the rabbit in a noncorrosive dish, pour in the lemon juice, and add enough cold water to come to the top of the dish. Cover and marinate in the refrigerator overnight. Drain rabbit and pat dry.

Preheat the oven to 350°F.

In a heavy ovenproof skillet, heat the olive oil, add the pancetta or prosciutto, and the rabbit pieces, and brown quickly on all sides. Remove rabbit and pancetta to a dish.

Add the onion to the skillet and sauté until soft. Add the garlic and also sauté until soft. Add the vinegar, tomatoes, and wine, mix well, then simmer the mixture for 5 minutes.

Add the sage, salt, and pepper to the skillet. Return the rabbit and pancetta to the pan, cover pan with foil, and bake for 35 to 45 minutes or until the rabbit is easily pierced with a fork. Serve with the sauce poured over the rabbit.

Note: Serve this dish with polenta and pour some of the sauce over the slices.

Anatra alla Griglia

Grilled Duck
Serves 4

The French claim duck with orange sauce as their creation. Italians argue that they, and particularly Catherine de Medici, introduced the French to good cooking and *anatra all'arancia*, or orange-sauced duck. In checking the work of Apicius, I found in Book IV, entitled "Fowl," six recipes for *anatem*, or duck. The sauces were made from spices, particularly coriander, cumin, celery seed, caraway, rue, and pepper. Herbs such as mint, oregano, lovage, and myrtle berries were added along with wine, honey, vinegar, mustard, and broth. Cooked down, this would taste like an *agrodolce*, or sweet-and-sour sauce. No oranges were listed.

My version borrows on the ancient work of Apicius. I use wild duck, which has a strong flavor and should be marinated a day before cooking, turned frequently in the marinade. Done on a grill, it is superb, but oven roasting is fine too.

1 3½-pound duck, boned	1 teaspoon black peppercorns
½ cup dry red wine	2 shallots, peeled and thinly sliced
¼ cup olive oil	
Juice of ½ lemon	2 tablespoons balsamic vinegar
Leaves from 3 sprigs rosemary	2 tablespoons honey
1 teaspoon fine sea salt	Cranberry, Pear, and Prune Sauce (page 286)

Wash and dry the duck pieces. Set aside.

In a glass dish large enough to hold the duck in a single layer, stir together the remaining ingredients except the sauce, and mix well. Add the duck, cover, and marinate in the refrigerator overnight. Baste the duck frequently with the marinade.

Heat a charcoal or gas grill. When coals are ready, drain the duck and wipe dry. Grill about 6 minutes on each side, turning frequently and basting with the marinade. Serve the duck immediately, accompanied by sauce.

Anatra con Pesche

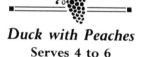

Duck with Peaches
Serves 4 to 6

I spent a few days visiting friends in Reggio Emilia, a city with a cuisine I can't get enough of. When I arrived at Lorenza's home, I was offered her mother's apartment. At first I was reluctant to call it home, because I felt it was an inconvenience. But the family insisted, shoving me in the door and showing me each room with pride.

The kitchen was filled with food for *prima colazione,* the Italian version of breakfast: biscotti, juice, coffee, and a large mound of very green peaches. The next morning, after jet-lag and a sleepless night, I made caffè latte, grabbed a biscotto, and decided to have a peach, unripe as they appeared. Surprise came in the first bite. The peach was sweet-tart, with a perfumed scent that I can't describe. The skin was fuzzless and I was in heaven. The depleting supply was replaced often.

When peaches are plentiful at home, I bake pies, make jam, and serve this duck dish with peaches. I also think how sensational this dish would be with those peaches in Italy.

1 4½- to 5-pound duck	4 cups hot Beef Broth (page 32)
Salt and pepper to taste	
1 bay leaf	2 tablespoons brandy
3 sprigs thyme	2 tablespoons dry white wine
3 sprigs marjoram	5 fresh peaches, peeled, pitted, and cut in half
1 sprig rosemary	
2 ribs celery, chopped	
2 medium carrots, peeled and chopped	1 small head radicchio, shredded
¼ cup unbleached all-purpose flour	

Wash and dry the duck, then rub inside and out with salt and pepper, rubbing it into the skin as well. Tie the herbs in a bunch with string and insert it into the duck cavity. Place the duck in a baking dish, breast side down, and surround with the celery and carrots.

Preheat the oven to 375°F.

With a whisk, dissolve the flour in the broth. Add the brandy and wine, and mix well. Pour the mixture over the duck, then roast for 25 minutes.

Baste duck with some of the pan juices, turn the duck breast side up, and continue roasting and basting for 30 minutes, or until the duck is fork-tender.

Remove the duck to a cutting board and cut into serving pieces. Rearrange the duck pieces in the baking dish and surround with the peach halves. Return to the oven to bake for about 5 minutes, basting the duck and peaches with the pan juices.

Arrange a bed of radicchio on a serving platter. Place the duck pieces on the platter, with the peach halves around it. Serve immediately with some of the pan juices.

Note: Chicken can be used instead of duck.

Pesce

Fish

Less is better. This is the lesson I learned from my grandmothers and mother about cooking fish. Their philosophy was that fish is delicate and only needs a touch of oil, herbs, and tomatoes, or a light sauce to complement its natural flavor.

My grandmothers and mother bought whole fish to retain freshness as long as possible. Arriving home from the market, they quickly went to work to scaling, gutting, and cleaning the fish. The head and trimmings were saved for making fish stock.

In those days we ate fish for dinner on Fridays like most Catholic families. Cod, perch, haddock, squid, and hake were the usual choices. The fish was dredged in flour, sautéed in olive oil, and then seasoned with salt, lemon juice, and a sprinkling of parsley—a simple preparation that I follow to this day. Squid was braised in tomato sauce and served over spaghetti, or mixed with broccoli and lightly tossed in olive oil and sprinkled with salt and pepper. Fish dipped in beaten egg, coated in freshly toasted bread crumbs, and baked in the oven was my favorite.

On Christmas Eve, all Italian families observed the *vigilia,* or the vigil of Christmas. The entire day was devoted to preparing at least seven fish dishes to be eaten that evening, one dish representing each day of the last week of Advent.

Today, the greater demand for fresh fish as part of a healthy diet has brought the fish market to the supermarket. Look for fish that has shiny skin and clear eyes, not eyes that are sunken or cloudy, or fish with a fishy odor. Already gutted and cleaned fish should be white and firm, not grayish white and soggy, a sign of frozen and thawed fish. Get to know the manager of your local market. He or she will gladly scale and gut the fish for you while you wait; this takes just a few minutes and ensures that you get the freshest fish available.

The firmness or delicacy of the fish determines how it should be cooked. Meaty and firm fish like swordfish, salmon, and halibut are good choices for the grill. Sole, flounder, and cod—more delicate in texture—are best when baked or pan-fried.

One of the most popular dishes to be found in Italy is *fritto misto di pesce,* or mixed fried small seafood such as sole, anchovies, squid, and cuttlefish. They are lightly dusted in flour and then plunged into hot oil and fried until golden brown. A dash of salt and a lemon wedge are all that are needed to accompany the dish.

I take every opportunity to taste the many fish dishes available in Italy, disappointed that I cannot duplicate many of them at home. The recipes in this chapter use fish readily available in the United States. With the exception of shrimp, all recipes call for fresh, not frozen, fish.

Merluzzo Gratinato

Baked Cod
Serves 2 to 3

My grandmothers prepared salted dried cod, or *baccalà,* on Fridays and during Lent. I was always fascinated at how they would rehydrate the cod. The stiff-as-a-board fish was placed in the sink; the faucet was turned on just to a slow drip, and the fish was left overnight to plump up as if by magic. The cod was rinsed several times in cold water and then baked or fried. In contrast, this recipe uses fresh cod that can be ready in twenty minutes.

3½ tablespoons olive oil

1 pound fresh cod fillets, cut into serving pieces

6 to 8 anchovy fillets with capers, packed in olive oil

1 tablespoon chopped fresh parsley

¼ teaspoon coarsely ground black pepper

2 tablespoons (¼ stick) butter

½ cup fresh bread crumbs

1 lemon, quartered

Use 1 teaspoon of the olive oil to grease an ovenproof dish large enough to hold the fish in a single layer. Set aside.

In a mortar with a pestle or in a food processor, mash the anchovies, parsley, remaining olive oil, and black pepper to a paste. Set aside.

Preheat the oven to 375°F.

In a small frying pan, melt the butter, add the bread crumbs, and sauté until browned. Set aside.

Place the fish pieces in the baking dish and spread the anchovy paste on the fish. Sprinkle on the bread crumbs. Bake for 15 to 20 minutes, or until fish easily flakes with a fork. Serve at once, garnished with lemon quarters.

Grigliata di Pesce Spada

Grilled Swordfish
Serves 4

Palermo still retains many of its Arab characteristics, most evident in its architecture, dialect, and food. The boisterous and crowded Vucciria, one of the grand outdoor markets of this ancient city, displays an enormous array of food and spices. Everything is exposed, an old Arabic custom that has been preserved. Swordfish has a place of honor in the market, and the Sicilians are masters at its preparation. Here it gets the full treatment: marinated, grilled, and then topped with a spicy sauce.

Marinade	*Sauce*
⅓ cup olive oil	¼ cup olive oil
⅓ cup dry white wine	2 cloves garlic, peeled and minced
1 teaspoon black peppercorns	¼ teaspoon hot red pepper flakes
½ teaspoon fine sea salt	½ teaspoon dried oregano
1 bay leaf	4 oil-packed sardines, mashed
1 small white onion, peeled and thinly sliced	¼ teaspoon fennel seeds
2 pounds swordfish steaks, cut into 4 pieces	2 tablespoons fresh lemon juice
	4 tablespoons dry white wine

In a glass dish, mix the marinade ingredients. Add the swordfish, turning several times to coat with the marinade. Cover the dish and refrigerate several hours before cooking. Baste the swordfish occasionally with the marinade.

In a saucepan, heat the olive oil, add the garlic, red pepper flakes, and oregano, and sauté for 2 to 3 minutes. Add the sardines and stir to dissolve in the olive oil. Add the fennel seeds and continue to sauté for 2 or 3 minutes. Remove the saucepan from the heat, add the lemon juice and wine, stir, and set aside.

Prepare a chargrill or grease an oven broiler pan with olive oil. Drain the swordfish and place on the grill or broiler pan. Grill or broil the fish, basting frequently with the marinade, until a fork can easily flake the meat. Depending on thickness, this will take anywhere from 7 to 12 minutes. Do not overcook the fish.

To serve, place the swordfish steaks on individual plates. Quickly reheat the sauce and spoon a little over each steak. Serve immediately accompanied by oven-roasted potatoes or rice.

Pesce Spada al Forno

Baked Swordfish
Serves 4

Many of the components of Sicilian cooking—capers, olives, and raisins—are evident in this treatment of baked swordfish. The sauce provides a slightly sweet finish to the dish.

4 swordfish steaks (about 2 pounds)	1 tablespoon salted capers, rinsed, dried, and chopped
¼ cup unbleached all-purpose flour	¼ cup diced pitted green olives
½ cup olive oil	2 tablespoons chopped raisins
2 ribs celery, diced	4 plum tomatoes, seeded and diced
1 medium onion, peeled and diced	Salt and pepper to taste
2 cloves garlic, peeled and minced	

On a sheet of waxed paper, dredge the swordfish in the flour, shaking off the excess. Set aside.

In a skillet, heat the olive oil, brown the fish on both sides until golden, then remove to a greased oven dish and set aside.

Preheat the oven to 350°F.

In the fish drippings, sauté the celery and onion until soft. Add the garlic and sauté until soft. Add the capers, olives, and raisins; continue to sauté for 3 to 4 minutes. Add the tomatoes, salt, and pepper and cook over medium heat for about 10 minutes.

Pour the sauce over the fish. Cover dish with foil and bake for 15 minutes, or until the fish is hot. Remove the foil and serve the fish immediately with some of the sauce.

Variation: Use salmon fillets or steaks in place of the swordfish.

Tonno alle Erbe

Tuna Steak with Herbs
Serves 4

While fish has become prohibitively expensive in Italy, it remains a very popular item in the markets and on most restaurant menus. Tuna, swordfish, and salmon are particularly good choices for this easy preparation—and one that you can get ready the night before. A hot cast-iron skillet cooks the fish best; if you do not have one, cook the fish on a hot grill.

1 clove garlic, peeled and minced	**Freshly ground black pepper to taste**
Leaves from 2 sprigs thyme	**1¼ pounds tuna steak, cut into 4 pieces**
3 tablespoons extra-virgin olive oil	**8 basil leaves, torn into pieces**
½ teaspoon fine sea salt	

In a glass casserole dish large enough to hold the fish, place the garlic, thyme, oil, sea salt, and pepper; mix well. Place the fish on top and turn to coat on both sides. Marinate the fish, covered, for 2 hours, turning the pieces occasionally.

Heat a cast-iron skillet until very hot. Add the fish and cook over high heat about 2½ minutes on each side.

Sprinkle the basil on top and serve the fish immediately.

Saor alla Venezia

Venetian Marinated Fish
Serves 4

During a recent stay in Venice I had an appointment to interview Venetian cooking teacher Fulvia Sesani. One regal red rose was waiting for me in my hotel room, with a note that said, "*Benvenuta a Venezia,*" or "Welcome to Venice."

Trying to find the Palazzo Morosini, where Fulvia lived and conducted cooking classes, was like wandering through a maze. Finally, arriving at the grand palace of her ancestors, I met Fulvia and was ushered into a splendid living room, where she and I talked about traditional Venetian cooking. One classic recipe called *saor* is a cooked then marinated fish dish. Fresh sardines are used in Venice, but flounder or sole works well, too. This is Fulvia's recipe for saor, which must be prepared a day in advance of serving. I particularly enjoy it on a hot summer day.

2 pounds sole or flounder fillets	**¼ cup red wine vinegar**
Flour, for dredging	**⅓ cup pine nuts**
½ cup olive oil	**⅓ cup golden raisins**
2 cups thinly sliced white onions	**3 tablespoons chopped candied citron**

Dredge the fish pieces in the flour, shake off the excess, and place on a plate.

In a skillet, heat the oil, then fry the fish on both sides until golden brown, about 5 minutes. Remove the fish to a serving dish.

In the same oil (add more if necessary), slowly brown the onions about 5 to 7 minutes, until almost caramelized or deep brown in color. Add the vinegar, pine nuts, raisins, and citron. Cook, stirring, for a couple of minutes, then pour the mixture over the fish.

Cover the fish with plastic wrap and refrigerate for 1 day before serving. To serve, bring the dish to room temperature.

Pesce Fritto

Fried Fish
Serves 4

Pesce *fritto* is a fish fry. For this recipe from home, I use firm fish like hake, haddock, monkfish, or cod. When several kinds of fish and seafood are used, the dish becomes a *fritto misto*. The batter is made at least 1 hour before frying the fish. Once the fish is fried, it must be served immediately, otherwise the coating becomes soggy. You can also use the batter for frying vegetables.

1½ cups unbleached all-purpose flour	4 cups vegetable oil
½ teaspoon active dry yeast	1¼ pounds firm white fish fillets, cut into 4 pieces
1½ cups beer, at room temperature	Lemon wedges
	Salt to taste

In a bowl, mix the flour with the yeast. Gradually add the beer, stirring with a wooden spoon until no lumps remain and the batter is like pancake batter. You can also use an electric mixer to beat the batter. Cover the bowl with plastic wrap and refrigerate the batter for at least 1 hour.

In a deep-fryer or heavy, deep pan, heat the oil to 375°F.

Dry the fish pieces with paper towels, then dip each piece in the batter, coating well on both sides, letting the excess drip back into the bowl. Fry the fish in hot oil until golden brown, about 3 to 4 minutes. Drain the pieces on a platter lined with brown paper.

Serve the fish immediately, accompanied by lemon wedges and a sprinkling of salt.

Polpette di Pesce

Fish Cakes
Serves 4

Fish cakes are a frequent meal at our house during Lent. You can vary the type of fish, but I like using monkfish, which is very firm. Other choices include haddock and cod or even leftover cooked fish.

1½ cups soft fresh bread crumbs

¼ cup milk

3 large eggs

½ teaspoon fine sea salt

½ teaspoon coarsely ground black pepper

2 tablespoons minced fresh parsley

2 tablespoons grated Pecorino Romano cheese

1 pound fresh monkfish, haddock, swordfish, or cod fillets

3 cups water

¼ teaspoon coarse salt

1 small carrot, peeled

1 small onion, peeled and quartered

¼ to ⅓ cup unbleached all-purpose flour

¾ cup fine bread crumbs

2 to 3 cups vegetable oil, for frying

Lemon wedges

In a bowl, moisten the fresh bread crumbs with the milk. Mix in 1 egg, sea salt, pepper, parsley, and cheese. Set aside.

Place the fish in a shallow pan with the water, coarse salt, carrot, and onion; simmer until fish easily flakes, about 8 to 10 minutes.

Carefully lift the fish out of the water with a strainer, place in a bowl, and cool to room temperature. Dice the carrot and add to the bread crumb mixture. Discard the water and onion. Flake the fish with a fork, then add it to the bread crumb mixture and mix well.

Have ready a plate with the flour, and one with the fine bread crumbs. In a small bowl, beat the remaining eggs.

Divide the fish mixture evenly into 8 balls, forming them with your hands. Roll each ball in the flour and shake off the excess. Coat the balls in the beaten egg, then roll them in the bread crumbs, coating them evenly. Place the balls on a plate and press down slightly with your hand to flatten a little.

In a deep skillet or deep-fryer, heat the vegetable oil to 375°F. Fry the fish cakes in the oil until golden brown, about 4 to 5 minutes. Drain on brown paper and serve hot, accompanied by lemon wedges.

Gamberi con Salsa di Pomodori Saporiti

Shrimp with Spicy Tomato Sauce
Serves 4

Creating recipes gives me great satisfaction, especially when the results are surprisingly good. When I cook I let my intuition take over, but I'm never sure until I add the final ingredient as to how the dish will taste. For this shrimp dish I wanted a spicy sauce. I had bits of limp herbs, leftover red wine, and a few black olives on hand. They went into a sauce that turned out very *piccante,* a perfect foil for the shrimp. Serve this over spaghetti or rice.

1 pound (about 30) medium shrimp, in the shell

Juice of ½ lemon

1 bay leaf

1 cup coarsely chopped onion

8 large basil leaves

2 cloves garlic, peeled

3 tablespoons olive oil

1 28-ounce can chopped plum tomatoes (3½ cups)

1 teaspoon fine sea salt

½ teaspoon coarsely ground black pepper

½ teaspoon dried oregano

½ cup dry red wine

¼ cup water

3 tablespoons diced oil-cured black olives

1 pound spaghetti

In a medium saucepan, bring about 2 quarts of water to a boil. Add the shrimp, lemon juice, and bay leaf. Boil just until the shells turn pink, about 2 to 3 minutes. Drain the shrimp, let cool, then peel, devein, and set aside.

Place the onion, basil, and garlic on a cutting board and, with a knife, chop the ingredients together until fine, making a battuto. Set aside.

In a saucepan, heat the olive oil, add the onion mixture, and sauté over medium heat until soft, about 3 minutes. Stir in the tomatoes, sea salt, pepper, oregano, wine, and water. Cover the pan, lower the heat, and simmer for about 25 minutes.

Uncover the pan, stir in the shrimp and olives, re-cover, and simmer for 5 minutes. Set the sauce aside and keep warm.

In a large pot, bring 4 to 6 quarts of water to a boil. Add the spaghetti and cook until *al dente*. Drain and place on a platter. Pour over the sauce, mix gently, and serve immediately.

Scampi con Linguine e Limone

Shrimp with Linguine and Lemon
Serves 4

This light and easy to prepare scampi and linguine says it all about Italian cooking; use fresh ingredients and keep the treatment simple.

1 pound large shrimp, in the shell	½ teaspoon fine sea salt, or more to taste
6 tablespoons extra-virgin olive oil	Freshly ground black pepper
1 large clove garlic, peeled and cut in half lengthwise	3 tablespoons fresh lemon juice
1 small dried hot red pepper, cut in half lengthwise	1 tablespoon grated lemon zest
¾ pound linguine	3 tablespoons finely chopped fresh parsley

In a medium saucepan, bring about 6 cups of water to a boil. Add the shrimp and cook just until the shells turn pink, about 2 to 3 minutes. Drain the shrimp in a colander and cool. Shell and devein the shrimp, then cut in half lengthwise, but not through the tail, and set aside.

In a large skillet, heat the olive oil with the garlic and red pepper. Sauté very slowly, pressing on the garlic and pepper with a wooden spoon to extract juice. Remove and discard the garlic when it starts to soften and turn golden. Remove the pepper when soft and discard. Set skillet aside.

In a large pot, bring 4 to 6 quarts of water to a boil. Add the linguine and boil until *al dente,* or firm but not mushy.

While the linguine is cooking, reheat the skillet, add the shrimp, and sauté for about 2 minutes. Sprinkle in the sea salt and pepper.

Drain the linguine in a colander and immediately add to the shrimp. Add the lemon juice, zest, and parsley and toss well. Transfer to a large platter and serve immediately.

Cappesante con Pesto

Scallops with Pesto
Serves 3 to 4

This scallop and pesto combination is a quick supper idea, assuming you have sun-dried tomatoes packed in olive oil and pesto on hand.

1½ pounds sea scallops

½ cup (3 ounces) sun-dried tomatoes in olive oil, drained and cut into strips, 2 tablespoons oil reserved

¼ cup diced onion

1 clove garlic, peeled and minced

3 tablespoons Pesto (page 92)

2 tablespoons chicken broth or water

Salt to taste

Place the scallops in a colander and drain throughly. Dry on a clean towel and set aside.

In a skillet, heat the oil from the sun-dried tomatoes, add the onion, and sauté until softened, about 1 minute. Add the garlic and continue to sauté for a couple of minutes. Put in the scallops and sauté for 3 minutes, or until they take on a whitish appearance. Keep warm.

In a small bowl, dilute the Pesto with the chicken broth or water and add to the scallops, coating and turning scallops well in the sauce. Add the tomatoes and continue cooking for 1 to 2 minutes. Add salt and serve immediately.

Calamari e Cappesante
al Forno

Baked Squid and Scallops
Serves 4

Here is a recipe I particularly love when fresh squid are available, although frozen squid may be used. Actually, there are two types of squid: *calamari* and *totani*. The calamaro is more tender than the totani. I use very small calamari for grilling and in seafood salads. Larger ones are stuffed and baked, or simmered in tomato sauce. For this recipe, use 5- or 6-inch-long calamari.

4 fresh or frozen squid,
about 6 inches long

½ cup olive oil

1 large clove garlic,
peeled and minced

1 medium onion, peeled
and minced

¼ pound bay scallops

1 teaspoon fine sea salt

1 teaspoon capers in
brine, drained

½ cup toasted bread
crumbs

2 plum tomatoes, peeled,
seeded, and diced

¼ cup dry white wine

Freshly ground black
pepper to taste

Clean the squid by pulling the head away from the body, removing the pen (plasticlike bone). Cut the tentacles below the eyes and save. Rinse the squid body clean and pull off the outer purple skin and discard. Drain the squid on paper towels and set aside. Rinse the tentacles, dice them, and set aside.

In a large skillet, heat ¼ cup of the olive oil. Add the garlic, onion, and tentacles and sauté the mixture for about 4 minutes. Add the scallops and continue sautéing for 3 minutes.

Transfer the mixture to a bowl; add the sea salt, capers, and bread crumbs and mix well. Divide the mixture and stuff into each squid body. Close the openings with a toothpick and set aside.

Heat the remaining ¼ cup olive oil in a large skillet, add the stuffed squid, and brown slowly over low heat for 5 minutes. Raise the heat to medium, add the tomatoes and wine, and cook for 2 minutes. Cover the skillet, lower the heat, and simmer for 15 to 20 minutes, or until the squid are easily pierced with a knife. Serve immediately with some of the pan juices poured over the top.

Verdure

Vegetables

s young women in Italy, both my grandmothers lived from and worked on the land. Nonna Galasso worked as an olive picker in Naples, and Nonna Saporito planted and picked vegetables to sustain her family in Caltinasetta, in Sicily.

When they came to America, they did not settle on a farm, but in neighborhoods where the houses had just about enough room to slither sideways between them. But nothing stopped them from raising the vegetables they were so fond of in Italy. A small patch of dirt, a container, even a homemade trellis was used to grow their beloved beans, plum tomatoes, basil, oregano, zucchini, grapes, and geraniums.

As I travel throughout Italy, I am reminded of my grandmothers' ingenuity when I see little gardens tucked in front and backyards, or terra-cotta pots brimming with oregano and basil, and tomatoes in window boxes on sunny balconies.

Around midday, you might be lucky enough to catch a glimpse of the cook's deft hand reaching out of a window to pinch off some sprigs of basil to add to her spaghetti.

My grandmothers would be very proud of my garden, in which grow primarily Italian vegetables. I buy seeds from mail-order companies that carry international vegetable varieties. Of course, the soil and climate are much different here, but I grow such things as *pane zucchero,* a bitter lettuce, as well as *cavolo nero,* a black cabbage from Tuscany that can almost outlast winter; the latter is used to make the classic ribollita, or twice-boiled soup. I also plant various types of zucchini, as well as fennel, plum tomatoes, basil, mint, radicchio (a regal purple-red chicory with white striping used in salads or oiled and grilled), and arugula (a pungent and peppery salad green). I must admit that I have very good luck . . . and a husband with a green thumb. Together we create a little bit of Italy right in our own backyard.

When it is harvest time, my vegetables are treated carefully and cooked with a few tricks I learned from my grandmothers. They never cooked vegetables in a lot of water, or for any great length of time, because that would deprive them of their vitamins. Green vegetables were always added to boiling water with a teaspoon of olive oil, which helped keep their vibrant color. A lid was never put over green vegetables, as this would cause the color to pale. Potatoes and dried beans were always started in cold water and brought to a boil.

When the vegetables were cooked, the cooking water was collected in glass jars and used for soup the next day.

Both my grandmothers revered the vegetables that they grew. In Grandma Galasso's bedroom dresser was a drawer full of little Italian books, mostly litanies to the saints. I once got into trouble for thumbing through the brown stained pages, accidently letting dried seeds spill onto the floor. These precious seeds had been carefully collected from Grandma's vegetable harvest and saved for the following spring's planting. I like to think that keeping the seeds in her prayerbook was a sign of renewed hope.

Carciofi in Tegame

Braised Artichokes
Serves 4

In the spring, wonderful varieties of artichokes begin to appear in Italian markets. Some are deep green with purple-tipped leaves; others are paler green with brownish tips. They come from Apulia, Sicily, and around Florence. When I ask the market vendors how they cook them, they just break off a few leaves and pop them into their mouths!

A popular way to have artichokes in Rome and Florence is deep-fried. In Liguria, they are slowly cooked in a little milk and white wine, and served as an accompaniment to veal cutlets.

2 large globe artichokes (about 1 pound)	2 cloves garlic, peeled and minced
Juice of 1 lemon	2 tablespoons minced fresh parsley
2 tablespoons (¼ stick) butter	¼ teaspoon salt
2 tablespoons olive oil	2 tablespoons milk
	¼ cup dry white wine

Wash and dry the artichokes. Roll them around on the countertop under your hand to loosen the leaves. Cut off the stems and remove the tough outer leaves at the base. Cut ¼ inch off the top of each artichoke and trim the thorns on the tips. Open the center of each artichoke and remove the fuzzy choke with a melon scoop or spoon.

Cut the artichokes in half, then in quarters. Place in a bowl of cold water and lemon juice. Let soak for several minutes, then drain and dry well. Set aside.

In a Dutch oven, heat the butter and oil. Add the garlic and sauté until it begins to soften. Add the parsley and continue to cook over low heat for 2 to 3 minutes. Put in the artichokes and coat well with the seasonings. Sprinkle the salt over the artichokes, cover the pot, and cook over low heat for about 5 minutes.

Add the milk and half the wine to the pot and continue to cook, covered, for 15 minutes. Add the remaining wine and cook until a knife is easily inserted into the leaves and heart. Serve immediately.

Carciofi Ripieni

Stuffed Artichokes
Serves 4

I served these artichokes to friends who were celebrating twenty-five years of marriage. Usually, I cook them the traditional way with butter, mint, and garlic, but I wanted to be creative so I stuffed them with acini di pepe, a tiny pasta usually used for soup. I used the smaller Australian artichoke, which has softer outer leaves and fewer thorns, but globe artichokes work just as well.

For the twenty-fifth-anniversary dinner, I served the Shrimp Cocktail (page 24) to start, Grilled Duck (page 135) with Cranberry, Pear, and Prune Sauce (page 286), the artichokes, Arugula, Avocado, and Dried Fig Salad (page 190), and Cooked Cream (page 298) with fresh Strawberry Amaretto Sauce (page 281).

2 medium artichokes
(about ¾ pound)

Juice of ½ lemon

2 tablespoons olive oil

2 cups water

⅛ teaspoon salt

½ cup acini di pepe or
pastina

2 tablespoons (¼ stick)
butter

3 ounces Asiago cheese,
minced

¼ teaspoon black pepper

1 tablespoon minced
fresh parsley

Cut off the stems and remove any tough outer leaves from the artichokes. Trim any needlelike thorns with a scissors. With a sharp knife, cut the artichokes in half lengthwise. Use a melon ball scoop to scrap out the fuzzy chokes and discard. Also discard the yellowish interior leaves.

In a saucepan just large enough to hold them, place the artichokes cut side down. Fill the pan with enough water to just cover them. Add the lemon juice and 1 tablespoon of oil. Cover the pot and bring to a boil. Lower the heat to medium-high and gently boil the artichokes for about 20 minutes, or until a leave is easily detached from the base. Carefully drain the artichokes in a colander and set aside to cool.

Bring 2 cups of water to a boil in a saucepan. Add the salt and pasta, and boil until tender, about 10 minutes. The pasta will absorb most of the water. Drain in a colander and place in a bowl. Add the butter, half the cheese, pepper, and parsley. Mix well.

Preheat the oven to 350°F.

With the remaining tablespoon of oil, grease a 7-inch casserole dish. Add the artichokes cut side up in a single layer. Fill each cavity with some of the pasta mixture, mounding it up slightly. Sprinkle the remaining cheese over the artichokes. Cover the casserole with aluminum foil and bake for 20 to 25 minutes or until hot. Serve immediately.

Verdure Miste

Mixed Vegetables
Serves 4

As soon as the danger of frost is past, I head for the garden and begin turning a muddy blanket of dirt into a patchwork of green hues. My husband prepares the soil while I sort the seeds. I covet the Italian seeds, taking extra care with them as I plant.

Months later, harvest time is a joy. I have no set plan as to how I will prepare some of the vegetables, like the deeply ridged dark green zucchini or the almost-black cabbage from Tuscany. I pick judiciously and then remember... simplicity is best. Like this fresh vegetable sauté, which just came together by accident. Swiss chard or spinach is substituted for the black cabbage.

¼ cup olive oil

1½ teaspoons garlic, peeled and minced

1 medium zucchini, cut into ¼-inch slices

1 medium yellow summer squash, cut into ¼-inch slices

2 plum tomatoes, diced

1 cup Swiss chard or spinach, torn in pieces

Salt and pepper to taste

¼ cup grated Pecorino Romano cheese

Place the olive oil and garlic in a skillet, and sauté until garlic is soft. Add the zucchini and summer squash, and sauté for 2 to 3 minutes. Add the tomatoes, cover the skillet, lower the heat, and cook for about 5 minutes.

Add the Swiss chard or spinach, salt, and pepper to the skillet. Stir the mixture, cover, and continue to cook until the chard or spinach has wilted. Transfer the mixture to a serving dish, sprinkle on the cheese, and serve at once.

Variation: Fry slices of Italian bread in olive oil on both sides. Place the bread on individual serving dishes and pour some of the vegetables over the bread. Serve immediately.

Fagiolini e Patate
con Pesto

Green Beans and Potatoes with Pesto
Serves 4 to 6

Many times at home I could look forward to a plate of green beans cooked with potato gnocchi and served with tomato sauce and fresh mint. Taking that old method, I have given it a new twist: beans and potatoes lightly coated in pungent pesto.

1 pound green beans, stemmed and rinsed	4 tablespoons Pesto (page 92)
1 pound potatoes, peeled and cut into 1-inch chunks	Salt to taste

Place the potatoes in a pot, cover with cold water, and bring to a boil. Cook the potatoes for 5 minutes, then add the beans and continue cooking the vegetables until tender but not mushy, about 5 to 7 minutes.

Drain the vegetables in a colander, reserving 3 tablespoons of the cooking water.

In a serving dish, mix the Pesto with just enough water to smooth out the sauce. Add the vegetables and gently toss with the sauce. Add the salt, toss, and serve immediately.

Coroncine di Carote agli Spinaci

Little Carrot and Spinach Crowns
Serves 6

The word *contorni* refers to the vegetables that accompany the main course. I made this colorful vegetable combination for my family to go with a roast pork. My son Chris, who is suspicious of all vegetables, actually enjoyed these. This is a beautiful company dish, easy to prepare ahead.

1 pound fresh spinach,
washed and stemmed

4 tablespoons olive oil

½ cup diced onion

1½ teaspoons salt

¼ teaspoon black
pepper

1¼ pounds potatoes,
peeled and quartered

1 pound carrots, peeled
and quartered

3 tablespoons butter

¼ plus 12 tablespoons
grated Parmigiano-
Reggiano cheese

½ teaspoon grated
nutmeg

Place the spinach in a skillet, cover the pan, and cook over medium-high heat for about 4 minutes, or until the spinach wilts. Drain the spinach in a colander, squeezing out as much water as possible. Place on a cutting board and cut it into strips.

Dry out the skillet, pour in and heat 3 tablespoons of the olive oil, then add the onion, sautéing until soft and golden. Add the spinach, ½ teaspoon salt, and the pepper. Stir, cooking the mixture for 2 to 3 minutes. Keep warm.

Place the potatoes, carrots, and remaining salt in a pot. Cover the vegetables with water and boil until very tender, about 15 minutes. Drain the vegetables in a colander. Return vegetables to the pot and "dry" them over low heat for 2 to 3 minutes.

Place the vegetables in a food processor, blender, or bowl. Add the butter and puree or mash by hand until very smooth. Transfer the mixture to a bowl, add ¼ cup of cheese and the nutmeg, and combine well.

Grease a large casserole dish with the remaining olive oil. Fit a 12- or 16-inch pastry bag with a star tip. Fill bag with some of the carrot-potato mixture, then pipe out twelve 2-inch circles into the prepared casserole dish. Using a circular motion, fill circles with the mixture to build up the sides so that they are about 1 inch high. If necessary, reheat circles in a 350° oven for about 8 minutes. Remove from oven.

Divide the spinach mixture among the circles, placing about 1½ tablespoons in the center of each. Sprinkle the remaining cheese over the tops and serve immediately.

Note: To make this ahead, grease a large casserole with 1 tablespoon olive oil. Form the circles, cover them, and refrigerate until serving time. Heat circles in a 350°F. oven for about 15 minutes or until hot. Serve immediately.

Manaste Patano

Greens and Potatoes
Serves 4 to 6

My mother tells the story of how her mother in early spring gathered bitter, wild endive (*cicoria*) and dandelions in her apron. She boiled them until tender, then tossed them into boiling chicken or beef broth, along with some potatoes. It was a very satisfying peasant dish, and for my grandmother, the greens were a gift from nature.

The combination of greens and potatoes has remained for me a culinary example of simplicity and frugality in the kitchen. The potatoes in this dish were lumpy, mashed with a fork, because Grandma had a weakness in her arm that sapped her strength. She always served them with meat drippings that she had saved, but I have left it out because of today's health consciousness.

1 pound escarole, dandelion greens, or chicory, washed	½ cup milk
	½ cup grated Pecorino Romano cheese
1 pound potatoes, peeled and cut into quarters	Salt to taste
6 tablespoons (¾ stick) butter plus 1 teaspoon	Ground black pepper to taste

Bring a large pot of water to a boil. Add the greens, and boil rapidly for 6 to 7 minutes, or until the greens are wilted and tender. Drain the greens in a colander, reserving 2 tablespoons of the cooking water.

With the back of a spoon, press as much water as possible out of the greens and place them on a cutting board. With a knife, coursely chop the greens into 1- to 2-inch pieces and place in a bowl.

Put the potatoes in a pot, cover with water, and boil until fork-tender, about 15 minutes.

Drain the potatoes well and place in a bowl. Add 4 tablespoons of the butter and the milk, and mash with a potato masher or an electric mixer until smooth (or leave them slightly lumpy). If the potatoes are too dry, add 2 tablespoons of the cooking water. With a spoon, mix in half the cheese and the salt and pepper. Add the chopped greens and combine.

Preheat the oven to 350°F.

Grease an 8-inch square baking dish with the 1 teaspoon butter, and spread the potato mixture in the pan. Melt the remaining 2 tablespoons butter and drizzle it over the top, then sprinkle on the remaining cheese and bake until hot, about 20 minutes. Serve immediately.

Fagiolini in Salsa di Pomodori

Green Beans in Tomato Sauce
Serves 4

Picture clean newspaper spread on a kitchen table and a large mound of tender green beans as the centerpiece. Next to them sits Grandma Galasso, pinching off the stem ends and putting the beans in a tub of cold water. This is what I recall every time I make the green bean and tomato dish that my grandmother made when beans were in season.

1 pound green beans, stemmed and washed	**2 cups peeled, seeded, and chopped plum tomatoes**
2 tablespoons olive oil	**½ teaspoon salt**
1 clove garlic, peeled and thinly sliced	**1½ cups diced mozzarella cheese**
1 tablespoon minced fresh mint	

Bring a large pot of water to a boil. Add the beans, and boil until tender, about 10 minutes. Drain the beans and set aside.

In a saucepan, heat the olive oil, add the garlic, and sauté until soft, then discard. Add the mint and swirl it in the oil until it is soft. Add the tomatoes and salt, stir the sauce, and simmer, covered, for about 15 minutes.

Add the beans to the sauce, mixing well and heating until the beans are hot. Stir in the cheese, turn off the heat, cover the pot, and let the beans sit for 3 to 4 minutes, or until the cheese has melted. Serve immediately.

Involtini di Melanzane

Eggplant Bundles
Serves 6

Stuffed and rolled, eggplant, called *involtini*, makes a light meal when served with a salad and crusty bread. Involtini are usually stuffed meat bundles, but this idea developed from when I had an armload of vegetables from my garden.

1 medium (1 pound)
eggplant, 7 inches
long

Salt

½ to ¾ cup peanut oil

1 tablespoon plus
1 teaspoon olive oil

1⅔ cups shredded
mozzarella cheese

Ground black pepper to
taste

2 ounces sun-dried
tomatoes packed
in oil

12 fresh basil leaves

Wash the eggplant, cut off the stem end, and slice lengthwise into twelve ¼-inch-thick slices. Layer the slices in a colander, sprinkling salt between each layer. Fill a heavy pot with water, sit it on top of the eggplant to act as a weight, and let the eggplant stand for about 1 hour. Then rinse and dry the eggplant, and set aside.

In a skillet, heat ½ cup of the peanut oil. Sauté the eggplant slices in batches on both sides, keeping them flat, until they are limp. *Do not overcook them or they will split.* Carefully remove eggplant to brown paper and let them drain. Add more oil as needed to finish sautéing the batches.

Grease a 14- x 9-inch oven dish with 1 teaspoon of the olive oil.

Lay each slice of eggplant flat on a work surface. Evenly divide and sprinkle each slice with the cheese. Sprinkle on salt and pepper to taste. With a scissors, snip a tomato and a basil leaf evenly over each slice.

Starting from one end of the slice, roll each one up like a jelly roll and place in the baking dish seam side down. Drizzle the remaining tablespoon of olive oil over the rolls.

Cover the dish with foil and bake for about 25 minutes, or until hot. Serve immediately.

Melanzane della Nonna

Grandma's Eggplant
Serves 6

This uncomplicated eggplant casserole is put together in no time at all. It is even good served cold, or as a filling for sandwiches with homemade bread. The skin is never removed because, according to my grandmother, it is the best part. The success of this dish depends on "sweating" the eggplant to remove its bitter juices.

2 small to medium eggplants (about 1½ pounds total), 6 or 7 inches long	3 tablespoons grated Parmigiano-Reggiano cheese
Salt	¼ pound Provolone, mozzarella, or Bel Paese cheese, diced
Juice of 1 large lemon	
½ cup unbleached all-purpose flour	¾ cup Fresh Tomato and Basil Sauce (page 85)
¾ to 1 cup peanut oil	
2 tablespoons (¼ stick) butter	

Remove the stem ends of the eggplant with a knife and cut the eggplants lengthwise into ¼-inch slices. You should have about 20 slices.

Place the slices in a colander in layers, sprinkling each layer with salt and a little of the lemon juice. Place a bowl filled with water on top of the eggplant slices and let them "sweat" for about 1 hour. Rinse and dry the eggplant and set aside.

Preheat the oven to 350°F.

Place the flour on a plate and lightly dredge each eggplant slice in flour on both sides. Shake off excess and set slices aside.

In a skillet, heat ¾ cup of peanut oil until hot. Add a few eggplant slices at a time and fry on both sides, just until they are wilted. Remove the pieces to brown paper to drain. Add more peanut oil as needed to fry remaining slices.

With 1 tablespoon of the butter, grease a 14- x 9-inch casserole dish. Layer in half the eggplant slices, overlapping them slightly. Sprinkle on the

Parmigiano-Reggiano cheese, then the diced cheese. Cover with the remaining slices of eggplant. Spread the tomato sauce evenly over the eggplant. Dice the remaining butter and scatter it over the sauce.

Cover the dish with foil and bake for 30 minutes. Remove the foil and serve immediately.

Patate in Padella

Potatoes in a Skillet
Serves 4 to 6

This potato recipe comes from Nonna Galasso and is easy to prepare, since most of the ingredients are already in your pantry. I like to use small baking potatoes about 1 inch in diameter, either red or white skin. This dish is a perfect accompaniment to spring lamb, roast pork, or chicken cutlets.

¼ cup olive oil

1 large clove garlic, peeled and minced

1 medium onion, peeled and diced

1 tablespoon fresh rosemary leaves, or 1 teaspoon dried

1 pound small potatoes, washed and cut in half

1 teaspoon fine sea salt

1 teaspoon coarsely ground black pepper

2 tablespoons red wine vinegar

In a large skillet, heat the olive oil, add the garlic, onion, and rosemary, and sauté for 1 minute. Add the potatoes, cut side down, in a single layer. Lower the heat to a simmer, cover the pan, and cook for 15 to 20 minutes, or until potatoes are tender.

Sprinkle on the sea salt and pepper, raise the heat to high, and add the wine vinegar. Stir the potatoes gently until the vinegar has evaporated and serve immediately.

Patate e Zucchini al Forno con Aglio

Oven-Roasted Potatoes and Zucchini with Garlic
Serves 4

In this recipe, garlic is minced with sea salt and fresh rosemary, and the vegetables are tossed in the mixture. Sometimes I vary this recipe by adding fresh tomato wedges about 10 minutes before the dish is done. Serve it with roasted chicken, fish, or meat. I like to serve this on Thanksgiving because it goes together so quickly and is easy to bake along with the turkey.

6 or 7 red-skin potatoes, washed	**½ teaspoon fine sea salt**
2 medium zucchini	**½ cup olive oil**
3 cloves garlic, peeled	**Coarsely ground black pepper to taste**
Leaves from 2 sprigs fresh rosemary, or 1 tablespoon dried	

Preheat the oven to 350°F.

Cut the potatoes and zucchini into 1-inch chunks, ½ inch thick. Put the zucchini in a bowl, cover, and set aside.

Mince the garlic with the rosemary and sea salt until the mixture is almost a paste. Set aside.

In a 14- x 9-inch baking dish, mix the olive oil and garlic paste. Add the potatoes and coat well with the mixture. Bake for 30 to 35 minutes, basting frequently with a brush.

Add the zucchini to the baking dish and toss the vegetables well. Bake an additional 20 to 25 minutes, or until the zucchini are soft but not mushy and the potatoes are golden brown. Sprinkle with pepper and serve immediately.

Peperoni Casalinghi

Homestyle Peppers
Serves 4 to 6

My husband grows both red and yellow peppers in our garden, and I treasure them because they are so expensive to buy. Peppers like hot weather, which is probably why they grow so prolifically in parts of Italy, especially in the south. Serve these peppers as an antipasto or as an accompaniment to grilled or baked fish.

¾ **cup olive oil**	1 **tablespoon tomato paste**
4 **to 6 slices Italian bread**	¾ **cup hot Chicken Broth (page 31)**
4 **medium (about 1¼ pounds) red bell peppers**	1 **tablespoon anchovy paste**
1 **large clove garlic, peeled and minced**	2 **tablespoons chopped fresh parsley**
1 **teaspoon fine sea salt**	2 **tablespoons diced oil-cured black olives**

In a frying pan, heat ½ cup olive oil, add the bread slices, and fry on both sides until golden. Add more olive oil as necessary. Drain the slices on brown paper and set aside.

Wash and dry the peppers, cut off the stem tops, then cut them in half lengthwise and remove the seeds. Cut each half into 5 or 6 lengthwise pieces. Set aside.

In the same frying pan, heat the remaining olive oil, add the peppers and garlic, and sauté over medium heat for about 4 minutes. Sprinkle the sea salt over the peppers.

Dilute the tomato paste in ½ cup of the broth and add to the peppers. Mix well, cover the pan, and cook peppers over medium heat for 20 minutes. Add more broth during the cooking if the pan seems dry.

Add the anchovy paste, stir to blend, cover the pan, and cook 5 minutes longer.

Place the peppers on a serving dish, sprinkle on the parsley and olives, and serve immediately over the fried bread.

Variation: Use a combination of red and yellow peppers for a nice visual effect.

Peperoni Rossi Ripieni

Stuffed Red Peppers
Serves 10

Preparing roasted peppers is easy. Use an outdoor grill, the broiler unit of an oven, or a charring grate placed over a stovetop burner.

These filled red peppers make a great buffet dish to go with any meat. Put them together early in the morning and bake just before serving. Make this dish when red peppers are in season; use a combination of red and yellow peppers also.

10 medium red bell peppers	2 tablespoons fresh bread crumbs
½ cup long-grain rice	¼ cup coarsely chopped pistachio nuts
1½ cups water	
2 tablespoons plus 1 teaspoon olive oil	2 large egg whites
	¼ teaspoon fine sea salt
1 medium zucchini, diced	¼ teaspoon coarsely ground black pepper
1 small onion, peeled and diced	⅔ cup grated Pecorino Romano cheese

Wash and dry the peppers. Place on a piece of foil on top of a broiler pan. Broil the peppers, turning them occasionally, until blackened all over.

Carefully transfer the peppers to a brown paper bag. Fold over the top, and let the peppers steam for 20 minutes.

Carefully remove the core, blackened skin, and seeds of the peppers; try to keep the peppers in one piece. Dry the peppers with paper towels and set aside.

In a saucepan, boil the rice in the water until cooked, about 10 to 12 minutes. Drain the rice well and place in a bowl.

In a skillet, heat 2 tablespoons of the olive oil, add the zucchini and onion, and sauté until the vegetables are soft, about 5 minutes. Transfer the mixture to the bowl. Add the remaining ingredients except the cheese, and mix well.

Preheat the oven to 350°F.

Grease a 14- x 9-inch baking pan with the remaining olive oil. Lay each pepper out flat and spread with ¼ cup of the filling. Roll the peppers up like a jelly roll. Arrange the peppers in the baking pan seam side down. Sprinkle the cheese evenly over the top of the peppers. Cover the dish with foil and bake for 25 minutes, or until the peppers are hot. Remove the foil, bake an additional 5 minutes, then serve warm.

Fiori di Zucchini Fritti

Fried Zucchini Flowers
Serves 8 to 10

It is common in outdoor markets in Italy to see carts of bright yellow-orange zucchini blossoms. They bring a tinge of nostalgia for me, because the blossoms were a familiar sight in our kitchen. I usually run to my garden when zucchini are plentiful and gather an apron full of blossoms. I don't know anyone with zucchini plants who, by mid-summer, would not love to give away some blossoms.

1 pound zucchini blossoms	**Flour, for dredging**
6 to 7 cups peanut oil	**4 large eggs, beaten**
	Salt and pepper to taste

Open the centers of the flowers gently, remove the pistils and stigmas, and discard. Put the flowers in a bowl of ice water for 1 hour.

Heat the oil to 375°F in a deep-fryer or heavy pot.

Dry the blossoms on paper towels; roll each in the flour and then the eggs. Fry the blossoms in oil until golden, about 2 to 3 minutes. Drain on brown paper, then sprinkle with salt and pepper. Serve immediately.

Torta di Patate e Spinaci

Potato and Spinach Pie
Serves 6 to 8

I almost forgot to include the recipe for my grandmother's spinach and mashed potato pie, until my mother reminded me. This vegetable and potato combination is delicious, and you can vary the cheese with whatever is on hand. I serve this with Chicken Roasted in Salt (page 126).

1½ pounds (4 to 5) medium potatoes, peeled and cut into 1½-inch chunks

4 tablespoons olive oil

½ teaspoon salt

1 large egg

6 ounces mozzarella, Asiago, or other cheese, cubed (1½ cups)

1 10-ounce bag fresh spinach, stemmed, washed, and drained

1 large clove garlic, peeled and cut in half

2 tablespoons pine nuts

1 teaspoon grated nutmeg

6 tablespoons (¾ stick) butter, diced

Place the potatoes in a 2-quart pot and cover with water. Bring water to a boil and cook the potatoes until tender, about 12 minutes. Drain the potatoes, but reserve ¼ cup cooking water.

Place the potatoes in a bowl. Add the cooking water, 1 tablespoon of oil, salt, and egg. With a potato masher or an electric mixer, beat the potatoes until smooth. If they seem too dry, add a little more water. Fold in the cheese and set the mixture aside.

Place the spinach in a dry skillet, cover with a lid, and cook until the spinach wilts, about 2 to 3 minutes. Drain the spinach in a colander.

In the same skillet, heat 2 tablespoons of olive oil, add the garlic, and press on the garlic with a wooden spoon to release its juice. When the garlic begins to turn color, remove and discard it.

Return the spinach to the skillet, add the pine nuts, and sauté the mixture for about 2 minutes. Turn off the heat, add the nutmeg, and blend. Set the mixture aside.

Preheat the oven to 350°F. With the remaining tablespoon of oil, brush the bottom and sides of a 9-inch round cake pan.

Place half the potato mixture in the pan, smoothing the top. Add the spinach mixture, spreading it evenly on top of the potatoes. Place the remaining potato mixture on top of the spinach, spreading to cover the spinach. Dot with the diced butter and bake for about 40 minutes, or until the top begins to crust over.

Place the pan under the broiler for 2 to 3 minutes to brown the crust. Let cool for about 3 minutes, then cut the pie into wedges and serve immediately.

Variation: Instead of making a pie, form balls from the spinach and potato mixture. Roll the balls in flour, beaten egg, and bread crumbs and fry in vegetable oil. Serve as an accompaniment to roasted meats.

Ubi Roma, Ibi Allium

Where There Are Romans, There Is Garlic

Almost everyone associates garlic with Italian cooking. In the ancient Mediterranean, garlic—a member of the lily family—was used mostly for medicinal purposes. One theory says that the ancient Romans disliked it, but ate it to stimulate hair growth. In the Middle Ages, garlic was considered a combative to the plague and was worn around the neck. Today it is used not only in culinary dishes, but also touted as a preventive for certain diseases. As a child, I remember being the brunt of ethnic jokes about garlic; if you ate garlic, you were looked down upon. Today it is not only wise but chic to eat garlic, raw and in pill form—something Europeans have been doing for a long time.

In Italy, garlic is used more abundantly in the central and southern regions than it is in the north. And every Italian cook you talk to will have instructions on the right way to cook with garlic. Some prefer to put it in at the last moment, thereby ensuring that it does not burn. Others, including myself, add garlic as one of the first ingredients when making a dish.

I grow my own garlic. It is the easiest thing to plant. Simply divide the bulb into individual sections and stick each clove in the ground with the pointed end up. Water well. In late summer, when the foliage has turned yellow and dropped down, pull the plants from the ground, shake off the soil, and tie the garlic plants into bunches with string. Hang the bunches in a dry place where there is good air circulation. It will take two to four weeks for the garlic to dry, depending on the air temperature and the place where you hang it. When the foliage stems are crackle dry, remove them. Place the garlic bulbs in a net bag and hang in your kitchen or keep in a cool place and use as needed.

To remove the thin paperlike skin from garlic, place a clove on a cutting board and press down on it with the flat side of a large knife, or use a meat pounder to press on it. The skin will slip off easily. Another method for removing the skin is to cover the garlic cloves with boiling water, then steep for one minute, and drain.

To roast garlic, leave the skin on for better flavor and moistness. Divide the bulb into sections and coat the cloves with olive oil. Place in a shallow baking pan and roast in a 350°F. oven for 25 to 30 minutes, or until a knife can easily pierce the clove. Serve as an accompaniment to roasted chicken, lamb, pork, or beef.

To make garlic paste for coating vegetables and meats before roasting, place three or four peeled cloves on a cutting board and sprinkle with ½ teaspoon of fine sea salt. Mince the garlic fine until it becomes a paste. Add a little more salt if the mixture seems too dry. Keep garlic paste in a jar in the refrigerator and use within two days, as the garlic tends to discolor and become very strong.

To make garlic oil, simply peel and partly slit two cloves of garlic, and place them in a 12-ounce bottle of olive oil. Store in the refrigerator, but bring to room temperature before using.

To make garlic-flavored vinegar, follow the procedure for garlic oil but add the garlic to wine or basil vinegar. Let it steep in a sunny spot for a week before using.

Scarola Ripiena alla Camille

Camille's Stuffed Escarole
Serves 4 to 6

This Old World recipe for *scarola,* or escarole, comes from Camille Guarino, a viewer of my television series. She, like me, hated this dish as a kid, but now is fond of it. Green, curly leaves of escarole stuffed with bread crumbs, anchovies, and raisins were a hallmark of my grandmother's cooking. Camille's recipe takes me back to Grandma's kitchen.

½ cup raisins	Coarsely ground black pepper
1 pound escarole	1 teaspoon dried oregano
⅔ cup fresh bread crumbs	1 tablespoon minced fresh basil
2 tablespoons grated Pecorino Romano cheese	5 tablespoons olive oil
2 cloves garlic, peeled and mashed	¼ cup water
	Salt to taste

Soak the raisins in water to cover in a small bowl for 15 minutes.

Rinse and drain the escarole well, but do not detach the leaves from the core.

In a small bowl, combine the bread crumbs, cheese, half the garlic, ¼ teaspoon pepper, oregano, basil, and 3 tablespoons of the olive oil.

Drain the raisins and add one fourth to the mixture. Reserve the remaining raisins.

Carefully spread the escarole leaves open to the center and stuff the filling in the middle. Close up the leaves and tie the escarole firmly with kitchen string so filling will not fall out.

Place the escarole bundles in a Dutch oven or slow cooker. Sprinkle on the remaining olive oil, garlic, and raisins. Add the water, cover the pot, and cook over low heat for 20 to 25 minutes, or until the leaves have wilted and are soft.

Carefully remove the escarole to a cutting board and cut off the strings. Cut the bundle into pieces and serve with pan juices, and salt and pepper to taste.

Torta di Porri, Carciofi, Finocchio, e Salsicce

Leek, Artichoke, Fennel, and Sausage Tart
Serves 8

One of the great culinary triumphs of the Renaissance was the great *torta,* or pie, stuffed with every imaginable ingredient, including live birds. I developed this recipe, taking my inspiration from a Renaissance pie called *de la torta parmesana,* filled with cheese, meats, herbs, vegetables, and almonds. Prepare the dough and vegetables the day before it is to be served.

continued

4 cooked medium
artichoke hearts

4 tablespoons olive oil

1 pound leeks, white
parts only, sliced into
thin rings

1 medium fennel, bulb
quartered and cut into
thin strips; tops
minced

¾ pound mild or hot
Italian sausage

1 teaspoon fennel seeds

1 teaspoon fine sea salt

½ teaspoon coarsely
ground black pepper

¼ cup toasted pine nuts

¼ cup grated
Parmigiano-Reggiano
cheese

1 recipe Pasta Frolla
(page 299), chilled

4 large eggs

¼ cup dry white wine

1 tablespoon water

Cut the artichoke hearts into small pieces and place them in a large bowl.

Heat 3 tablespoons of olive oil in a skillet and sauté the leeks for
about 3 minutes or until wilted. Add leeks to the artichokes.

Add the remaining tablespoon of oil to the skillet and sauté the fennel
for about 4 minutes or until it begins to soften. Add the fennel to the bowl
with the artichokes.

In the same skillet, brown the sausage, adding no additional fat; add
a little water if the sausage is lean. When the sausage is browned, drain
off the fat, transfer sausage to a cutting board, and let cool for 10 minutes.
Cut the sausage into ¼-inch slices, then add them to the bowl.

Toss 2 tablespoons fennel leaves, fennel seeds, sea salt, pepper, pine
nuts, and cheese into the artichoke mixture and set aside.

Preheat the oven to 425°F.

Divide the dough into 2 pieces. Roll each piece on a lightly floured
surface into a 14-inch circle, then use 1 piece to line a 9-inch tart pan
with a removable bottom. Let the excess dough hang over the edges. Place
the filling in the tart shell, smoothing it out but not compacting it.

In a small bowl, whisk 3 eggs with the wine and pour the mixture
into the tart shell. Place the second piece of dough over the top, letting
the edges hang over. With a rolling pin, roll over the edges of the pan to
cut off the excess dough.

Re-roll the pastry scraps and make a decorative pattern of vines and
leaves over the top of the tart. In a small bowl, beat the remaining egg
with the water and brush the mixture evenly over the top of the tart. Bake
the tart for 35 to 40 minutes, or until the top is golden brown.

Remove the tart to a rack and let cool slightly. Remove the sides of the tart pan, and place the tart on a serving dish. Slice into wedges to serve.

Note: To prevent the edges of the tart from browning too much, cover them loosely with a piece of aluminum foil.

Torta di Pomodori ed Erbe

Tomato and Herb Tart
Serves 4 to 6

I love making this colorful tart with ripe tomatoes and fresh herbs from my garden. It is similar to a quiche, but contains no eggs. It is perfect as a luncheon course, and I also often serve it for dinner with soup or salad. You can vary the cheese filling, combining favorites, and change the herbs to suit your fancy. Store-bought puff pastry speeds the preparation time.

3 fresh plum tomatoes, sliced in thin rounds

Salt

2 cloves garlic, peeled

3 tablespoons fresh thyme leaves

3 tablespoons fresh parsley leaves

3 tablespoons fresh oregano leaves

1 small onion, peeled and quartered

Freshly ground black pepper

3 tablespoons extra-virgin olive oil

1 sheet prepared frozen puff pastry from a 17¼-ounce package, thawed

1 tablespoon Dijon mustard

½ pound Swiss cheese, diced

continued

Layer the tomato slices in a colander, sprinkling each layer with salt. Let the tomatoes "sweat" while preparing the other ingredients.

With a knife, mince together the garlic, thyme, parsley, oregano, and onion. Place the mixture in a small bowl and blend in the pepper and olive oil. Set the mixture aside.

Preheat the oven to 425°F. Lightly grease the bottom of a deep 10½-inch tart pan with a removable bottom. Set aside.

On a floured surface, roll the puff pastry into a 14-inch circle and line the bottom and sides of the tart pan, cutting off any overhanging dough. Prick the dough uniformly with a fork, or line the shell with dried beans to keep it from puffing up. Bake the shell for 10 minutes, watching carefully so that it does not brown too much.

Remove the shell from the oven, and remove and discard the beans, if used. Immediately brush the bottom of the tart shell with the mustard. Fill the shell evenly with the cheese. Rinse and dry the tomato slices, then place them in overlapping circles over the cheese. Spread the garlic and herb mixture evenly over the tomatoes. Place the tart in the oven and bake for 25 minutes.

Cool the tart slightly on a rack, then carefully remove the sides of the pan. Place the tart on a serving dish and cut into wedges. Serve warm.

Insalate

Salads

The one dish that was regularly served at every lunch and dinner in our house was a salad dressed with oil and vinegar, or sometimes lemon juice. My grandmothers insisted that eating *insalata* after the main course was a *digestivo*, or a healthy way to settle one's stomach.

They preferred bitter greens, which they called *cicoria*, a term for wild kinds of greens. They both picked dandelion greens for salads; their bitter flavor was similar in taste to the greens they were used to in Italy. The dandelion greens were boiled and served cold with oil and vinegar. For me, having to eat this was worse than being sent to confession every Saturday afternoon! At my friends' homes, I always ate iceberg lettuce.

I still serve a green salad to my family after every meal. A few basic rules ensure that my salads will be perfect: Do not buy limp lettuce or lettuce that has yellow leaves or dark brown spots at the top; this is an indication of old age. Fresh lettuce is uniformly green and almost stands up on its own. The leaves are springy when shaken and the head feels solid. Most supermarkets irrigate their produce several times a day to ensure crispness. If what you see in the supermarket does not satisfy you, ask the produce clerk to open a new box from the back room. Many people do not know enough to do this, and often wind up taking the second best home and paying top dollar.

When I make salad I vary the ingredients, often combining romaine, radicchio, and arugula; or I mix endive and spinach leaves. Never wash lettuce leaves until you are just about to make the salad. Drain the leaves well in a colander, then gently roll them in paper or cloth towels to absorb the excess water. If the lettuce is wet, the oil will not adhere to the leaves.

I serve *insalata verde* ("basic green salad") or *insalata mista* ("mixed green salad containing raw vegetables") when I have a meat or poultry course. For fish dishes, I often serve my Grandmother Saporito's simple combination of orange slices, fennel, and black olives lightly drizzled with olive oil.

Of course, there are many salads that are served *before* the meal as antipasti. These can include anything from olives and beans in olive oil to one of my favorites—*insalata Russa,* or Russian salad, which is a composite of vegetables in a mayonnaise dressing.

Insalata d'Indivia

Endive Salad
Serves 4

It's spring in Italy when I see wooden crates full of artichokes, asparagus, and leafy endive lined up against the walls of small produce shops. This springtime salad uses the milder, pale Belgian endive found in U.S. markets.

2½ tablespoons fresh
   lemon juice

½ teaspoon grainy
   mustard

½ teaspoon salt

½ cup extra-virgin
   olive oil

6 baby potatoes, about 1
   inch in diameter,
   scrubbed

3 ribs celery, sliced

½ pound (2 medium
   heads) Belgian endive,
   washed and drained

In a small bowl, whisk the lemon juice, mustard, and salt together. Gradually whisk in the olive oil until a smooth emulsion is obtained. Set aside.

In a small saucepan, boil the potatoes until tender, about 10 minutes. Drain and let cool completely, then peel and cut into ¼-inch slices.

Place potatoes in a salad bowl with the celery. Cut the endive into thin strips and add to the potatoes.

Whisk the salad dressing until smooth again, pour over the salad, and mix gently. Serve immediately.

Note: Line the salad plates with the reddish-purple leaves of radicchio for a color contrast.

Insalata di Varie Crudità

Mixed Raw Salad
Serves 4 to 6

Here is a salad that can be served as antipasto or after the main course. Vary the salad depending on what's in season. This composition is a variation on the classic *pinzimonio,* or raw vegetable salad, served in Tuscany, but here various lettuces are used for a mix of flavor. You can omit the fresh mozzarella if unavailable. It's a great salad for a buffet.

8 ounces fresh mozzarella cheese (*fior di latte*), cut in strips

¼ pound romaine lettuce, washed and drained

¼ pound radicchio, washed and drained

¼ pound chicory, washed and drained

1 cup sliced fresh mushrooms

¼ pound ham, cut in strips

2 scallions, white parts only, cut in thin rounds

1 ripe avocado, peeled and cut in thin slices

1 rib celery, thinly sliced

Juice of 1 large lemon

½ teaspoon salt

Freshly ground black pepper

6 tablespoons olive oil

On a large serving plate, arrange the cheese, lettuces, vegetables, and ham attractively in bunches.

In a bowl, whisk together the lemon juice, salt, and pepper. Slowly whisk in the olive oil until a homogeneous dressing is obtained. Drizzle the mixture over the salad ingredients and serve immediately.

Note: You may want to toss the sliced avocado slices in lemon juice to prevent discoloration.

Insalata di Arucola, Avocado, e Fichi Secchi

Arugula, Avocado, and Dried Fig Salad
Serves 4

The addition of dried figs gives this salad an interesting texture.

1 bunch arugula,
cleaned, dried well,
and torn into pieces

½ small head romaine
lettuce, cleaned,
dried well, and torn
into pieces

1 medium avocado,
peeled, pitted, and
cut into small pieces

1½ tablespoons fresh
lemon juice

½ cup dried figs, sliced
¼ inch thick

¼ cup extra-virgin
olive oil

2 tablespoons balsamic
vinegar

½ teaspoon salt

Toss the arugula and romaine together in a salad bowl. Set aside.

Toss the avocado with 1 tablespoon of the lemon juice in a small bowl; add along with the figs to the salad greens.

In another small bowl, whisk together the olive oil, vinegar, salt, and remaining lemon juice. Pour the dressing over the salad ingredients, toss well, and serve immediately on individual plates.

Insalata di Spinaci e Patate

Spinach and Potato Salad
Serves 4

Here is an adaptation of a fresh spinach salad that I had in Boston. I liked the flavor combination of the potatoes sautéed in duck fat and the fresh spinach leaves. Here, I have substituted bacon fat for duck fat.

1 10-ounce bag fresh spinach, washed, stemmed, and drained

¼ to ½ cup bacon or duck fat

2 medium red potatoes, peeled and thinly sliced

3 tablespoons extra-virgin olive oil

2 tablespoons balsamic vinegar

Salt and pepper to taste

1 small black truffle, shaved, optional

Dry the spinach leaves well, place in a salad bowl, and refrigerate.

In a large skillet, heat ¼ cup of the bacon fat. Add some of the potato slices and sauté in batches until nicely browned on both sides, about 5 to 7 minutes. Drain the potatoes on brown paper and keep warm.

Toss the spinach leaves with the olive oil and balsamic vinegar, and season with salt and pepper.

Distribute one third of the spinach leaves among 4 salad plates. Top each with a layer of potatoes, a layer of spinach, another layer of potatoes, and another layer of spinach. Scatter the truffle shavings on the salads and serve immediately.

Insalata di Mozzarella
e Peperoni

Mozzarella and Pepper Salad
Serves 4

Fresh mozzarella made from cow's milk (*fior di latte*) and sliced tomatoes are a popular item in American restaurants. For variety, try making this fresh pepper and mozzarella salad.

2 red bell peppers	½ teaspoon salt
2 yellow bell peppers	¼ teaspoon coarsely ground pepper
½ pound (2 balls) fresh mozzarella cheese (*fior di latte*), sliced into ¼-inch rounds	3 or 4 fresh basil leaves, cut into thin pieces
½ cup extra-virgin olive oil	

Preheat the broiler.

Wash and dry the peppers. Place on a broiler pan and broil until blackened all over, about 12 to 15 minutes. Place peppers in a paper bag, close bag, and let steam until cool.

Remove the pepper stem tops, outer skins, and seeds. Wipe the peppers free of seeds with a paper towel. Cut the peppers into ¼-inch strips. Set aside.

On a serving platter, arrange a row of alternating colored pepper strips, slightly overlapping. Next to them, arrange a slightly overlapping row of mozzarella. Continue with another row of peppers and cheese, until all are used.

Drizzle the oil over the peppers and cheese. Sprinkle on the salt, pepper, and basil. Cover the platter loosely and let the salad marinate several hours at room temperature.

Variation: Add ¼ cup pitted, diced oil-cured black olives.

Insalata di Barbabietola

Beet Salad
Serves 4

Nothing could get me to eat my grandmother Galasso's beet salad. Her purple stained fingers were a tipoff that boiled beets were in the refrigerator. And now, I have trouble getting my family to eat them, so I've dressed them up in a zippy dressing that is very refreshing. Baking instead of boiling the beets prevents the juices and color from leaching out.

2 pounds (4 to 6) beets

⅓ cup extra-virgin olive oil

1 teaspoon crushed garlic

2 tablespoons balsamic vinegar

1 teaspoon sugar

1½ tablespoons minced fresh mint

Salt to taste

2 hard-boiled eggs, sliced

1 small head red-leaf lettuce, cleaned and separated into leaves

Mint sprigs, for garnish

Preheat the oven to 375°F.

Remove any leaves from beets and cut the stems, leaving about 2 inches of stem attached. Wash and dry the beets well. Wrap each in aluminum foil and bake for 20 to 25 minutes, or until a knife can easily be inserted. Unwrap and let cool.

In a flat shallow serving dish, mix the remaining ingredients except the eggs, lettuce, and mint sprigs.

Peel the beets, cut off and discard the remaining stems, and slice the beets into ¼-inch rounds. Place beets in the marinade and gently toss with a spoon. Cover the dish and let beets marinate at room temperature for at least 2 hours.

To serve, divide the lettuce leaves among 4 salad plates. Place some of the beets on top of each dish and garnish with a few egg slices. Add a mint sprig to each plate, if you wish. Serve immediately.

Insalata di Broccoli e Borlotti

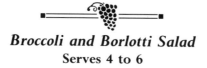

Broccoli and Borlotti Salad
Serves 4 to 6

It always puzzled me as to why I did not see broccoli in many markets in northern and central Italy. I learned that broccoli is regarded as a southern Italian vegetable, appearing in the cooler months of the year.

In this recipe, broccoli is boiled and then served cold, combined with borlotti beans. You can also use chickpeas in place of the borlotti. Soak the beans the night before you plan to make the salad; otherwise they will take about an hour to cook.

½ cup borlotti
(cranberry) beans or
chickpeas, soaked in
water overnight

½ cup extra-virgin
olive oil

3 tablespoons fresh
lemon juice

¼ teaspoon hot red
pepper flakes

½ teaspoon salt

Black pepper to taste

1 tablespoon chopped
fresh parsley

1 pound broccoli, cut
into 1-inch florets

Drain the beans, rinse, place in a pot, and cover with cold water. Bring the beans to a boil and cook for about 35 to 45 minutes, or until tender but not mushy. They should remain firm to the bite. Drain the beans and set aside.

While the beans are cooking, make the dressing. In a serving dish, large enough to hold the beans and broccoli, mix 7 tablespoons of olive oil, lemon juice, red pepper flakes, salt, and pepper.

Place the broccoli in a large pot of boiling water. Add the remaining tablespoon olive oil. Do not cover the pot. Cook the broccoli until a knife is easily inserted into the stem end, about 5 to 7 minutes. Carefully drain the broccoli and cool to room temperature.

Drain the beans and add along with the broccoli to the dressing. Toss gently to coat vegetables well. Cover the dish and let the vegetables marinate at room temperature for several hours, stirring often.

Note: Adding a little olive oil to the cooking water when boiling green vegetables helps retain their color.

Insalata d'Aragosta e Pere

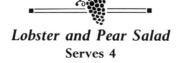

Lobster and Pear Salad
Serves 4

Turning forty was not hard, because celebrating this milestone in Italy made it all the easier. Mine was a working birthday, in the teaching kitchen of chef Mario Ragni, where students prepared crostini, crespelle, two types of veal, trout, and a memorable Lobster and Pear Salad. In the evening, we enjoyed the wonderful array of the chef's talents. The finale was a joyous musical rendition of *"Buon Compleanno,"* or "Happy Birthday," sung between bites of a dense chocolate cake. Every birthday since then, I remember that special day by making that salad . . . and growing older seems more digestible. I have changed the recipe slightly, adding fresh thyme and lemon juice to the pears. Serve this elegant salad as a special luncheon treat or as the first course to a company meal.

½ cup extra-virigin olive oil

1½ tablespoons red wine vinegar

2½ tablespoons fresh lemon juice

1½ tablespoons fresh thyme leaves

1 tablespoon sweet grainy mustard

¼ teaspoon salt

1 tablespoon minced fresh chives

2 ripe Bartlett pears, cut into ¼-inch slices

7 or 8 romaine leaves, washed, dried, and torn into pieces

12 ounces cooked lobster meat, cut in pieces

In a jar, combine the olive oil, vinegar, 1 tablespoon lemon juice, 1 tablespoon thyme, the mustard, salt, and chives. Shake well and let rest at room temperature for 2 hours.

In a glass dish, blend the remaining lemon juice and thyme. Add the pear slices and coat with the mixture. Cover the dish and marinate 1 hour.

Arrange the lettuce leaves around the edges of a serving platter. Place the lobster meat in the center and arrange the pear slices in a border around the lobster. Shake the dressing and pour over the lobster and pears. Serve.

Coppette Tonnate

Tuna Cups
Serves 4

This interesting salad combines tuna with chicken and makes a nice antipasto or an easy lunch. Be sure to use tuna packed in olive oil.

2 cups water

1 rib celery, cut in half

1 shallot, peeled and halved

½ cup plus 3 tablespoons dry white wine

⅛ teaspoon salt

½ pound boneless chicken breast

3 tablespoons olive oil

1 small onion, peeled and minced

1 6-ounce can tuna in olive oil, flaked

2 teaspoons capers in vinegar, drained

¼ head romaine lettuce, cleaned and torn into pieces

1 cup mayonnaise

Place the water, celery, shallot, ½ cup of the wine, salt, and the chicken breast in a medium pot. Bring to a boil and cook until the chicken is tender, about 25 minutes. Drain the chicken and cool. Cut the chicken into thin slices and refrigerate. Discard the cooking water and ingredients.

In a skillet, heat the olive oil and add the onion. Mince half the capers and add to skillet along with the tuna. Sauté over medium-high heat for 2 to 3 minutes, then add the remaining wine and cook until evaporated. Remove the skillet from the heat, place the mixture in a bowl, cover, and chill.

When ready to serve, place the lettuce in 4 dessert goblets. Divide the chicken among the dishes. Place one fourth of the tuna mixture on the chicken, and garnish with the remaining whole capers. Pass the mayonnaise on the side.

Le Erbe Fresche

Fresh Herbs

Bunches of herbs tied with string and hung from nails were a familiar sight in my grandmothers' pantries. They would never think of serving a dish without proper seasoning. Mint, parsley, basil, oregano, and fennel were used fresh whenever possible. Others, like rosemary, marjoram, and thyme, were used dried. It all depended on which herbs my grandmothers could coax to grow from the ground and which were just too stubborn to send up their fragrant shoots.

In my own cooking, I shy away from dried herbs except for oregano and occasionally, rosemary, because when dried, most herbs loose a significant amount of their natural oils and most of their taste. Instead, I prefer to grow my herbs, most of which are perennials and therefore come up each year. I usually start basil plants from seed, as well as parsley, but I grow the flavorful Italian flat-leaf parsley, not curly parsley, which has little flavor.

I keep pots of my most frequently used herbs on the windowsill, and at the height of the summer, I preserve basil and sage in salt or freeze them. To freeze basil, remove the leaves from the stems, wipe them well with a damp paper towel, and layer them flat in plastic bags. Before sealing the bag, make sure that all the air is out by pressing on the bag. Place the bags in your freezer and then take out the leaves as you need them. While the flavor will be fresh, the leaves will have darkened in color, so you won't be able to use them when presentation is important but they are just fine for soups, stews, and sauces and for roasting with meats, fish, and poultry.

Another method for preserving sage and basil is to layer the leaves in coarse sea salt in clean jars. Store the jars in the refrigerator. Be sure the herbs are perfectly dry after you wash or damp-wipe them before layering them in salt. I have more success with this method if I use herbs with large leaves.

Certain herbs are synonymous with specific regions. In the northern regions like Liguria, marjoram and basil are frequently used. Tuscan and Umbrian cooking favors rosemary, wild fennel, and sage, especially with grilled meats. These herbs are tied together in a bunch and used as a basting brush. Southern Italians use oregano on pizza, in sauces, and with vegetables. Unfortunately, most people associate this herb with all Italian cooking!

Mint is frequently found in Roman dishes, especially those containing artichokes. Likewise, green bean salad Sicilian style always has a refreshing mint flavor. Parsley, like basil, is used extensively in all regions of Italy. Bay leaf is used in stews and some sauces and should always be added whole, not chopped, because jagged edges could catch in one's throat. Use it sparingly because adding too much bay leaf can ruin a dish, and impart a medicinal flavor. At home, fennel was considered to be a digestivo. Eating thin slices of the bulb after the meal settled your stomach. It is used in soups, with meats and fish, and in the classic blood orange and fennel salad from Sicily.

When visiting Italy, I buy herbs found only there, such as nepitella, a type of wild mint used with porcini mushrooms, sautéed zucchini, and artichokes. I like droga di arrosti, which is a combination of rosemary, bay leaf, fennel seeds, oregano, juniper berries, and parsley used to rub into meats before roasting.

Cooking with aromatic herbs is part of Italy's culinary tradition, and can easily be duplicated in your own kitchen. Just be sure to use fresh herbs when possible and, as my grandmothers would caution, "Far man frugale." ("Use them sparingly.")

Pomodori Ripieni di Tonno

Tomatoes Stuffed with Tuna

Serves 4

Chervil and tarragon are not found in many Italian dishes, but just recently I met up with these two pungent herbs in Siena, at Ristorante al Marsili, on Via del Castoro. They were used very sparingly in a light tomato sauce served over thin slices of veal. They were also used to flavor bulging, ripe tomatoes stuffed with tuna. This is a good summertime salad when fresh tomatoes and herbs are at their peak.

4 ripe medium tomatoes

1 6-ounce can tuna packed in water, drained

1 tablespoon capers in brine, drained and minced

1 small onion, peeled and diced

1 tablespoon minced chervil leaves

1 tablespoon minced tarragon leaves

4 tablespoons mayonnaise

Salt and pepper to taste

Cut ¼ inch off the stem end of each tomato and reserve. Squeeze each tomato gently to remove the seeds. Use a spoon to remove most of the flesh, which can be saved for soup. Salt the interior of each tomato, then turn it upside down and let drain on paper towels for about 20 minutes.

In a bowl, stir the remaining ingredients until well blended. Stuff each tomato with some of the filling. Replace the tops of the tomatoes, place on individual serving plates, and serve.

Pizza

I did not include any recipes for tomato-based pizza in my first book, *Ciao Italia,* because I assumed that most people knew not only how to make it but also knew that there were many other types of *pizze,* called by other names in Italy. What amazed me was how many people thought that pepperoni pizza meant a disk of dough topped with cooked tomato sauce, cheese, and hard, spicy sausage, all smothered under a medicinal layer of dried oregano. Not at all Italian. Ask for pizza with pepperoni in Italy, and you will get pizza topped with Italian peppers, because that's what *peperoni* means in Italian.

Although pizza is made all over Italy, the concept for baking flat disks of dough is not Italian, but dates from the Neolithic age, when grain and water was mixed into a paste, patted into flatbread, and cooked on hot stones.

Italian pizza today is baked in hot brick or stone ovens with temperatures that reach 650°F. The toppings are as varied as the regions of Italy. Some pizzas are topped with mushrooms, others with just olive oil and slivers of garlic; some are dressed with mussels and squid tentacles, others with onions and olives or a composite of garden vegetables; some are pungent like pesto pizza and others have nothing more than olive oil and ground black pepper over the top. In Naples, where the best pizza is claimed to be made, one of the most popular is pizza margherita, and it was created by a *pizzaiolo* ("pizza maker") named Raffaele Esposito. Another classic of Naples is pizza napoletana. Of course, my grandmothers and mother made their versions of pizzas, but I ate it in its purest form the first time I went to Italy at a family-run trattoria called El Condor. I watched the pizzaiolo quickly shape a formless mass of dough into a free-form oval or round shape and then sprinkle it with a little olive oil. Peeled and seeded fresh tomatoes were spread thinly over the top, along with a few anchovies. The pizza was placed into the hot brick oven to bake on the oven floor. What emerged was a true Neapolitan culinary masterpiece, flavorful and well balanced. When I tasted it, it was so light, so delicious and so unlike what I was expecting that I had no doubt that the Neapolitans had the corner on the art of making pizza.

Three key ingredients identify the success of pizza in Naples: fresh tomatoes, fresh basil or oregano, and fresh cheeses called *fior di latte* and *mozzarella di bufala*. *Fior di latte* is a whole-milk mozzarella, which is very delicate in flavor, and *mozzarella di bufala* is cheese made from the milk of the water buffalo.

I make my pizza using a *cresciuta*, or "growth." After the first rising of the yeast dough, I pinch off a piece about the size of a small orange and place it in an oiled jar and store it in the refrigerator.

When I am ready to use my cresciuta, I bring it to room temperature. In a bowl, I mix warm water and a little dry yeast to give added fortification to my dough. Next, I add the cresciuta and mix the two together before adding the flour. When using the cresciuta, make sure to allow the dough to rise slowly for several hours. This will help to develop the dough's full flavor. I use the cresciuta for bread as well, and I bake it on my baking stone. It produces a dense, chewy loaf that is good for *bruschetta* ("grilled bread") rubbed with garlic and drizzled with olive oil.

A unique hostess gift is a freshly baked loaf of bread made with the cresciuta, as well as a small jar of the growth with instructions and your recipe on how to use it.

If you do not want to make pizza with a cresciuta, then use the recipe for Pasta per Pizza on page 203. This basic dough requires less time.

Pasta per Pizza

Pizza Dough
Makes 1½ pounds

Here is a basic pizza dough that is made without the cresciuta (page 204). Good on its own or as an alternative to making a starter dough. This dough will not be as chewy or tangy as that made with a starter.

1½ teaspoons active dry yeast

1½ cups warm water (110° to 115° F.)

3½ to 3¾ cups all-purpose unbleached flour

½ teaspoon salt

1 teaspoon olive oil

In a large bowl, dissolve the yeast in ½ cup warm water. Allow the yeast to proof until it is foamy, about 10 minutes.

Add the remaining 1 cup of warm water, combining it well with the yeast. Add 3 cups of the flour and the salt. Mix the dough with your hands or use a mixer with a dough hook, adding the remaining flour as needed to make a dough that holds together.

Place the dough on a floured surface and knead it for about 10 minutes, or until the dough is soft and not sticky. Grease a bowl with the olive oil. Put the dough in the bowl and turn a few times to coat with the oil. Cover the bowl tightly with plastic wrap and let it rise for 2 hours in a warm place.

Punch down the dough and knead it for a few minutes on a lightly floured surface. Use the dough to make one large thick pizza or divide it in half to make two small thin ones.

Pizza with Cresciuta

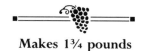

Makes 1¾ pounds

Now let me get you started on making pizza with a cresciuta. Use fresh, active dry yeast. I buy it loose in bulk; it is cheaper and fresher, and I use a lot of it. Store it in a jar in the refrigerator.

I use filtered water in this recipe because it is purer than tap water and I do think it makes a difference in taste, especially if your water is heavily treated with chemicals and high in sodium. I also spoon the flour into my measuring cup instead of scooping it from the bag or flour bin. This ensures that I have 4 ounces to my cup instead of the 5 for the scooped method.

Cresciuta	*Second Dough*
¾ teaspoon active dry yeast	1 teaspoon active dry yeast
½ cup warm water (110° to 115° F.)	1½ cups warm water (110° to 115°F.)
½ cup plus 2 tablespoons unbleached all-purpose flour	3½ to 4 cups unbleached all-purpose flour
	⅛ teaspoon salt

For the cresciuta: In a small bowl, dissolve the yeast in the warm water. Let it rest, covered, for 10 minutes. Stir in the flour with a spoon and blend well. Cover the bowl tightly with plastic wrap and let it rise in a warm place for 3 to 4 hours.

For the second dough: In a large bowl, dissolve the yeast in the warm water. Add the cresciuta to the second dough and mix well with your hands.

In a separate bowl, mix 3⅓ cups of the flour and the salt and add to the large bowl. Mix with your hands until you have a ball of dough. Add up to ⅔ cup additional flour as needed to make a dough that is soft and slightly sticky. Turn the dough out onto a floured surface and knead for about 10 minutes, adding additional flour as needed, to make a smooth and elastic ball.

Grease a large bowl lightly with olive oil; add the dough, turning it in the bowl to coat it with the oil. Cover the bowl tightly with plastic wrap and let rise in a warm place for 2 to 3 hours.

Turn the dough out onto a floured surface. Pinch off a piece of dough about the size of a small orange, roll it into a ball, and place it in a small jar that has been lightly brushed with olive oil. Cap the jar and store in the refrigerator. This is your cresciuta and next time you make pizza you will only need to make the second dough and add the saved cresciuta. Make sure you always tear off a piece of dough and save it for the next time you make the dough.

Knead the remaining dough for 3 to 4 minutes. Divide the dough in half and use as directed in pizza recipes.

Note: Wrap the dough well and freeze for future use.

Pizza Casalinga

Homestyle Pizza
Makes one 16- x 15-inch pizza

I make pizza at least once a week because it is my son Chris's favorite food. The topping for this pizza was invented when I found some odds and ends of cheese in the refrigerator and vegetables from my garden. When I took my creation out of the oven, it was so beautiful to look at that I snapped a picture of it. To me it was a good example of the create-with-what's-on-hand style of home cooking I grew up with, and made me feel very close to my roots. In this recipe, I have used Swiss chard, but you can use spinach as well. As for the cheeses, use what you have on hand.

1 recipe Pizza with Cresciuta (page 204)

Topping

1 pound Swiss chard, cleaned, stems removed

6 tablespoons olive oil

2 cloves garlic, minced

1 medium yellow squash, cut into 4- x ¼-inch strips

½ teaspoon salt

¼ teaspoon black pepper

1 medium white onion, thinly sliced

½ cup grated Asiago cheese

½ cup grated ricotta salata cheese

Freshly ground black pepper

Place the Swiss chard leaves in a skillet and add 1 cup water. Cover and cook over medium heat for 7 to 10 minutes, or until the leaves are tender. Drain the Swiss chard well in a colander, using your hands to squeeze out the excess water. When cool, chop coarsely and set aside.

In the same skillet, heat 3 tablespoons of the olive oil, add the onions and cook slowly over medium-low heat until translucent. Remove the onions to a dish. In the same pan add the Swiss chard, minced garlic, and 2 tablespoons of olive oil. Sauté the Swiss chard for 3 to 4 minutes, add the salt and pepper, and mix well. Remove to a dish and set aside.

Preheat the broiler.

In a small bowl, toss the squash with 1 tablespoon of the olive oil. Place the squash on a broiler pan lined with foil and broil for 5 minutes, or until they start to brown. Remove the squash to a dish.

Preheat the oven to 375° F.

Lightly brush a 15- x 14-inch cookie sheet with 1 tablespoon of olive oil. Roll the dough into a 16- x 15-inch rectangle. Place the dough on the cookie sheet. Create an edge by turning the edges in toward the center and pinching the dough with your fingers.

Spread the Swiss chard on top. Sprinkle on the onions and the squash. Sprinkle the cheeses over the top. Drizzle on the remaining 1 tablespoon of olive oil and add the pepper.

Bake the pizza for 25 to 30 minutes, or until it is a golden brown. Cut into squares with kitchen scissors and serve immediately.

Note: This makes a nice party appetizer when cut into small squares.

La Passeggiata

The Stroll

The passeggiata *is the Italian pastime. Calling the steady, measured stroll done by family, friends, business acquaintances, and, of course, lovers "taking a walk" is to underestimate its significance.*

The passeggiata is treasured time, not measured time; simply put, it is relaxation. Like food and the family dinner, the passeggiata is some of the glue that binds Italian people to one another. The passeggiata is most evident on weekends and weeknights, when Italians seem to come out of everywhere to walk arm-in-arm to the center of the piazza. As they walk and talk, they eat gelato or nibble on folded wedges of pizza. Sometimes the passeggiata is temporarily interrupted with a stop for a drink of Campari or una limonata.

Sometimes the attention of strollers is diverted to a demonstration for some social cause or sports event; there are often artists selling their wares, and occasionally music resounds in the street. I giovani ("teenagers"), walking with their own gender, are linked in groups of four or six. Smartly dressed couples stop now and then to admire the stylishly arranged window displays of pastry, clothing, jewelry, and objects of art. Waiters in their whites dash down the street balancing trays of pasta and pyramids of just-made dolci, gaily wrapped in bright colored paper and ribbon, to deliver to local customers. The clergy is very much in evidence too, asking patrons at the numerous bars that line the piazza for donations for the poor.

Not too long ago, an Italian student from Emilia-Romagna came to stay with us. His name was Massimiliano, but we all called him Max. He quickly became a member our family, even sharing the same interest in sports as my son Christopher. Every night after dinner, Max had what we thought was a curious request: Could we please drive him into town to the shopping plaza? Of course, we complied, but it took a couple of dropoffs for us to realize that Max was taking the passeggiata. Other visiting Italian students would meet at the plaza and socialize at a fast-food restaurant. They identified it as the counterpart to their piazza at home. Even when away from home, the tradition is a strong one.

I envy this time-honored tradition. Whenever I am in Italy, I stroll arm-in-arm with people I care about, treasuring the time spent in relaxation.

Pizza con Porcini

Pizza with Porcini
Makes one 17- x 11-inch or two 13-inch pizzas

Porcini, also known as cepes, are the kings of Italian mushrooms. These woodsy mushrooms grow wild in oak and pine forests and can be dried very successfully. I use them sparingly in sauces, stews, and on this pizza. You need only a few, and the amount given here after soaking in water will equal about 1 cup of fresh mushrooms. I make this pizza on a 17- x 11-inch jelly-roll pan, which produces a thick-crusted pizza, or divide the dough in half and use two 13-inch round pizza pans. Cut into small squares or wedges and serve this pizza as an antipasto.

1 ounce (30 grams) dried porcini mushrooms	3 tablespoons olive oil
	½ teaspoon coarsely ground black pepper
12 ounces button mushrooms, sliced	1 recipe Pizza with Cresciuta (page 204)
3 tablespoons butter	

Preheat the oven to 375° F.

In a bowl cover the porcini with cold water and let them soak for 30 minutes. Drain well, chop the mushrooms, and set aside. Reserve the liquid for another use.

In a skillet, melt the butter and 1 tablespoon of the olive oil. Add the sliced mushrooms and sauté until all the liquid has evaporated. Add the porcini and sauté for an additional 2 minutes. Sprinkle the mushrooms with the pepper and set aside.

Punch down the dough and roll to fit your pan size. Brush the pan or pans with the remaining olive oil and place the dough on top, stretching it to fit. Turn any excess dough inward to form an edge.

Scatter the mushrooms over the top. Bake the pizza for 30 to 35 minutes, or until the crust is nicely browned. Serve immediately.

Pizza con Salsicce e Cipolle

Pizza with Sausage and Onions
Makes one 13-inch pizza

This pizza, made with fresh homemade sausage (page 124) and onions, is one of my favorites. Sausage perfumed with fennel seeds and slowly cooked onions are a tasty combination. I use half the recipe of dough for Pizza with Cresciuta (page 204). If you wish to make two pizzas, double the topping ingredients. Buy good-quality sausage if you don't make your own. To round out the meal, a mixed salad and fresh fruit are sufficient.

4 tablespoons olive oil

1 large onion
(5 ounces), sliced
into thin rounds

¾ pound mild or spicy
Italian sausage

2¼ cups (10 ounces)
chopped mozzarella
cheese

1 tablespoon freshly
minced sage

Grinding of black pepper

½ recipe Pizza with
Cresciuta (page 204)

Preheat the oven to 375° F.

In a skillet, heat 3 tablespoons of the olive oil. Add the onions and sauté slowly over medium heat until they are soft and golden. Remove the onions to a dish. In the same skillet, brown the sausage over medium-high heat for 20 to 25 minutes. Drain off any excess fat that accumulates. Remove the sausage to a cutting board and let it cool about 10 minutes. Cut the sausage into ½-inch pieces and set aside.

Brush the pizza dough with the remaining 1 tablespoon of olive oil. Scatter the onions evenly over the dough. Lay the sausage pieces over the onions. Sprinkle on the cheese, sage, and pepper.

Bake the pizza for 20 to 25 minutes, or until the crust is nicely browned. Cut into wedges and serve at once.

Variation: Sauté 1 sweet red pepper cut into thin strips with the onions.

Pizza Chena

Serves 10 to 12

Every Good Friday afternoon I could look forward to two things: spending a good part of the day in church, and watching my grandmother and mother make an enormous pie for Easter, called *pizza chena*. I never knew what that meant in Italian until many years later, when studying the language, I realized that pizza chena was dialect for *pizza piena,* which meant "a very full pie." And it was—chock-full of meats, cheeses, and a dozen eggs! While I have reduced the number of eggs, this still remains a substantial and memorable pie. It looks impressive when made in a round or rectangular pan at least 2½ inches deep.

Dough

1 tablespoon active dry yeast

2½ cups warm water (110° to 115° F.)

5½ to 6 cups unbleached all-purpose flour

1 teaspoon salt

3½ teaspoons olive oil

Filling

¾ pound mozzarella cheese, thinly sliced

½ pound ham, thinly sliced

½ pound Provolone cheese, thinly sliced

½ pound Genoa salami, thinly sliced

½ pound Swiss cheese, thinly sliced

½ pound capocollo, thinly sliced

7 large eggs

½ cup grated Parmigiano-Reggiano cheese

⅓ cup minced fresh parsley

Salt to taste

Grinding of black pepper

In a large bowl, dissolve the yeast in 1 cup of the warm water. Allow the yeast to proof for 5 minutes, or until it is foamy. Add the remaining water and stir well.

In a separate bowl, mix 5 cups of the flour with the salt and add to the yeast mixture with 1 teaspoon of the olive oil. Using your hands, work in the flour until a ball of dough is obtained. Add additional flour if necessary to achieve a soft but not sticky dough. Place the dough on a floured surface and knead it until smooth and elastic. Grease a bowl with 1 teaspoon of olive oil. Put the dough in the bowl and toss a few times to coat with the oil. Cover tightly with plastic wrap and let it rise until doubled in bulk.

Remove the dough from the bowl, punch it down, and knead it on a floured surface for 3 to 4 minutes. Divide the dough in half. Brush the bottom and sides of a 15- x 13-inch rectangular baking dish or a 10¼-x 3-inch springform pan with the remaining olive oil and set aside.

With a rolling pin on a floured surface, roll 1 piece of dough 2 inches larger in length and width than the pan size. Fit the dough in the pan, stretching the dough up the sides.

Place alternating layers of cheeses and meat on the dough until all the ingredients are used up. You should have at least 9 layers.

In a bowl, whisk together 6 of the eggs with the Parmigiano-Reggiano cheese, parsley, salt, and pepper. Pour the mixture evenly over the layers.

continued

Preheat the oven to 375° F.

Pinch a piece of dough about the size of a lemon from the dough and set aside. Roll out the second piece of dough to fit the top of the pan, leaving an overhang of at least ½ inch. Place the dough on top of the ingredients and seal the edges all around the pan by pinching the dough and rolling the edges underneath with your fingers.

Divide the lemon-size piece of dough in half and roll each piece under the palm of your hand to form a rope. Make a cross with the pieces and center it on top of the pizza.

In a small bowl, mix the remaining egg with 1 teaspoon water. Brush the top of the pizza evenly with the egg wash. Bake for 35 to 40 minutes, or until the pizza is nicely browned. Remove from the oven and let cool completely. If using a springform pan, release the spring and transfer the pizza to a serving dish. Cut into wedges to serve. For a rectangular pan, cut the pieces in the pan, then remove and place them on a serving dish.

Note: This pizza will keep for 1 week in the refrigerator. It is best served at room temperature or just slightly warm.

Pizza Margherita

Makes two 13-inch pizzas

This pizza was created around 1890 for Queen Margherita of Italy and was said to be one of her favorites, so it bears her name. The rolled dough is topped with paper-thin slices of fresh plum tomatoes, chunks of creamy fresh mozzarella cheese, and whole leaves of fragrant, peppery basil. It is baked quickly in a hot stone oven and is a triumph of Neapolitan cooking.

1 recipe Pizza with Cresciuta (page 204)

3 tablespoons olive oil

4 ripe plum tomatoes, cut into thin rounds

2 cups diced fresh *fior di latte* mozzarella cheese

12 fresh basil leaves

½ teaspoon fine sea salt

continued

Preheat the oven to 425° F.

Divide the dough in half and roll each piece out on a floured surface into a 13½-inch round and place the rounds on lightly oiled 13-inch pizza pans. Turn in the overhanging edge ½ inch to form a rim. You can stretch the dough to fit an even larger pan if you wish. Place the dough on 2 wooden peels, dusted with cornmeal, if you plan to use baking stones to bake the pizza.

Brush each round with 1 tablespoon of the olive oil. Divide the tomato slices between the rounds. Divide the cheese and sprinkle it on top of the tomatoes. Divide the basil leaves and sprinkle them on top of the cheese. Divide and sprinkle on the salt and the remaining 1 tablespoon of oil.

Bake the pizzas for 25 to 30 minutes, or until the top and bottom crusts are nicely browned. Cut into wedges and serve immediately.

If using baking stones, preheat the stones in a 450° F. oven for 20 minutes. Just before placing the pizza on the stone from the baking peel, sprinkle each stone with a handful of cornmeal. Bake for 20 to 25 minutes, or until the crust is nicely browned on the bottom.

Scacciata con Olive

Square Pizza with Olives
Makes one 17- x 11-inch pizza (1¾ pounds dough)

I was amused and delighted when a friend of mine sent me a food clipping from Florida showing a woman cutting into *scacciata*. She wanted to know if I had ever heard of it. Yes, my grandmothers and my mother made this thick egg-dough–based pizza. It is usually baked in a square or rectangular pan and cut into squares. The word *scacciata* is derived from *scacco*, which means "square." There are infinite toppings for this chewy pizza, and probably as many names. *Scacciata con Olive* ("squares with olives"), which is a family favorite, can be cut into tiny squares for appetizers, or it can be the centerpiece for lunch or a simple supper.

Dough

1½ cups warm water (110° to 115° F.)

1 teaspoon active dry yeast

1 teaspoon sugar

2 tablespoons plus 1 teaspoon olive oil

1 egg, at room temperature

4¼ to 4½ cups unbleached all-purpose flour

⅛ teaspoon salt

Topping

2 cups prepared tomato sauce

1 tablespoon dried oregano

⅓ cup (about 14) oil-cured black olives, pitted and halved

½ cup freshly grated Pecorino Romano cheese

In a large bowl, dissolve the yeast and sugar in ½ cup of the water. Allow the yeast to proof, covered, for about 10 minutes. Add the remaining water, 1 tablespoon of the olive oil, and the egg and beat with a whisk to blend.

Add 4 cups of the flour mixed with the salt to the yeast mixture and mix with your hands to form a soft ball. Add additional flour as needed.

Place the dough on a floured surface and knead it for 5 minutes, or until very soft. Grease a bowl with 1 teaspoon of olive oil, add the dough, and toss it in the oil. Cover the bowl tightly with plastic wrap and let it rise in a warm place until doubled, about 1 hour.

Preheat the oven to 425° F.

Grease a 17- x 11-inch jelly-roll or other pan with the remaining olive oil. Set aside.

Punch down the dough on a floured surface and, with a rolling pin, roll it out to fit the pan. Fit the dough in the pan, bringing the edges up the sides.

Spread the tomato sauce evenly over the dough. Sprinkle the oregano over the sauce. Evenly space the olives, cut sides down, over the top. Sprinkle on the cheese.

Bake the pizza for 35 to 40 minutes, or until the bottom crust is nicely browned. Cool slightly for even cutting, then cut into squares and serve.

Pizza di Nonna Saporito

Grandma Saporito's Pizza
Makes two 13-inch round pizzas

My dad loved the pizza that his mother, my grandma Saporito, made. It was nothing more than her all-purpose yeast dough, which she also turned into bread and rolls. After rolling out the dough, she placed it on a rectangular pan, dimpled it with her fingers, and spread on some olive oil, sea salt, and butcher's black pepper. That was it. For Grandma, this typified the food of her native Sicily.

1 recipe Pizza with
  Cresciuta (page 204)
  or 1 recipe Pasta per
  Pizza (page 203)

½ cup plus 2 teaspoons
  extra-virgin olive oil

Coarse sea salt to taste

Coarsely ground black
  pepper to taste

Preheat the oven to 425° F.

Divide the dough in half and roll each piece on a floured surface into a 13½-inch round, or roll the dough to fit two 15- x 10½-inch rectangular pans. Brush each pan with 1 teaspoon of the olive oil.

With your fingers, spread the dough in the pan and dimple the surface. Divide the remaining olive oil and drizzle it over each pizza. Sprinkle on the salt and pepper.

Bake the pizza until the bottom and top crusts are golden brown. Let them cool slightly, then cut into pieces and serve.

Variation: Press tiny slivers of fresh garlic into the dough or add fresh herbs such as basil, oregano, rosemary, or mint.

Pizza Napoletana

Neapolitan Pizza
Makes two 13-inch pizzas

Ask for pizza Napoletana in Naples and you will be served a crisp disk of dough with a layer of freshly chopped and seeded plum tomatoes, fresh buffalo mozzarella cheese, anchovy fillets, and a sprinkling of oregano. Since buffalo mozzarella is very perishable and rarely available, substitute fresh-whole milk *fior di latte*.

1 recipe Pizza with Cresciuta (page 204)	8 salted anchovies, cut into small pieces
3 cups (about 2 pounds) seeded and drained plum tomatoes	2 teaspoons dried oregano
1 pound *fior di latte* mozzarella cheese, sliced	¼ cup extra-virgin olive oil

Preheat the oven to 425° F.

Divide the dough in half and roll each piece out on a floured surface into a 13½-inch round. Place the rounds on each of two lightly oiled 13-inch pizza pans. You can stretch the dough to fit an even larger pan, if you wish. Turn in the overhanging edge ½-inch to form a rim. Or place the rounds on 2 wooden peels, sprinkled with cornmeal, if you plan to bake the pizza on baking stones.

Divide the tomatoes and spread them evenly on each pizza. Divide and layer on the cheese. Divide the anchovies and scatter them over the top. Divide and sprinkle on the oregano and olive oil.

Bake the pizzas for 25 to 30 minutes, or until the bottom crusts are nicely browned and the cheese is melted on top. Cut the pizzas into wedges and serve immediately.

If using baking stones, preheat the stones for 20 minutes, then sprinkle them with cornmeal and transfer each pizza from the peel onto a hot stone. Bake until the crusts are nicely browned, about 25 minutes. Cut the pizzas into wedges and serve immediately.

Pizza con Pesto

Pizza with Pesto
Makes two 13-inch pizzas

A layer of pesto gives this pizza a distinctive taste. I also add leftover vegetables and cheeses. If you do not want to make two, divide the amount of topping in half. Freeze half of the prepared dough for a later use.

1 recipe Pizza with
    Cresciuta (page 204)

Topping

¾ cup Pesto (page 92)

3 cups thinly sliced
    yellow squash

3 cups diced Fontina or
    Bel Paese cheese or a
    combination

Salt to taste

Ground black pepper to
    taste

Preheat the oven to 425° F.

Divide the dough in half and roll each piece out on a floured surface into a 13½-inch round. Place each piece on a lightly oiled 13-inch pizza pan. Roll the edges in to create a rim.

Divide the pesto between the two doughs, spreading it evenly over the tops. Divide the remaining ingredients and place over the pesto in the order listed.

Bake the pizzas for 25 to 30 minutes, or until the bottom crusts are nicely browned and the cheese has melted. Cut into wedges and serve immediately.

Pane

Bread

Breadmaking is an old tradition in my family, and for me is the most enjoyable form of cooking. Recollections of both grandmother Galasso and my mother making bread in our large, old kitchen with a wooden counter at one end are very vivid.

Grandma Galasso rose early to stoke the stove and start the bread dough for the evening meal. Her silver hair was piled high atop her head, held there in a bun with silver pins. Her robust figure sported a snowy white apron, and her flour bin and clean towels were ready for the day's work.

From my bedroom I could hear the clatter of mixing bowls being readied for the dough, and I knew by heart all the succeeding noises for the process to begin: The unwrapping of the yeast cakes and the clang of the sugar bowl told me that a pinch of sugar was being added to speed the proofing of the yeast.

By the time I was dressed and ready for school, the dough was already rising under an old blanket, in Grandma's yellow spongeware bowl. When I arrived home from school, I inhaled the welcoming smell of freshly baked bread, even before getting through the front door!

I learned how to make bread just by watching the process. There were no written recipes, only wit and intuition. There were no fancy bread machines or food processors to do the mixing and kneading: My grand-mother and mother made bread by feel, and that is still my technique.

Bread always took form in a "well," not a bowl. The flour was put on the wooden counter in a pile, and Grandma bored down into the center with her fist. There, the water and yeast would rest, until the flour from the sides of the well would slowly be incorporated with her fingers and a ball of dough was formed. The dough was kneaded so quickly that you could hardly see her hands moving. Then it rested under the blanket.

Within seconds, basic bread dough could change character with the addition of fruits, nuts, cheese, or olives. At holiday time, all the traditional breads were made, including Colomba di Pasqua (Easter Dove Bread, page 244) and panettone, a Christmas bread from Milan.

The breads in this chapter represent some of my favorites and are not difficult to make. I use unbleached all-purpose flour unless otherwise noted, because its higher gluten content allows the dough to be easily stretched or rolled. Like my grandmother, I start my breadmaking early in the day, often making two kinds.

Freshly baked bread should be allowed to cool completely. For a few days' storage, do not use plastic bags; they do not allow the bread to breathe. Wrap the loaves in waxed paper first, then store in a paper bag. For freezing, wrap the bread well in aluminum foil.

For best results when making bread dough, lightly spoon the flour into your measuring cup. Do not compact it.

Pane Integrale

Whole Wheat Bread
Makes 1 large loaf

I developed this wheat bread using the Basic Dough recipe from my book *Ciao Italia*. I have simply changed the ratio of unbleached flour to whole wheat flour, and added malt barley because the sugars in it cause rapid multiplication of yeast cells. Malt barley is used by many bread bakers in Italy to help give color and rise to their breads. You can find it in health food stores or by mail order (page 323.) Add an equal amount of sugar if malt barley is not available.

1 tablespoon active dry
    yeast

1¾ cups warm water
    (110° to 115°F.)

2 teaspoons malt barley
    or sugar

1 cup whole wheat
    flour

3 cups (12 ounces)
    unbleached all-purpose
    flour

½ teaspoon salt

1 teaspoon olive oil

1 large egg, slightly
    beaten

1 tablespoon
    wheat bran

In a large bowl, dissolve the yeast in ¼ cup of the warm water. Allow the yeast to proof until it is foamy, about 10 minutes. Add the remaining 1½ cups water and malt barley or sugar and mix well. Set the bowl aside.

In a separate bowl, mix the whole wheat flour, 2 cups of the all-purpose flour, and the salt. Add to the yeast mixture and mix with a wooden spoon. At this point, the mixture will be very soft. Add the remaining flour and mix with your hands until a ball of dough is formed. Add additional all-purpose flour as needed to make a soft dough.

Place the dough on a floured work surface and knead it for 5 to 10 minutes, folding the dough over on itself several times, until it is shiny and elastic. Let the dough rest, covered, on a floured surface for 5 minutes.

Grease a bowl with the olive oil. Put the dough in it and turn the dough a few times to coat with the oil. Cover the bowl tightly with plastic wrap and then a towel, and let it rise in a warm place until doubled, about 1 hour.

Punch the dough down and knead it a few times on a floured surface. Shape the dough into a round, oval, or braid and place on a baking sheet. Cover the bread and let rise about 20 minutes.

Preheat the oven to 375°F. Grease a baking sheet.

Just before baking, brush the top of the dough with the beaten egg and sprinkle on the wheat bran. Bake for 30 to 35 minutes, or until the top and bottom are nicely browned. Remove the bread to a rack to cool completely.

Panetti di Nonna Tavino

Grandma Tavino's Little Buns
Makes 2 dozen

The recipe for these charming little buns is the handywork of Giuseppina Tavino, grandmother of Rose Tavino Manes, a friend of the family from Benevento, Italy, and an Italian author of a book about life in Benevento. While her recipe does not call for whole wheat flour, I have added it for its nutritive value and the rustic look it gives the bread. A basketful of these warm gems on your kitchen table won't last long. To ensure a light texture, lightly spoon the flour into your measuring cup; do not pack it.

½ cup scalded milk,
    cooled to warm (110°
    to 115°F.)

2 tablespoons warm
    water (110° to 115°F.)

1 teaspoon active dry
    yeast

3 tablespoons sugar

¼ cup vegetable oil

2 large eggs

3¼ to 3½ cups
    unbleached all-
    purpose flour

1 cup whole wheat
    flour

½ teaspoon salt

1 teaspoon ground
    cinnamon

1 teaspoon grated
    nutmeg

½ cup raisins

In a large bowl, mix the milk and water. Sprinkle on the yeast and stir to dissolve. Add the sugar and blend well. Cover the bowl tightly with plastic wrap and let yeast proof for 10 minutes.

In a small bowl, whisk together the oil and eggs. Add to the yeast mixture and blend well.

In a separate bowl, mix 3 cups of the all-purpose flour with the whole wheat flour, salt, cinnamon, nutmeg, and raisins. Add to the yeast mixture and work with your hands until a ball of dough is formed. Add additional flour as needed to prevent the dough from sticking.

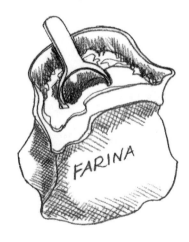

Turn the dough out onto a floured surface and knead until smooth and elastic. Let dough rest, covered, on a floured surface for 10 minutes. Place the dough in a lightly greased bowl, cover tightly with plastic wrap, and let rise in a warm place until doubled in size.

Preheat the oven to 375°F. Grease 2 baking sheets.

Punch the dough down and roll it on a floured surface into a 24-inch-long rope. Cut twenty-four 1-inch pieces and roll each piece into a rope about 8 or 9 inches long. Form a knot with each piece. Space the buns on baking sheets and bake for 12 to 15 minutes, or just until nicely browned. Let the buns cool slightly on racks, then serve immediately.

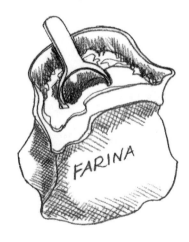

Crescia

Makes 1 large, round loaf

This recipe comes from an old friend of my mother, Rena Petregani. Rena came from the village of Famo, in the Marches. She prepared all the food for my mother's wedding over fifty years ago. Her son Oscar gave this recipe to my mother, who gave it to me. It is a very old bread made for Easter and eaten with sausage. It was originally made in a large, deep round pan, but I shape it in a round loaf or tube pan. *Crescia* means "to grow," and this dough grows into a beautiful round loaf.

¼ cup warm water (110° to 115°F.)	7 large eggs, at room temperature
1 tablespoon active dry yeast	1 cup grated Pecorino Romano cheese
¼ cup warm milk (110° to 115°F.)	1 teaspoon black pepper
8 tablespoons (1 stick) butter or margarine, softened	6½ to 7 cups unbleached all-purpose flour
	1 teaspoon olive oil

Place the water in a small bowl, sprinkle the yeast over it, and stir to dissolve. Let the yeast proof, covered, for about 10 minutes or until foamy. Add the milk.

In a large bowl, beat the eggs with a whisk until well blended, then add the yeast mixture. Stir in the cheese, pepper, and flour 1 cup at a time until a soft ball of dough is formed. Add more flour if the dough is sticky. Turn the dough out onto a floured surface and knead until smooth, about 5 minutes. Let dough rest, covered, on a floured surface for 10 minutes.

Pour olive oil into a large bowl, place the dough in the bowl, and turn to grease it. Cover the bowl with a towel and let dough rise until doubled in size, about 1½ hours.

Punch the dough down and place on a lightly floured work surface. Knead into a smooth ball, then place the bread on a greased baking sheet or in a greased tube pan. Let the dough rise until doubled again, about 30 minutes.

Preheat the oven to 375°F.

Bake the bread for 30 to 35 minutes, or until nicely browned. Let cool slightly if using a tube pan, then carefully remove to a cooling rack. Serve the Crescia warm, cut into slices.

Taralli di Elena Julian

Helen's Taralli
Makes about 2½ dozen

These are not the traditional ringlike *taralli;* instead, they are shaped as twists, and the dough has cheese in it. As these bake, the smell of black pepper and cheese permeates the house. They are served at Eastertime and disappear very quickly in my house. The original recipe came from Helen Julian, whose ancestral home is Cumblebas, Italy.

3½ to 4 cups unbleached all-purpose flour	5 large eggs
2 teaspoons baking powder	¼ cup sugar
¼ teaspoon coarsely ground black pepper	1 tablespoon olive oil or lard
	¼ cup grated Pecorino Romano cheese

In a large bowl, combine 3 cups of the flour with the baking powder and pepper, and set aside.

In another large bowl, beat the eggs, sugar, olive oil, and cheese with a whisk. Add the flour mixture and mix to form a firm dough. Add more flour as needed to keep dough from getting sticky. Knead until smooth and pliable.

Roll the dough out on a floured surface. Breaf off small balls of dough about 1 inch in diameter and roll into ropes 10 inches long and ½ inch wide. Hold the rope in the middle with your fingers and twist the 2 ends together, forming a twist about 4 inches long. Place the twists on towels.

Preheat the oven to 350°F. Lightly grease a baking sheet.

In a large pot of boiling water, drop the twists a few at a time and let come to the surface. They will rise to the surface in about 1 minute. Remove with a slotted spoon and place on brown paper to drain. Arrange the twists on baking sheet and bake for about 30 to 35 minutes, or until golden brown. Cool on a rack.

Gnocco

Makes 1 round or rectangular loaf

Gnocco means "dumpling," but in Modena, where this recipe originated, it refers to a delicious yeast dough embedded with *ciccioli* ("cracklings") of rendered pig fat. My grandmother used bits of pork rind, but if you want to cut down on fat, substitute prosciutto. Whatever you use, these are delicious appetizers or snacks.

½ **pound prosciutto, diced**	2 **eggs, at room temperature, beaten**
¾ **cup warm water (110° to 115°F.)**	4 **tablespoons (½ stick) plus 1 teaspoon butter, diced**
1 **teaspoon active dry yeast**	
3¼ **to 3½ cups unbleached all-purpose flour**	1 **teaspoon coarse salt**

In a frying pan, sauté the prosciutto until it begins to render its fat and start to curl. Drain the prosciutto on brown paper, and cool any drippings to lukewarm. Set aside.

In a large bowl, combine the warm water and yeast and let proof, covered, for 10 minutes.

Add the flour, eggs, 4 tablespoons butter, reserved drippings, and half the prosciutto. Mix to form a ball of dough, adding more flour if necessary, then knead until smooth. Let dough rest, covered, on a floured surface for 10 minutes.

Lightly grease a 17- x 11¼-inch jelly-roll pan or large pizza pan with the remaining butter. Set aside.

Roll the dough out evenly on a floured surface and place in the prepared pan, bringing the dough up along the rim of the pan. Sprinkle the top with the remaining prosciutto and salt, and lightly press into the dough. Let dough rise in a warm place for about 30 minutes.

Preheat the oven to 375°F.

Bake the loaf for 30 minutes, or until nicely browned. Cut into pieces and serve immediately.

Pane di Miele

Honey Bread
Makes 1 large loaf

*M*iele, or honey, is an ancient sweetener. The Egyptians, Greeks, and Romans all used it, not only as a sweetener but also as a preservative. Apicius, the knowledgeable Roman gourmand, tells us that vegetables, herbs, and fruits were preserved by covering them with a combination of honey and vinegar. Meat, including sides of pork or beef, could be preserved by "placing them in a pickle of mustard, vinegar, salt and honey, covering the meat entirely. And when ready to use you'll be surprised."

continued

Honey was also put in bread and what were called "honey cakes," not so much for the sweetness it afforded but because it kept the bread fresh for a long time. This honey bread, which is a family heirloom, probably has a pedigree traceable to the ancients; it too keeps well. When I am in the small towns of Italy, especially Montalcino, I bring back colorful ceramic jars of honey, exotically flavored with the essence of orange, lavender, thyme, and whatever else the bees feed on.

This is an impressive-looking bread for any holiday meal.

½ cup warm water (110° to 115°F.)

1 teaspoon active dry yeast

1 cup warm milk (110° to 115°F.)

¾ cup plus 2 tablespoons honey

2 tablespoons (¼ stick) butter, melted and cooled

2 tablespoons plus 1 teaspoon extra-virgin olive oil

1 large egg, at room temperature

1 teaspoon salt

2 teaspoons anise seeds

1 tablespoon grated lemon zest

4½ to 5 cups unbleached all-purpose flour

1 cup finely chopped walnuts

½ cup raisins, finely chopped

½ cup finely chopped dried pitted prunes

Place the water in a large bowl, sprinkle on the yeast, and mix to dissolve. Let the mixture proof for about 10 minutes, or until foamy. Add the milk, ¼ cup of the honey, the butter, 2 tablespoons of the oil, egg, salt, anise seeds, and lemon zest. Stir the ingredients well. Add 4 cups of flour and mix with your hands or a bread mixer to obtain a ball of dough. Add additional flour until you have a nonsticky ball of dough.

Turn the dough out onto a floured board and knead until smooth and elastic, about 5 minutes. Let dough rest, covered, on a floured surface for 10 minutes. Grease a large bowl with the remaining olive oil and turn the dough in it, coating it on all sides. Cover the bowl tightly with plastic wrap and let the dough rise in a warm place until doubled, about 1½ hours.

In a small bowl, mix the walnuts, raisins, and prunes. Set aside.

Punch the dough down and turn it out onto a floured surface. Knead for 2 to 3 minutes, then pinch off an orange-size piece of dough and set aside. With a rolling pin, roll the remaining dough out into a 16-inch circle.

With a brush, spread ½ cup of the remaining honey over the dough. Reserve ¼ cup of the filling and sprinkle the remainder evenly over the dough. Roll the dough up as for a jelly roll, tucking in the edges as you roll. The loaf will be about 16 inches long and 3 inches thick. Place the roll on a lightly greased large baking sheet. Set aside.

Roll the remaining piece of dough into a 10-inch circle and cut ten ½-inch strips with a pastry wheel. Make 5 crisscross designs on top of the bread using 2 strips each. Tuck the ends underneath the loaf. Cover with a towel and let dough rise until doubled in size, about 30 minutes.

Preheat the oven to 350°F.

Bake for 30 to 35 minutes, or until the bread is golden brown. Remove immediately to a cooling rack. With a brush, spread the remaining 2 tablespoons of honey over the top of the loaf and sprinkle on the remaining filling. Let the bread cool before cutting.

Il Convento

The Convent

On a recent visit to Assisi, the pastoral homeland of St. Francis, my husband and I, and our friends Wayne and Paulette, decided to stay in a convent run by the Sisters of Saint Brigida. Tired of overpriced hotels, we were yearning for simplicity and some adventure as well. The price was right—$42 a day per person, which included a simple breakfast of coffee and panini ("small rolls"), and a few prayers thrown in by the good sisters for our souls.

The pink and gray stone convent was perched high on a hilltop; from its vantage, the plains of Assisi and Mount Subasio, veiled in fine mist, formed the landscape below. As one would expect, the rooms were sparsely furnished: low ceilings, white-washed walls, bare floors, cots with paper-thin mattresses, and a large crucifix in each room, a reminder of one's mortality. From our window I could see neat rows of gnarled olive trees and the narrow dirt road where a steady stream of sinners and would-be saints made their way each day to the Basilica of St. Francis.

The Sisters of Saint Brigida ran a tight ship greeting, feeding, and housing travelers, but always with an air of profound reverence. Their steel-gray habits were in sharp contrast to their red and pink rose gardens, graceful fruit trees, and thick greenery.

After a day spent studying Giotto's frescoes of the life of St. Francis in the upper church of the Basilica, the four of us decided to do something un-academic and head for the piazza. The activity and noise in the main square was in sharp contrast to the quiet of the basilica, just a few steps away. Somehow we lost track of time as we browsed in all the shops, stopped to admire the Temple of Minerva, and had a late dinner at Pozzo della Mensa, a small trattoria off the main square. As we made our way back to the convent, only the stars were our guide. Groping in the dark, we arrived at the front door of the convent to discover that it was locked. We had no key and there was no sign of light or activity coming from any of the windows. I rang the bell, but no one came. The thought of sleeping on the rough cobblestone courtyard didn't bother me; it wouldn't have been much worse than sleeping on our penitential cots. On the side of the convent, I noticed a shining light casting a glow on the lawn below. Moving around the corner, I saw that it came from another traveler's window. After throwing a few stones at the window to catch attention, an elderly Dutch woman appeared and we motioned to her in loud whispers to let us in. In halting English, she yelled down that the sisters always locked the door from the inside before retiring for the night and took the key. Our Dutch friend made her way down to the second floor, opened a window, and threw out a chair for us to use to climb in through the window. The men went first, climbing onto the feeble chair and hoisting each other up amidst loud groans.

Once inside the window, they motioned to Paulette and me to climb onto the chair and grab their hands, but being considerably shorter than our husbands, we had a hard time scaling the wall. After helping to hoist Paulette up, it was my turn, and as my feet left the chair beneath me, I prayed that my husband and Wayne would not loose their grip on me. Finally we were inside. We tiptoed to our rooms like midnight intruders, said a prayer of thanks to St. Francis for coming to our rescue, and went to sleep.

The next morning, while sipping coffee and eating our meager ration of bread, a stern Mother Superior appeared at our table. Towering over us and shaking her head from side to side, she delivered a sound scolding for last night's disturbance. It made me feel like a schoolgirl. We all said "Mi dispiace ("I'm sorry") in unison and hoped that this would suffice. The convent, we were tersely informed, closes at 10 P.M., and if one plans to be out later, a request must be made to take along a key. Ho capito ("I understood"). Adventure was one thing, but staying in a convent meant playing by the rules.

Schiacciata di Vendemmia

Grape Harvest Bread
Makes 1 large loaf

S chiacciare means "to crush or flatten," and *schiacciata* is a flatbread that can change character depending on the toppings and season of the year. At home, the dough was prepared weekly and topped with oil and herbs, or sometimes vegetables and onions. But in the fall, when grapes were plentiful, Grandma Galasso would sweeten the dough with sugar, then crush the grapes with her fingers and spread them on top of the dough. A second sheet of dough was placed over the top of the grapes and the Schiacciata was baked.

I use red seedless grapes, but I don't crush them. The result is a sweet-tart harvest bread, with the grapes almost protruding under the blanket of dough as it bakes. It is best served the day it is made, either for dessert or as a snack.

1 teaspoon active dry yeast

1 cup warm water (110° to 115°F)

6 tablespoons sugar

4 tablespoons plus 1½ teaspoons extra-virgin olive oil

2½ to 2¾ cups unbleached all-purpose flour

⅛ teaspoon salt

2½ pounds seedless red grapes, stemmed, washed, and dried

1 large egg, beaten

In a large bowl, dissolve the yeast in the warm water and let proof for 5 minutes. Stir in 2 tablespoons of sugar and 2 tablespoons of the olive oil.

In a small bowl, mix 2½ cups of the flour with the salt and add to the yeast mixture. Work the dough with your hands until a smooth ball of dough is formed. Add additional flour as needed, but do not make the dough too stiff. Knead the dough for a few minutes.

Grease a large bowl with ½ teaspoon of the olive oil and turn the dough in it. Cover the bowl tightly with plastic wrap and place in a warm place to rise until doubled, about 1 hour.

Brush a 17½- x 11¼-inch baking pan with 1 teaspoon of the olive oil. Place a piece of parchment paper, cut to fit the bottom and set aside.

Preheat the oven to 375°F.

After the dough has risen once, punch it down and turn it out onto a floured surface. Knead the dough a few times, then with a rolling pin, roll it into a 20- x 16-inch rectangle. Place the dough in the pan, stretching it a little over the sides of the pan. Brush the dough with 2 tablespoons of the olive oil, then scatter the grapes evenly over the top. Sprinkle 2 tablespoons of the sugar evenly over the grapes.

Bring the overhanging dough from the 2 longest sides toward the middle and pinch the seam together. Cut most of the excess dough off the 2 remaining short sides, leaving about ½ inch extending. Then fold the dough in on itself, pinching the ends closed. Using a fork, crimp the 2 short ends. The finished size should be about 15 x 8 inches.

Re-roll the scraps of dough and make a decorative pattern on top. I like to cut out vines and leaves, and makes small bunches of grapes, but a crisscross pattern is nice too. Gently brush the top all over with the beaten egg and sprinkle the remaining 2 tablespoons of sugar evenly over the top. Bake on the middle rack for 30 to 35 minutes, or until the dough is golden brown on top and browned on the bottom.

Let the Schiacciata cool for 30 minutes. Then carefully lift it out, with the parchment paper. Let it cool to warm, then carefully pull the parchment paper away from the bottom, or leave the parchment paper in place and remove after cutting the Schiacciata into serving pieces. This is best served warm the day it is made. It does not freeze well.

Pane all'Uvetta

Raisin Bread
Makes 1 loaf

I make this bread all the time for breakfast. It is similar to one found in Assisi. If you cannot get fine semolina flour, then use all all-purpose flour.

½ cup raisins

½ cup warm water (110° to 115°F.)

1 tablespoon active dry yeast

1 cup scalded milk, cooled to lukewarm

1 tablespoon sugar

1 cup fine semolina flour

2¼ cups unbleached all-purpose flour

1 teaspoon salt

1 teaspoon olive oil

1 large egg, slightly beaten

2 tablespoons turbinado (raw sugar) or coarse brown sugar

In a small bowl, soak the raisins in enough water to cover. Set aside.

In a large bowl, dissolve the yeast in the ½ cup warm water and milk. Add the sugar, mix well, and let yeast proof for about 5 minutes.

In a separate bowl, mix the semolina and all-purpose flours with the salt. Add to the yeast mixture and work with your hands until a ball of dough is formed. Place the dough on a floured surface and knead for 5 to 10 minutes, or until the dough is elastic and shiny. Add additional flour as needed to keep dough from being sticky. Let the dough rest for 5 minutes, covered.

Drain the raisins. Dry them on a towel, then dice them. Set aside.

On a floured surface, roll the dough into a 10-inch round. Sprinkle on the raisins and fold the dough over to enclose them. Knead the dough into a ball.

Grease a bowl with the olive oil. Add the dough and turn it in the oil to coat it. Cover the bowl tightly with plastic wrap, and let the dough rise in a warm place until doubled, about 1 hour.

Punch the dough down on a floured surface and shape it into an oblong loaf 12 inches long and 4 inches wide. Place the loaf on a greased baking sheet. Cover with a towel and let rise for about 20 minutes.

Preheat the oven to 375°F.

Brush the top of the loaf with the egg and sprinkle on the sugar. Bake for 30 to 35 minutes, or until loaf is nicely browned on the top and bottom. Remove to a rack and cool completely.

Schiacciata Dolce

Sweet Flatbread
Makes 1 loaf

In the tombs of the Etruscans, early inhabitants of Italy, there are curious drawings of daily activities, including depictions of pasta making and bread-making. One such bread was Schiacciata, a flat bread that today has many different versions, depending on where you are in Italy. In Siena, it is a flat Easter cake with confectioner's sugar on the top; in Florence, an hour's drive away, it is a flat pizza with herbs or onions. This recipe, an old version of Schiacciata, is made with a batterlike dough and baked in a rectangular pan. It has a slightly sweet flavor and is perfect for breakfast or tea.

⅔ cup plus
   2 tablespoons warm
   water (110° to 115°F.)

1 tablespoon active dry
   yeast

2 cups unbleached all-
   purpose flour

1 teaspoon olive oil

1 large egg, slightly
   beaten

5 tablespoons butter,
   melted

¼ cup granulated sugar

1 tablespoon grated
   orange zest

⅛ teaspoon powdered
   saffron

1 tablespoon vanilla
   extract

Confectioner's sugar, for
   sprinkling

Pour the warm water into a bowl, sprinkle on the yeast, and stir to dissolve. Gradually add the flour and mix with your hands until a ball of dough is formed. Knead the dough on a floured surface. Oil a bowl with 1 teaspoon of olive oil, add the dough, and turn the dough in the oil to coat it. Cover the bowl tightly with plastic wrap and place it in a warm place to rise until doubled, about 1 hour.

Remove the plastic wrap. Do not punch the dough down. Add the egg and all but 1 tablespoon of the melted butter, the granulated sugar, zest, saffron, and vanilla. Using an electric mixer with a dough hook, beat the ingredients on high for about 2 minutes. Or use a wooden spoon, and beat the ingredients by hand into the dough using a circular motion. Beat for about 10 minutes to incorporate enough air into the dough. It will be very soft and sticky.

Use 1 teaspoon of the remaining butter to grease a 12- x 10-inch baking sheet. Using a rubber spatula, pour the dough onto the sheet and smooth it out to the edges. Brush the remaining melted butter over the top. Let the dough rise in a warm oven for about 2 hours.

Preheat the oven to 325°F.

Bake the bread for 15 to 20 minutes, or until the top is nicely browned. Let the Schiacciata cool completely, then cut into squares and dust with confectioner's sugar.

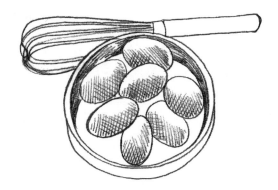

Panini di Ciliege

Cherry Rolls
Makes 30 rolls

July 4 was an important date in our Italian-American household, not only because of U.S. independence but because the day signaled our annual summer event—picking cherries. My parents packed us into the car and off we went, bemoaning the task that lay ahead. We picked bushels of the ruby red fruit, some to give to relatives, a lot to preserve in canning jars or dry, and some to eat. At Christmastime my mother used the dried fruit to make her cherry cookies, which I would snitch from wherever they were hidden. Their tart-sweet flavor made my lips pucker, yet I crave those cookies every year. I also crave these sweet rolls, which I serve for breakfast on Christmas morning. Dried cherries are readily available, though a bit on the expensive side.

⅔ cup nonfat dry milk

1⅓ cups warm water (110° to 115°F.)

1 tablespoon active dry yeast

½ cup plus 1 teaspoon granulated sugar

4½ tablespoons butter or margarine, at room temperature

1 large egg plus 2 large egg whites

5 to 5½ cups unbleached all-purpose flour

Filling

1 cup granulated sugar

2 teaspoons ground cinnamon

1 cup dried tart red cherries, diced

Glaze

1½ cups confectioner's sugar

4 tablespoons milk

½ teaspoon almond extract

Place the dry milk in a large bowl and add the warm water. Stir to dissolve. Sprinkle the yeast over the milk, add the teaspoon of granulated sugar, and stir to dissolve. Let the mixture proof for 10 minutes, covered.

Add 2½ tablespoons of the butter or margarine, the egg and egg whites, and remaining granulated sugar to the mixture and whisk until well blended. Add the flour gradually, until a ball of dough is obtained that is not sticky. Turn the dough out onto a floured surface and knead until smooth, about 10 to 12 minutes. Place the dough in a lightly greased bowl, cover tightly with plastic wrap, and let rise until doubled in bulk, about 1 hour.

Preheat the oven to 375°F. Grease two 15- x 11-inch baking sheets.

Mix the sugar and cinnamon together for the filling and set aside.

Punch the dough down and divide in half. Knead each half until smooth, about 5 minutes. Roll 1 piece on a floured surface into a 16-inch circle. Brush the dough with 1 tablespoon of the remaining butter. Sprinkle on half the sugar and cinnamon, and then half the cherries. Roll the dough up from the widest side into a tight jelly roll. Cut the roll into fifteen 1-inch slices and place them on baking sheet, spacing them close together. Repeat for the second piece. Let rise, covered, for 15 minutes.

Bake for 25 to 30 minutes, or until nicely browned. Let the rolls cool until warm on a cookie rack.

In a small bowl, mix the confectioner's sugar with the milk and almond extract until smooth. Drizzle a little of the glaze over the tops of the rolls. Serve warm.

Note: These can be frozen unglazed.

Pane di Pasta Reale

Almond Paste Bread
Makes 1 large bread

My mother is very fond of using almond paste in her baking. Almond paste is found in many Italian cakes and cookies. It is easy to make from ground almonds, sugar, and egg whites. I developed this sweet bread using prepared almond paste, sold in cans. (Do not use the almond paste sold in a cellophane tube, because there is too much water in the mixture.) This is the perfect bread for Sunday morning or any holiday.

Dough
- 1 tablespoon active dry yeast
- 1½ cups warm water (110° to 115°F.)
- 3 large eggs
- ⅓ cup plus 2 tablespoons sugar
- 4 tablespoons (½ stick) butter
- 5 to 5¼ cups unbleached all-purpose flour

- 1 teaspoon olive oil
- 1 8-ounce can almond paste

Glaze
- ½ cup confectioner's sugar
- 1½ tablespoons half-and-half or milk

In a large bowl, sprinkle the yeast over ½ cup of the warm water, stir, and let proof for 5 minutes, or until foamy. Add the remaining water and blend.

In a separate bowl, beat 2 eggs, 1 egg yolk (reserve the white), ⅓ cup sugar, and the butter with a whisk until blended. Add to the yeast mixture along with the flour, 1 cup at a time, until a ball of dough is formed. Add additional flour if needed to keep dough from being sticky.

Sprinkle a work surface with flour and knead the dough until it is soft and elastic. Let dough rest, covered, on a floured surface for 10 minutes. Grease a large bowl with the olive oil, add the dough, and turn to coat it with the oil. Cover the bowl tightly with plastic wrap and let dough rise in a warm place for 1 hour, or until doubled in bulk.

In a separate bowl, with an electric mixer, beat the almond paste, egg white, and remaining 2 tablespoons of sugar until smooth. Cover and set aside.

Turn the dough out onto a floured surface, punch it down with your fist, and knead it for a few minutes. With a rolling pin, roll out the dough to an 18- x 12-inch sheet. Spread the almond paste mixture in a thin layer over the surface of the dough to within ½ inch of the edge. Starting at the longer side, roll the dough up as for a jelly roll, and tuck in the ends.

Preheat the oven to 350°F. Grease a baking sheet with the remaining butter.

Place the dough on the baking sheet, and form an *S* shape with your hands. With a scissors, make 1½-inch-long slits crosswise around the edges of the bread. Cover the bread and let rise a second time for about 25 to 30 minutes.

Bake the bread for 35 to 40 minutes, or until nicely browned on the top and bottom. Carefully remove the bread to a rack and place a piece of waxed paper underneath the rack. Let the bread cool for 10 minutes. In a small bowl, mix the confectioner's sugar and milk until thin. Spread the glaze over the top, letting the excess run down the sides.

To serve, cut into slices and serve warm.

Note: Divide the dough in half to make 2 smaller breads.

Colomba di Pasqua

Easter Dove Bread
Makes 1 loaf

The Colomba is a sweet bread similar to panettone but it is shaped like a dove and made during Easter all over Italy, most of it commercially these days. This bread along with many others was prepared on Good Friday and Holy Saturday, and eaten during Easter week. The recipe has come down through the Galasso family.

¼ cup warm water (110° to 115°F.)

1 tablespoon active dry yeast

½ cup warm milk

⅔ cup sugar

8 tablespoons (1 stick) butter or margarine, melted

1 tablespoon grated lemon zest

1 tablespoon vanilla extract

3 large eggs, at room temperature

3 large egg yolks, at room temperature

4½ to 5 cups unbleached all-purpose flour

¾ teaspoon salt

1 large egg white, slightly beaten

1 tablespoon turbinado (raw sugar) or coarse brown sugar

In the large bowl of an electric mixer, put the warm water and yeast and stir to dissolve. Let the mixture proof for 10 minutes. Add the milk, sugar, butter, lemon zest, vanilla, whole eggs, and egg yolks and beat on low speed to blend well. Then beat on medium speed for 3 minutes. Add 4 cups of the flour and beat on medium speed. Gradually add the remaining flour a little at a time, until a soft dough is formed. You may not need all the flour.

Turn the dough out onto a floured surface and knead until smooth and elastic, about 8 to 10 minutes. Place the dough in an oiled bowl. Cover and let rise until doubled in bulk, about 1 hour.

Punch the dough down, divide it in half, and form 2 balls. Place 1

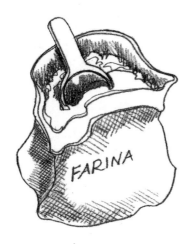

ball width-wise on a greased baking sheet and gently flatten it into a cylinder 10 inches long and 5 inches thick. Curve the dough slightly in the center.

Pat the other ball of dough into a triangle with 14 inch sides and a 7 inch base. This forms the dove's body. Place the triangle over the cylinder to form a T. Twist the top third of the body to the right; pinch and shape to form the dove's head, neck, and beak. Twist the bottom third to the left; pull and stretch it into a fan shape to form the tail. With a scissors, cut deep slashes in the wings and tail to resemble feathers.

Cover the dove with a sheet of buttered waxed paper and a towel. Let the bread rise in a warm place until almost doubled, about 20 minutes. Do not let it overrise or the shape will be lost in baking.

Preheat the oven to 350°F.

Gently brush the dove all over with the egg white and sprinkle the wing tips and tail section with the brown sugar. Bake for about 50 minutes, or until the bread is golden brown. Carefully transfer the bread to a rack to cool.

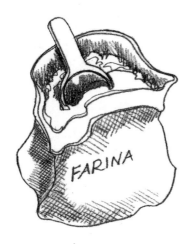

Gallette Dolci

Sweet Biscuits
Makes 1 dozen

Tourists visiting Italy are often surprised to find that breakfast is no more than *panini* ("rolls"), *caffè latte* ("coffee with hot milk"), and a copy of *il giornale* ("newspaper"). Many hotels now serve a full American breakfast. While staying at the Sistina in Rome, I was surprised to find, of all things, corn flakes and Rice Crispies! I stuck with tradition and ordered these wonderful biscuits, which Italians eat with jam. Be sure to lightly spoon the flour into your measuring cup; if you dip and pack it, your biscuits will be hard as bricks.

2 cups unbleached all-purpose flour	6 tablespoons sugar
⅛ teaspoon salt	1 large egg
1 teaspoon baking powder	¼ cup milk
4 tablespoons (½ stick) butter, cut in small pieces	1 tablespoon vanilla extract

In a large bowl, mix the flour, salt, and baking powder. Add the butter and work it into the flour mixture with a fork or your fingers. Set aside.

In a separate bowl, whisk together the sugar, egg, milk, and vanilla. Add the egg mixture to the flour mixture and mix with your hands until a smooth ball of dough is formed. Wrap the dough in plastic wrap and chill for 10 minutes.

Preheat the oven to 375°F. Grease 2 baking sheets.

On a lightly floured surface, roll out the dough to an 11-inch circle ¼ inch thick. Using a 3¼-inch biscuit cutter, cut rounds from the dough and place on baking sheets, spacing them ½ inch apart. Re-roll the scraps and cut more rounds.

Bake the biscuits for about 12 to 15 minutes, or until lightly browned. They should remain somewhat pale in color. Remove the biscuits to a cooling rack. Serve warm with jam or marmalade.

Note: These can be frozen for a couple of months. When ready to use, defrost and reheat them before serving.

Zaples di Zia Baratta

Aunt Baratta's Fritters
Makes about 3 dozen

These raisin fritters, or *zaples,* from Calabria come from my friend Marie Rogers's aunt, Jessie Baratta. The dough is very sticky and the fritters take on rustic shapes as they puff up in hot oil. They are best served warm.

2¾ cups warm water (110° to 115°F.)

1 yeast cake (0.6 ounces) or 1 package dry active yeast

1 tablespoon olive oil

5¼ cups unbleached all-purpose flour

2 tablespoons sugar

1½ teaspoons salt

¾ cup seedless raisins

8 cups vegetable oil, for deep-frying

Confectioner's sugar

Place ½ cup warm water in a large bowl and crumble in the yeast cake or sprinkle on dry yeast. Stir to dissolve, then let proof, covered, for 10 minutes. Add the remaining warm water and the olive oil. Set aside.

Lightly spoon the flour into a measuring cup and place in a medium bowl. Add the sugar and salt, and blend with a spoon.

Add the flour mixture to the yeast and water, and beat with a wooden spoon until the mixture is smooth. It should be a loose batter but not runny. Add the raisins and mix well. Cover the dough with plastic wrap and let rise in a warm place until doubled, about 1 hour.

Heat the vegetable oil to 375°F. in a deep-fryer or large, heavy pot.

Using 2 soup spoons, drop rounds of batter into the hot oil and fry until golden brown, about 4 minutes. Drain the fritters on brown paper. Sprinkle with confectioner's sugar and serve.

Variation: Heat 2 cups of honey in a saucepan and drizzle over the fritters. Serve warm.

Biscotti

Cookies

I'm a cook, but I am also a people watcher, especially when visiting Italy. In fact, people watching in Italy is almost a commandment. One of my favorite places to do this is at the Piazza del Popolo in Rome. Walking into the piazza for the first time, you will encounter an elegant architectural surprise. At one end are almost twin baroque churches: Santa Maria di Monte Santo on the left with its oval dome, and Santa Maria de'Miracoli on the right with its round dome. Looking at these two magnificent buildings side by side one gains a wonderful sense of harmony and power.

One lazy Sunday morning, I wandered into the piazza and up the steps of Santa Maria de'Miracoli. As I stood there, a fairytale event began to unfold: Out of nowhere, a group of glitterati began to congregate at the entrance to the church. Shortly thereafter, a sleek white Rolls-Royce stopped in front of the church. When the door of the car opened, out stepped the most beautiful bride I have ever seen. Her voluminous white gown seemed to float, carrying her like a giant frilly cloud. Sacred music resounded from the church, and the bride along with family and friends slowly negotiated the old steps into the church. As I moved toward the back of the group, I noticed a slightly bent woman in tattered gray clothes slouching near the entrance to the church, holding a sign that read "*Vi prego, ho fame*" ("I implore you, I am hungry"). I slipped some lire into her plate and moved inside. Standing in the back of the church, I saw the bride reach the front altar where her parents were waiting, facing her. In a show of respect, she bowed deeply to each of them and the ceremony began. Like a wise dinner guest who knows when to leave, I departed this beautiful scene.

As I walked back to my hotel, I remembered my own wedding. The centerpiece of our reception was a wedding cookie cake that resembled an edible Egyptian pyramid. It sat proudly on a snowy white tablecloth, watched over by Nonna Saporito. Alongside it sat the large decorated box that would receive the gift envelopes of money from the invited guests. I wondered if the wedding I just "attended" would have such a cake, or was such a tradition just an Italian-American invention?

At another wedding in Italy, where again I was a "guest" before the invited guests arrived, I wanted to see how Italians set up for a wedding. Some friends arranged for me to see the preparations being held in an old castle called Villa Oscano, just a short drive northwest of Perugia.

It was a huge house surrounded by lush gardens with commanding views of the countryside. Inside, waiters in starched white jackets readied the banquet tables. The decorations were a beautiful blending of fruits, plants, and flowers. The dinner tables were set with flowers and fruits and pink linen.

I peeked in the kitchen, where roast pork with rosemary and fresh pasta were in various stages of preparation. On a side table were those familiar pyramids of cookies, with the more delicate cookies resting on top. The guests would take these home later, as well as handpainted and dated ceramic plates from nearby Deruta, as momentos of the happy occasion. Reassured that tradition was alive and well, we quietly took our leave.

You don't have to wait for a wedding to make the *biscotti* ("cookies") in this chapter. While *biscotti* is a generic word for cookies, it also refers to the twice-baked cookies that are so popular now. By following these helpful reminders, your cookies will turn out perfectly every time you bake.

- Read the recipe before you begin and assemble all the ingredients. Do not make substitutions in the recipes unless indicated.
- Unless otherwise stated, use unbleached all-purpose flour.
- For delicate cookies that might stick to the cookie sheets, line sheets with parchment paper.
- Measure accurately. Do not scoop flour with your measuring cup, as this will compact it and give you more flour than the recipe calls for. Lightly spoon the flour into the cup and level it off at the top.

- If a recipe calls for eggs, they should be at room temperature.
- Use heavy-duty cookie sheets. I prefer T-Fal nonstick sheets, and I have them in many sizes, including 14½- x 10½-inch, as well as 15- x 10¼-inch jelly-roll pans.
- Do not form cookies on warm cookie sheets from which you have just removed cookies. The dough will spread and, in some cases, even begin to bake.
- Invest in a few cookie spatulas. They are smaller in size and make it easier for you to remove cookies.
- If the recipe requires cooling the cookie completely, do so on cooling racks. For cookies that need a glaze, wait until the cookie is warm to the touch but not hot; otherwise the glaze will drip off.
- Bake cookies on the middle rack of the oven. This allows more control for cookies that need to be light in color, not browned.
- Preheat the oven and make sure that your oven temperature is accurate. Check it with an oven thermometer.
- In the case of meringue-based cookies, make sure the egg whites are at room temperature before beating. Use a copper bowl to beat them in, if possible.
- If you want to create a cookie pyramid cake for a wedding or other celebration, you will need a round decorative serving dish. The larger the dish the wider will be the finished cake. I use a 16-inch dish and start with firmer cookies like Taralli and Anise Biscotti in alternating layers. I continue building, putting more delicate cookies on top. Try to fit the cookies together as snugly as possible so that no open spaces remain. If there are open spaces, insert small paper lace dollies. Place a bow with long streamers on top of the cookie cake, or an appropriate bride and groom decoration.

The first time I made this, I did not think about the logistics of moving it to the final destination. I suggest you assemble the cake where it will be presented, or use a basic confectioner's sugar frosting to "glue" the cookies in place.

Il Campanile

The Bell Tower

I stood amid the baptistry, the duomo, and the campanile—the leaning bell tower of Pisa—scribbling notes in a raw wind as my Italian guide fired off facts about the importance of Pisa as a strategic Roman military port on the Arno River, and a place where grains and exotic spices were shipped during the Crusades. While Pisa's importance as a naval port is somewhat diminished today, it is known the world over for its architectural wonder—the Leaning Tower, built in the twelfth and thirteenth centuries. It is now closed to tourists until city officials can come up with a plan to save the monument from collapse.

As I listened to my guide, I suddenly realized that there is a striking similarity in composition among Italian cities and towns. The main square or piazza in these cities all have three things: a baptistry; a duomo, or cathedral; and a campanile, or bell tower. The baptistry stands in front of and a short distance from the cathedral, and the bell tower is to the side of the cathedral. This sequence follows a person's induction into the Catholic church. First there is initiation by baptism in the baptistry, which confirms a child as a member of the church with the right to enter it. The duomo is the center of religious activity, where members carry out their religious observance. Duty to the church is reinforced by the daily resonating sounds of the bells, calling members to prayer and to the reflection of people's mortal moments on earth.

All this made perfect sense when I stopped to think about it. According to my enthusiastic guide, the bell tower is also the messenger of the city, tolling the time of day, and reminding one of the allegiance, or campanilismo, shared among members of the community. In the case of Pisa as in every other town in Italy, one is a citizen of the city first, then an Italian.

Biscotti al Cioccolato

Chocolate Cookies
Makes 1 bushel

I grew up surrounded by a neighborhood network of Italian-American women. They did what was women's work in those days: cooking, cleaning, and raising *bambini*. They worked hard with their hands; they also talked hard with their hands. On any given day of the week, I could expect to see one or more of them visiting my grandmother, and bringing with them something homemade like these chocolate cookies. The recipe has not been altered or rewritten, in order to give you some idea of the quantities of food these women made.

20 cups flour	**2 tablespoons baking powder**
½ pound baking cocoa	**1 teaspoon salt**
4 cups sugar	**1 tablespoon allspice**
4 cups lard or shortening	

Work as piecrust.

Grind

2 pounds shelled nuts, 3 oranges with juice, and 2 pounds raisins.

Mix

1 dozen eggs, 1 quart milk, and 2 tablespoons vanilla.
350 F. 10 to 15 minutes.

Frosting

4 pounds confectioner's sugar and milk for desired consistency. Frost while hot.

Biscotti d' Anice

Anise Biscuits
Makes about 3½ dozen

Here is a twice-baked cookie, or *biscotto,* that comes from the files of Marian Sterling, a broadcast personality whose roots are Italian. This cookie was a favorite in her household and is a good example of the many variations of biscotti that are part of the culinary tradition. This cookie has an anise flavor imparted by using both the extract and the seeds.

6 large eggs plus 1 egg white	2 tablespoons baking powder
1½ cups sugar	1 tablespoon anise seeds
1¼ cups vegetable oil	1 teaspoon water
1½ tablespoons anise extract	Colored sprinkles
7 cups unbleached all-purpose flour	

Preheat the oven to 425°F. Grease 3 or 4 cookie sheets.

In a bowl, beat the 6 eggs with an electric mixer on high speed for 1 minute. Gradually add the sugar and continue to beat for 1 minute. Add the oil and anise extract, and beat another minute. Set the mixture aside.

In another bowl, mix 6 cups of the flour with the baking powder. Stir in the anise seeds. Add the flour mixture to the egg mixture and mix with a wooden spoon until the ingredients are well blended. Add the remaining flour as needed to produce a dough that is stiff enough to shape.

Divide the dough into 3 or 4 pieces. With floured hands, shape each piece into a loaf 11 x 4 inches. Place the loaves on baking sheets. Beat the egg white with the water and brush the tops of the loaves. Sprinkle on the colored sprinkles.

Bake for 20 to 25 minutes, or until a wooden pick inserted in center comes out clean. The loaves should be rich brown in color. Remove from the oven and cool about 10 minutes.

Reduce the oven temperature to 375°F.

With a sharp knife, cut each loaf into approximately 1-inch-thick diagonal slices. Lay the slices on their sides on the cookie sheet and return them to the oven to toast for about 5 minutes on each side. Remove the biscotti to racks to cool completely. Store in an airtight container or freeze for up to 6 months. These are perfect with wine or coffee.

Biscotti di Vincenza

Vincenza's Cookies
Makes about 30 cookies

This recipe bears the name of Vincenza Salierno, who was born in San Leulcio del Sannio, and came to America in 1955 with her four children. This is a twice-baked cookie. It keeps well and was often served as breakfast food with strong coffee.

8 tablespoons (1 stick) butter or margarine	**½ teaspoon salt**
1 cup sugar	**1 teaspoon ground cinnamon**
1 large egg	**½ cup fresh orange juice**
2 cups unbleached all-purpose flour	**1 cup chopped walnuts or hazelnuts, or a combination**
1 teaspoon baking soda	

Preheat the oven to 350°F. Lightly grease a cookie sheet.

Sift the dry ingredients together 3 times. Set aside.

In a bowl, cream the butter or margarine with an electric mixer. Add the sugar gradually, beating well, then add the egg and blend thoroughly. Gradually add the sifted ingredients and orange juice. Fold in the chopped nuts.

Spread the dough on the cookie sheet to form a 9½- x 5-inch loaf. Bake for 30 minutes, or until the dough is firm. Remove the cookies from the oven and let cool about 5 minutes. Cut the cookies into 1-inch crosswise slices.

Lower the oven temperature to 300°F.

Place the cookies back on the cookie sheet on their side and return to the oven to toast about 5 minutes on each side. Cool the cookies completely on a rack.

Biscotti di Mamma

Ma's Cookies
Makes about 3½ dozen

I own three faded black notebooks containing handwritten recipes from home. Many of them are very sparse, with ingredients listed but giving no specific amounts. Some of these culinary treasures belonged to my Grandmother Saporito, and one recipe is entitled Ma's Cookies. I remember eating these at Grandma's house, but I never knew how they were made. When they first came out of the oven, they were delicate and cakelike in texture, but as they cooled, they became crisp. My mother said they were made with a funnel attached to an old-fashioned meat grinder, and came out shaped like Ss, or 8s. They can also be shaped as ladyfingers. I have reduced the original recipe considerably and have also eliminated the lard. To form the cookies, use a 12-inch pastry bag with a ½-inch nozzle. Or use a ¼-inch nozzle for smaller cookies and a larger yield.

3½ cups unbleached all-purpose flour

3 teaspoons baking powder

½ teaspoon baking soda

1 teaspoon salt

4 large eggs

2 cups sugar

1 cup melted and cooled solid vegetable shortening

2 tablespoons lemon juice

1 tablespoon vanilla extract

In a bowl, sift together the flour, baking powder, baking soda, and salt.

In another bowl, whisk the eggs with the sugar until light and lemon colored. Add the shortening, lemon juice, and vanilla and whisk in well. Gradually add the flour mixture to the egg mixture, mixing well to blend the ingredients. Let the batter sit, covered, for 5 minutes.

Preheat the oven to 350°F. Lightly grease several cookie sheets.

Fill a tipless pastry bag two-thirds full with some of the batter. Form 3-inch-long Ss or 8s on the cookie sheets, spacing them about 1½ inches apart, as the batter will spread some. Refill the pastry bag and continue to make more cookies until the batter is used up. Or shape them by hand, using 2 spoons.

Bake the cookies for about 10 to 12 minutes, or until pale golden in color. Watch carefully and rotate the trays to prevent cookies from burning. Let cool slightly on the tray before removing them to cooling racks.

Note: These are wonderful with coffee or tea—a great after-school cookie. They can be frozen, but will be softer in texture.

Biscotti di Noci

Nut Cookies
Makes about 30 Cookies

This rich-tasting butter and nut cookie is from Marian Sterling. They make a nice hostess gift when placed in small, decorative cupcake papers. These are a must at holiday time, and can be made ahead and frozen if you do not roll them in confectioner's sugar.

8 tablespoons (1 stick) butter or margarine, at room temperature

2 tablespoons granulated sugar

1 teaspoon vanilla extract

1 cup unbleached all-purpose flour

1 cup finely chopped walnuts

½ cup confectioner's sugar

In a bowl, cream the butter or margarine and the sugar with an electric mixer until light colored. Mix in the vanilla. Blend in the flour and the nuts. Wrap the dough in waxed paper and chill for about 1 hour for easier handling.

Preheat the oven to 375°F.

Break off 1-inch pieces of dough and roll into balls with floured hands. Place the balls on ungreased cookie sheets and bake for about 14 minutes or until lightly browned.

Place the confectioner's sugar in a shallow dish. Remove the cookies carefully with a spatula and gently coat the warm cookies with the sugar. Let cool completely on wire racks. You may need to coat them a second time to get the sugar to adhere well.

Biscotti Ripieni al Cioccolato

Filled Chocolate Cookies
Makes about 5 dozen

These delectable cookies require a little time to put together, but the job can be made easier if you bake the cookies one day, and fill them the next. I usually make these at Easter, but they know no season. Use good-quality chocolate for melting and coating the cookies. I usually coat just the top, but the entire cookie can also be covered in chocolate.

3 cups unbleached all-purpose flour, plus additional for rolling out the dough

1 teaspoon baking powder

8 tablespoons (1 stick) butter, softened

2 large eggs, slightly beaten

¾ cup sugar

⅓ cup finely chopped blanched almonds

¾ cup cherry or raspberry jam

4 ounces bittersweet or semisweet chocolate, or additional if coating cookies completely

In a large bowl, sift the flour with the baking powder. Add the butter and work in with your hands until the mixture is coarse. Add the eggs and sugar, and mix with your hands until a ball of dough is formed.

Sprinkle a work surface with flour and knead the dough until smooth. Wrap the dough in plastic and refrigerate for 1 hour.

Preheat the oven to 350°F. Lightly grease some cookie sheets.

Return the dough to the floured work surface. Flatten the dough a little with a rolling pin, sprinkle the nuts over the surface, and knead them into the dough with your hands.

Roll the dough into an 18- x 20-inch rectangle. Trim the edges so they are even. With a fluted pastry wheel, cut the dough into 13 crosswise rows 1½ inches wide, and 7 lengthwise rows 2 inches wide. The cookies should be 1½ by 2 inches. Re-roll and cut the scraps.

Place the cookies ½ inch apart on cookie sheets. Bake for 10 to 12 minutes or until lightly browned. Remove the cookies to a rack to cool completely.

Sandwich the cookies by spreading about ½ teaspoon jam between pairs of cookies. Set aside.

Fill the bottom of a double boiler half-full of water and bring to a boil. Turn off the heat and add the chocolate to the top portion of the double boiler. Cover the pot and let stand until the chocolate is melted.

With a small spoon, spread a little of the chocolate evenly over the top of each cookie. Place on a rack and let the chocolate dry completely. Or, using small tongs, coat the cookies in the chocolate and then dry on a rack.

Note: These will keep a few days before serving if they are stored in single layers between waxed paper and kept covered in the refrigerator.

Biscotti di Ciliegie

Cherry Cookies
Makes 4½ to 5 dozen

Dried cherries soaked in almond liqueur, and spooned between my mother's cookie dough, produced the most delicious of her dozens of Christmas cookies. I loved them so much that I could not wait for Christmas. When the need to bite into one of these came on strong, I quietly entered the back room where these cookies were stored in large gleaming tin cans and helped myself. These are good keepers and can be made 2 weeks ahead. Dried cherries are available in gourmet food shops. Sour cream has been substituted for Italian heavy cream, *panna doppia,* which has a thicker consistency.

Dough

6 cups unbleached all-purpose flour

1 teaspoon salt

1 teaspoon baking soda

1 cup (2 sticks) butter or margarine

2 cups sugar

1 tablespoon almond extract

Grated zest of 1 large lemon

1 cup sour cream

Filling

2½ cups (10 ounces) dried tart cherries

¼ cup Amaretto liqueur

Sift together the flour, salt, and baking soda, and set aside.

With an electric mixer, cream the butter or margarine, sugar, and extract until light colored. Add the lemon zest and sour cream, and beat until well blended. Add the flour mixture a little at a time, mixing well until a ball of dough is formed. (You may need to finish mixing by hand since this is a heavy dough.) Wrap the dough in plastic and chill for 2 hours.

In a bowl, marinate the cherries in the liqueur for at least 30 minutes. In a food processor, blender, or by hand, grind the cherries to a paste and set aside.

Preheat the oven to 350°F. Lightly grease 4 cookie sheets.

Divide the dough into 4 pieces. Working with one piece at a time on a floured board, roll out to an 18-inch circle. Use a 3-inch round or fluted cookie cutter to make circles. Use a 1-inch round cookie cutter to cut out a hole in the center of half the circles.

Place about 1½ teaspoons of the filling in the center of each whole circle, spreading it slightly. Top each with a circle with the hole. Seal by pressing all around the cookie with a fork. Transfer to a cookie sheet.

Repeat with remaining pieces of dough and re-roll the scraps to make more cookies.

Bake cookies for 20 minutes or until delicately browned. Remove the cookies to cooling racks, then store in airtight containers or freeze for up to 2 months.

Note: These are great for Valentine's Day too; use heart-shaped cutters.

Amaretti

Almond Cookies
Makes 2½ dozen

Almonds have been essential to Italian cooking for centuries. They were used to make sauces during the early Renaissance, especially during Lent. Today, as then, they are used in sauces and in fillings for meats; for stuffings for tortellini and vegetables, for marzipan, in cakes, breads, and of course, in biscotti. These Amaretti are just one of many kinds to be found all over Italy. In Italy, Amaretti are made with sweet and bitter almonds, but only sweet almonds are used in this recipe. Bitter almonds are not available in the United States because they contain prussic acid, a toxin that is believed harmful if ingested in large quantities.

1 pound shelled almonds	**1 teaspoon baking powder**
2¼ cups confectioner's sugar, sifted	**4 large egg whites, at room temperature**

Preheat the oven to 375°F. Cut sheets of parchment paper to fit 4 cookie sheets.

In a food processor or by hand, finely chop the almonds and place them in a large bowl.

In a medium bowl, mix the confectioner's sugar and baking powder. Add to the almonds and mix well.

In a separate bowl (preferably copper), beat the egg whites until stiff. With a rubber spatula, gently fold the egg whites into the almond and sugar mixture a little at a time until the mixture is well blended.

Using 2 soup spoons, shape the batter into small balls about 2 inches in diameter, and place them about 1 inch apart on the cookie sheets. They will spread while baking.

Bake the Amaretti for 10 to 12 minutes, or until they are firm to the touch and golden brown. Let the cookies cool completely on the parchment paper before removing; otherwise, they will break. Store the cookies in an airtight container.

Dolci Ripieni

Filled Sweets
Makes 9 dozen

My friend Rose Tavino Manes's ancestral home is in Benevento. For this recipe, an old family favorite, the cookies are fashioned much the same as for ravioli. The dough is springy and not too sweet; apricot or peach jam makes a nice filling, but almond paste and cooked prunes are also delicious. The only change I have made in the recipe is in the amount of oil and milk.

6 cups unbleached all-purpose flour	¾ cup sugar
6 teaspoons baking powder	½ cup milk
⅛ teaspoon salt	½ cup vegetable oil
6 large eggs	Juice of ½ lemon
	2¼ cups apricot or peach jam

In a bowl, sift the flour, baking powder, and salt together 3 times, and set aside.

In a separate bowl, beat the eggs with the sugar until light and fluffy. Add the milk, oil, and lemon juice, and blend well. Add the flour mixture slowly to the egg mixture, and mix with your hands until a ball of dough is formed. Add a little more milk if the dough seems dry. This will be a sticky and heavy dough. Knead the dough on a floured surface until smooth. Cover the dough with a bowl and let rest for 15 minutes.

Preheat the oven to 350°F. Lightly grease some cookie sheets.

Divide the dough into 4 pieces. Work with 1 piece at a time, keeping the remainder covered. Roll the dough out on a floured surface into a 16- x 14-inch rectangle. Using a pastry cutter, cut lengthwise into four 3½-inch strips, then cut each strip into 3½ x 2-inch rectangles. Place 1 teaspoon of jam in the center of each piece and fold over. Pinch the ends closed and seal with the tines of a fork.

Place the cookies on cookie sheets and bake for 15 to 20 minutes or until delicately browned. Remove the cookies to a rack to cool.

Variation: The dough can be rolled out, covered with filling, and rolled up as for a jelly roll. Cut the dough into ¼-inch rounds and bake as directed.

Ossi dei Morti

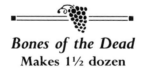

Bones of the Dead
Makes 1½ dozen

These cookies are brittle and dry like old bones. They are made all over Italy around November 1 and 2 to celebrate All Souls' Day, in remembrance of deceased relatives. Don't let their name turn you off. They are unusual to look at, delicious to eat, and a real conversation piece.

2 large egg whites, at
room temperature

⅔ cup confectioner's
sugar

¼ cup plus
2 tablespoons fine
semolina flour

⅔ cup coarsely chopped
semisweet or milk
chocolate

¾ cup coarsely chopped
blanched almonds

Frosting

⅔ cup coarsely chopped
semisweet chocolate

2 tablespoons (¼ stick)
butter

Preheat the oven to 300°F. Generously grease and flour your cookie sheets, or line with parchment paper.

In a glass or copper bowl, whip the egg whites until stiff peaks begin to form. Slowly add half the sugar a little at a time, beating until well incorporated and the whites are stiff and shiny. With a spatula, sprinkle the remaining sugar, semolina flour, chocolate, and almonds over the egg whites and fold in with a rubber spatula.

Using 2 teaspoons, use a small portion of batter to form bone-shaped cookies about 3 inches long and 1½ inches wide. (I use a cardboard template of a bone and trace it with a pencil onto the parchment paper, then fill in the space with the batter.) Space the cookies about 1 inch apart.

Bake for 30 to 35 minutes or until the cookies are fairly dry but still pale looking. Cool on the sheets, then transfer carefully to a cooling rack.

Fill the bottom of a double boiler with water and bring to a boil. Turn off the heat, add the chocolate and butter to the top of the double boiler, cover, and let stand for 10 to 15 minutes or until the chocolate and butter are melted.

Stir the frosting well. Dip the underside of each cookie into the frosting and, while still wet, make wavy lines through the chocolate with a fork or a frosting comb. Let the cookies dry completely.

Dolci con Melassa

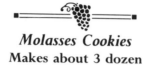

Molasses Cookies
Makes about 3 dozen

I don't often come across Italian cookie recipes containing molasses, so when I tested this spicy molasses cookie laden with hazelnuts from the family files of Rose Tavino Manes, I gave it two thumbs up. Once these are cut into strips, they harden up a bit, making them good keepers.

6 tablespoons solid vegetable shortening	¼ teaspoon ground ginger
7 tablespoons dark brown sugar	½ teaspoon ground cloves
2 cups molasses	1 tablespoon ground cinnamon
2 medium oranges	
1 tablespoon baking soda	½ teaspoon salt
7 cups unbleached all-purpose flour	2 cups chopped hazelnuts

Preheat the oven to 350°F. Grease and flour 2 cookie sheets.

In a medium saucepan, combine the shortening, brown sugar, and molasses. Bring to a boil and stir with a wooden spoon until the shortening melts. Set the mixture aside to cool.

Grate the oranges and set the zest aside. There should be about 3 tablespoons. Cut the oranges in half and squeeze the juice. There should be ½ cup juice. Add the zest, juice, and baking soda to the cooled molasses mixture, stir, and set aside.

In a large bowl, mix the flour with the spices and salt. Add the nuts and stir well with a wooden spoon. Make a well in the center and pour in the molasses mixture. Stir with a wooden spoon to blend, then use your hands to form a ball of dough.

Divide the dough in half and shape each piece on a cookie sheet into an oblong approximately 12 inches long and 4 inches wide. Bake the loaves for 40 to 45 minutes, or until they are nicely browned and a cake tester inserted in the center comes out clean. They should be firm to the touch.

Let the loaves cool for 1 minute on the cookie sheets. Gently remove them to a cutting board with a wide spatula. Cut each loaf into ¾-inch-wide diagonal strips. Allow the cookies to cool on racks. They will harden as they cool. Store in an airtight container.

Sfinci di Lucia

Lucy's Fried Puffs
Makes about 2 dozen

I love to search for old forgotten recipes, just for the pleasure of bringing back memories. This one originated in a small community not too far from Benevento, and was passed down by Lucia DiMicco's mother, a friend of Rose Tavino Manes. True, there are many versions of Sfinci, or fried puffs of dough. I like the texture and lightness of this one, which uses ricotta in the batter. These are quick snacks or a great breakfast treat. You can make the dough the night before.

2 large eggs

¼ cup granulated sugar

2 cups ricotta cheese, well drained

1 tablespoon vanilla extract or favorite liqueur

2 cups unbleached all-purpose flour

1½ teaspoons baking powder

⅛ teaspoon salt

3 cups vegetable oil

Confectioner's sugar

In a bowl, mix the eggs, sugar, ricotta, and vanilla until smooth and creamy.

In a separate bowl, sift the flour, baking powder, and salt, then add to the egg mixture, blending well until a heavy, sticky batter is formed. If the batter seems too dry, add a little milk.

In a heavy, deep pan or deep-fryer, heat the vegetable oil to 375°F.

Using 2 soup spoons, drop heaping tablespoons of batter into the hot oil and fry until deep golden on both sides. Sometimes the puffs will flip over by themselves; if not, turn them with a slotted spoon. Remove the puffs with a slotted spoon to brown paper to drain.

Place the puffs on a serving dish and sprinkle all over with confectioner's sugar. These are best served warm.

Savoiardi

Savoy Biscuits, or Italian Ladyfingers
Makes 4½ dozen

*S*avoiardi are ladyfingers. The name comes from the Savoy dynasty, one of Europe's oldest, which guarded the passes of the western Alps between southeastern France and northwestern Italy. Savoy is northwest of Turin, in the Piedmont. The House of Savoy ruled unified Italy from 1861 until the advent of the republic in 1946.

Ladyfingers are used for a number of desserts, including tiramisù. The trick to making good ladyfingers is to have the eggs at room temperature, blend the yolks well with the sugar, and stiffly beat the whites (preferably in a cooper bowl with a hand-held beater). Ladyfingers should have a light, airy, and dry texture.

2½ tablespoons confectioner's sugar

½ cup plus 3 tablespoons granulated sugar

6 large eggs, separated and at room temperature

1 cup unbleached all-purpose flour

⅛ teaspoon salt

Preheat the oven to 350°F. Line the cookie sheets with parchment.

In a small bowl, mix the confectioner's sugar and 2 tablespoons granulated sugar and set aside.

In a large bowl, beat the yolks and 9 tablespoons granulated sugar with an electric mixer until yolks are pale yellow and very thick. Lightly spoon the flour into a 1-cup measure, then place in a sifter and gradually sift a small amount at a time over the yolk mixture, blending well. Continue adding flour and blending. Set aside.

In a deep 10-inch copper or stainless-steel bowl, beat the egg whites with the salt until stiff peaks form. Gradually fold the egg whites a little at a time into the yolk mixture.

Fill a tipless pastry bag with some of the mixture and pipe out 1½-inch-wide and 3-inch-long fingers 1 inch apart on the cookie sheets. With a small sieve, sprinkle the tops of the ladyfingers with the sugar mixture. Bake the cookie sheets on the middle and top rack of the oven for about 15 minutes or until nicely browned. Switch the cookie sheets during baking to ensure even browning.

Let the ladyfingers cool about 5 minutes, then carefully remove to a cooling rack.

Note: These may be made ahead and frozen in single layers between sheets of waxed paper. They will keep for 2 months.

Biscottini Glassati al Cioccolato

Chocolate-Glazed Little Cookies
Makes 3 dozen

Not only do I drool at pastry windows all over Italy, I make notes on what I see, then go in and ask the *pasticcino* ("pastry cook") how the things that tantalize my sweet tooth are made. These buttery *biscottini* are bite-size cookies that are easy to make, but look impressive.

2¼ cups unbleached all-purpose flour	⅓ cup finely chopped almonds or hazelnuts
¼ teaspoon salt	1 extra-large egg, slightly beaten
12 tablespoons (1½ sticks) cold butter, cut in small pieces	2 ounces semisweet chocolate
½ cup granulated sugar	2½ tablespoons confectioner's sugar
¼ cup baking cocoa	

Preheat the oven to 400°F. Line cookie sheets with parchment paper.

In a bowl, mix the flour and salt, then cut in the butter with your fingers until the mixture is the texture of coarse granules.

Add the granulated sugar, cocoa, nuts, and egg, mix with your hands until the dough holds together and is well blended. Add a little water if the dough seems too dry.

Break off small pieces of the dough and roll them into 1-inch balls. Space the balls on parchment lined cookie sheets. Bake the cookies for about 13 minutes, or until just firm to the touch. Remove the cookies to a rack to cool completely.

Half-fill the bottom of a double boiler with water, bring water to a boil, turn off the heat, add the chocolate to the top of the double boiler, cover with a lid, and let the chocolate melt.

With a small spoon, glaze the bottom of each cookie with a little of the melted chocolate. Place the cookies, glazed side up, on a rack to dry.

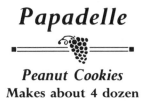

Turn the cookies right side up and, with a small sifter, sprinkle with confectioner's sugar.

Note: These cookies can be frozen unglazed and unsugared. Simply save these steps until the cookies have been defrosted.

Papadelle

Peanut Cookies
Makes about 4 dozen

This recipe for a peanut and molasses cookie with a long Italian family tradition was given to me by Marie Rogers, whose family came from Campobasso. In dialect, these cookies are called Papadelle.

4½ cups unbleached all-purpose flour	1 cup molasses
1 cup sugar	3 large eggs
½ teaspoon baking soda	1 cup chopped peanuts
1 teaspoon baking powder	Grated zest and juice of 1 orange
12 tablespoons (1½ sticks) margarine or butter, at room temperature	Colored sprinkles

Preheat the oven to 350°F. Lightly grease the cookie sheets.

In a large bowl, sift the flour, sugar, baking soda, and baking powder together. Set aside.

In a separate bowl, cream the margarine with an electric mixer until smooth. Add the molasses and 2 of the eggs, and beat together until smooth. Add the peanuts, orange zest, and juice; mix with a spoon until a soft dough forms.

On a floured surface, divide the dough into 4 pieces. Roll each piece into a rope about 12 inches long. Place the ropes on cookie sheets, patting them down a little with your hand.

In a small bowl, lightly beat the remaining egg with a fork, and brush the top of each rope. Decorate the tops with sprinkles. Bake for 15 to 20 minutes, or until firm to the touch. Remove the ropes to cooling racks. Let them cool for 30 minutes, then slice into ¼-inch pieces.

Caffè Italiano

Italian Coffee

I was sitting in the lounge of the Hotel Brunelleschi in Florence, staring out the window and wondering when the torrential downpour would end, so that I could continue my love affair with the sights of the city.

To take the chill off, I ordered a cappuccino. It came covered with its usual mound of foamed milk and a generous dusting of shaved chocolate. As I sat sipping sublimely, I noticed several people wander in, cursing the weather and shaking the rain from their clothes. They made themselves comfortable and called the waiter over. "Can we get coffee?" "Si, signori," was the reply. The waiter then proceeded to rattle off the choices of espresso, espresso con panna, espresso macchiato, caffè latte, latte macchiato, and cappuccino. "We just want American coffee" came the determined reply, and off went the waiter to satisfy yet another tourist reluctant to leave the habits of home behind.

Italians are passionate about their coffee, which was made popular in Europe by the Arabs in the seventeenth century. Espresso was invented in Italy in the early twentieth century so many cups of coffee could be brewed quickly in order to meet growing demands. Espresso is a method of brewing coffee in which steam is forced through ground coffee beans, which results in a thick, strong drink made palatable with sugar. With the addition of hot steamed milk and grated chocolate, it becomes cappuccino. There are also many other inventive ways to have this brew. Caffè latte, usually served for breakfast, is made with equal amounts of hot coffee and hot milk. Espresso macchiato has just a bit of milk, and espresso con panna is coffee with a dollop of whipped cream. Caffè Americano is just what its name implies. Espresso with a shot of whiskey, grappa, or Anisette was served by my grandmother at home. It had the ability to get you through anything.

Stelline d'Oro

Little Stars of Gold
Makes 4½ to 5 dozen

It was literally Christmas in July when I was asked to develop a cookie to fit an Italian folktale storyline by the well-known children's illustrator and author Tomie de Paola. With Italian Christmas music in the background to inspire me, I started baking immediately, and created these Stelline d'Oro. The frosting, tinted with saffron and bits of the threadlike stigmas, give this cookie its name and its starlike glow.

Dough	Frosting
2 cups unbleached all-purpose flour	4 to 5 saffron threads, crushed
½ teaspoon salt	3 tablespoons warm water (100° to 115°F.)
½ teaspoon baking powder	1¼ cups confectioner's sugar, sifted
1 cup granulated sugar	1 to 2 tablespoons orange flower water or orange juice
8 tablespoons (1 stick) butter or margarine, softened	
1 large egg	
1 tablespoon orange flower water, or 2 tablespoons fresh orange juice	

In a bowl, sift the flour, salt, and baking powder together. In a separate bowl, beat the granulated sugar and butter until creamy. Add the egg and flavoring, and mix well. Add to dry ingredients and mix well. Wrap the dough in waxed paper and refrigerate until firm, about 2 hours.

In a small bowl, soak the saffron threads in warm water until the water turns bright yellow. Add the confectioner's sugar and enough orange flower water to make a thin glaze. Set aside.

continued

Preheat the oven to 375°F. Grease the cookie sheets.

Divide the dough into 4 pieces. Work with 1 piece at a time on a floured surface. Roll out the dough until about ⅛ inch thick. Use a small star-shaped cookie cutter to cut out stars. Place the stars about 1 inch apart on cookie sheets.

Bake the stars about 7 to 8 minutes. Do not let edges brown; they should remain pale. Remove the cookies to cooling racks and frost while still warm.

Frutte e Salse di Frutte

Fruit and Fruit Sauces

For the most part, Italians eat fruit fresh off the tree or vine, and I can understand why. The natural flavors are intensely sweet owing to a long growing season with sunny days, rich soil, and generations of farmers who understand the land.

The flavor and quality of American-grown fruit was always a topic of conversation with my grandmothers, who stubbornly insisted that fruit in America did not have any taste. But they made do and looked forward to summertime, when availability and variety increased. Fruit was so cherished that when they visited their friends, they often took a few peaches or some cherries as a gift.

When fresh fruit season arrived, we made family trips throughout the summer to orchards to handpick peaches, cherries, and apples. We also bought Concord grapes for making juice and bushels of plum tomatoes for tomato sauce at outdoor markets. Canning days found my mother, grandmother, and me in the basement kitchen, each of us with more than one arduous task. My job was to wash all the canning jars and lids in scalding, soapy water in the large stone sink that doubled for doing laundry. Grandma sat on an old stool, slowly peeling peaches, newspapers spread on the floor around her to catch the peach skins and stones. Nearby, at a steaming stove, my mother scalded and peeled tomatoes. Apples also waited to be turned into applesauce. Squeezing hot, cooked apples by hand through rough sieves was grueling work. By the end of the day, there was not only a bushelful of apple skins, but skinned knuckles as well. And the smell of tomato sauce cooking and peaches in a cinnamon-sugar syrup filled the house. After everything was cooked and ready for winter storage in the fruit cellar, my job was to line up the jars in neat rows according to contents.

I can honestly say that I hated canning season. I would much rather have been riding my bike or reading Nancy Drew mystery stories. Perhaps that is why I have never continued this tradition, even though in the winter months there was nothing like the fruits we canned. I do make applesauce, but I use my food processor. I don't even remove the skins, and I freeze what we cannot eat. What I wind up with is something that my mother and grandmother would be proud of; a ruby red sauce with a tart-sweet cinnamon and clove flavor.

On one of my trips to Italy, I returned to a wonderful restaurant in Foligno, called Villa Roncalli. The specialty is spit cooking. As I walked up the jagged stone path lined with huge clay pots of red geraniums, I noticed an ancient-looking building to the left that I had not remembered seeing before. The door was ajar. Curiosity got the best of me, so I wandered over. There was a very familiar smell coming from inside. I walked in and saw a small elderly woman clad in black, with a bright red scarf almost covering her gray hair. She was stirring a huge black cauldron with a large wooden paddle. In my stumbling Italian I asked her if she was making tomato sauce. "*Ma no, signora, questa è la salsa di mele.*" She was making applesauce! For a moment, I was back in the days when this was done in my home and I perceived it as unnecessary and exhausting work. But now it seemed a comfort to know that I had been exposed to many of the elements of traditional cooking that survive in Italy today.

Besides eaten fresh, fruits are turned into sauces, added to puddings and semifreddi, and even fried.

Bavarese alle Banane

Banana Cream Pudding
Serves 6

A *bavarese* is a rich molded pudding made with cream and milk. It is one of my favorite desserts and very easy to make, lending itself to a variety of flavors. This one is made with very ripe bananas, which minimizes the amount of sugar needed. Make this early on the day you plan to serve it.

¼ cup water	1 large well-mashed
2 teaspoons unflavored gelatin	banana (⅔ cup)
4 large egg yolks	½ cup heavy cream
½ cup plus 2 tablespoons sugar	1 pint strawberries, stemmed and wiped clean
1 cup boiled milk	2 tablespoons brandy

Pour the water into a medium bowl, sprinkle the gelatin over it, stir, and let dissolve. Set aside.

In another bowl, beat the egg yolks and ½ cup of sugar with an electric mixer until the mixture is lemon colored. Set aside. Gradually stir the milk into the gelatin mixture, blending well. While beating, slowly pour the milk and gelatin mixture into the egg mixture. Add the banana and the cream, and continue to beat until smooth.

Pour the mixture into a 4-cup mold. Cover the mold with foil or plastic wrap and refrigerate for at least 4 hours or until firm.

In a food processor or blender, puree the strawberries with the brandy and remaining sugar until smooth. Set aside.

To serve, unmold the bavarese by placing a serving dish larger than the mold on top and carefully turning the dish over. Holding the sides of the plate and the mold, shake the mold gently to release it. If it does not come out easily, quickly dip the bottom of the mold in hot water and repeat the process.

Cut the mold into serving pieces and pour some of the sauce over the top.

Variation: Make individual molds. Spoon some of the sauce over each mold after unmolding.

Fichi Secchi in Vino

Dried Figs in Wine
Serves 4

One of the best fruit desserts is simply a bowl of fresh figs. I only see them in the market occasionally. When I do, I serve them as a first course with prosciutto or as a dessert with a dollup of sweet and creamy mascarpone on the side. When fresh figs are not available, I rely on this old family recipe that utilizes dried figs.

1 teaspoon butter	1 cup dry red wine
12 large dried figs (½ pound)	¼ cup honey
⅓ cup chopped walnuts	1 tablespoon grated orange zest

Preheat the oven to 350°F. Lightly grease a deep 6-inch round casserole dish with the butter.

With your fingers, open each fig at the stem end to form a small hole. Stuff some of the walnuts into each fig and place filled side up in a single layer in the casserole.

In a small pot, heat the wine and honey, stirring until the honey dissolves. Pour the mixture over the figs. Sprinkle on the zest, cover the casserole tightly with a lid or foil, and bake for 30 minutes.

Let the figs cool to room temperature in the casserole. To serve, place 3 figs on each of 4 small dessert dishes and pour over some of the wine sauce. Serve immediately.

Mele Fritte

Fried Apple Slices
Serves 4 to 6

This easy dessert from the region of Emilia-Romagna is the perfect thing to make when apples are in season, although it can be enjoyed year-round. If you wish, you can marinate the apple slices first in a little brandy. I use Yellow Delicious or Cortland apples. These are best served warm.

- 1 teaspoon active dry yeast
- ½ cup warm water (110° to 115°F.)
- ½ cup plus 2 tablespoons sugar
- 1 large egg, slightly beaten
- 3 tablespoons olive oil
- ¼ cup dry white wine
- ⅛ teaspoon salt
- 1 cup unbleached all-purpose flour
- 1 pound apples, peeled, cored, and sliced into ¼-inch rounds
- 4 cups vegetable oil, for deep-frying

In a bowl, dissolve the yeast in the warm water, then add 2 tablespoons of the sugar, egg, olive oil, and wine. Blend well.

In a separate bowl, mix the salt with the flour and add to the yeast mixture. Beat with a whisk until it is like pancake batter. If the batter seems too dry, add a little more wine or water. Set the batter aside.

Place the remaining sugar on a plate and set aside.

In a heavy pot or deep-fryer, heat the vegetable oil to 375°F. Coat a few apple slices at a time on both sides with the batter, letting the excess drain off. Fry the slices until golden brown, about 3 to 4 minutes.

Drain on brown paper. When cool enough to handle, gently press the apple slices into the sugar on each side. Arrange slices on a platter and serve immediately.

Pesche e Fragole
in Marsala

Peaches and Strawberries in Marsala
Serves 4

Frest fruit bobbing in bowls of in water are usually brought to an Italian table as the finale to a meal. This fresh fruit dessert goes one step further with the addition of confectioner's sugar and Marsala wine. Simple but elegant, it is a good ending to a company meal, especially when served in fancy wine or fruit goblets.

2 ripe medium peaches, peeled, pitted, and sliced	6 tablespoons confectioner's sugar
1 pint ripe strawberries, stemmed, wiped, and cut in half	½ cup sweet Marsala wine

In a bowl, gently mix the peaches, strawberries, sugar, and wine. Cover the bowl and let the fruit macerate at room temperature for at least 1 hour.

To serve, divide the fruit among wine or fruit goblets, and accompany with biscotti, if you wish.

Variation: Eliminate the sugar and Marsala. Mix the fruits together, place them in wine or fruit goblets, and pour Asti Spumante into each, filling it to the top. Let stand 5 minutes before serving.

Salsa di Fragole con Amaretto

Strawberry Amaretto Sauce
Makes 1 cup

This quick-to-make strawberry sauce can be used over *gelato* ("ice cream"), *semifreddi* ("partially frozen desserts"), and rich *panna cotta* ("cooked cream").

1 pint ripe strawberries, cleaned, stemmed, and cut in half

½ cup sugar

4 tablespoons Amaretto liqueur

1 tablespoon orange juice

Place the strawberries and sugar in a saucepan. Stir well and cook over medium heat until the berries begin to soften, then thicken, about 10 minutes, stirring often.

Pour the berry mixture into a sieve over a bowl. With a wooden spoon, press the berries through the sieve, extracting as much juice as possible. Discard the solids.

Add the liqueur and orange juice, and blend well. Let the mixture cool to room temperature.

Melegrane per Natale

Pomegranates for Christmas

On the day before Christmas Eve, Grandma Galasso put on her black coat, reached for her pocketbook, and said she wanted to pay a few outstanding bills. Heavy snow had begun to fall that day, making it difficult to walk, so Grandma asked me to go with her. I was caught up in Christmas and really didn't want to go, but reluctantly I accompanied her. As we slowly walked arm-in-arm to Mack Brindis's store, Grandma didn't say much, her breathing seemed strained as she made carefully executed steps in the snow. Finally arriving at the store, she was greeted with "Buon Natale" and "Good to see you, Mrs. Galasso." I shook the snow from my hair and made myself scarce between the grocery aisles, looking at all the special Italian foods imported for the holiday season. I especially eyed the ruby red pomegranates that Grandma always bought for us this time of year. I expected that she would bring some home, but she bought nothing. She paid her bill, put her receipt in her pocket, and motioned for me to come along. I thought it odd that she did not buy any pomegranates.

It seemed to take forever to walk home. The snow was falling harder and the walks were very slippery. When we got to the door, Grandma asked me to brush the snow from her boots. Then she went slowly to her room and closed the door.

I went back to wrapping presents. Later in the day there was much commotion in Grandma's room. She wasn't feeling well, and the doctor was called. When he arrived, the worried look on his face told me that this was serious. No sooner had he examined her than he was on the phone, calling the hospital, an ambulance, and Monsignor Bernardo, our parish priest.

Now the lump of anxiety began to form in my throat. All Grandma's children were also called. Everything from that moment on happened so quickly. The doorbell rang and in came the monsignor, carrying sacred round hosts and blessed oil under his snow white vestments. Grandma's room was very small, so I stayed out beyond the doorway, trying to absorb what was going on. I could see candles flickering and hear prayers being said in Latin. No sooner had the monsignor prepared my grandmother to take her leave from us than the ambulance appeared and she was whisked away to the hospital.

I never saw my grandmother alive again, and I regret that I didn't have the chance to say good-bye. I wish that I hadn't been so reluctant that wintry day to take her to the store; she wasn't going to die until all her affairs were in order.

That Christmas Eve was very hard on everyone. I went to church but I couldn't keep the tears from welling up. Gently sung Christmas carols only made it worse. I knew in my heart that my grandmother was in a good place. I just wish that I had appreciated her more, spent more time with her, and told her how much she was loved.

Now at Christmastime when I put a bowl of pomegranates on the table I am reminded of my good, gentle grandmother. I can never eat pomegranates without telling my family some wonderful stories about Grandma Galasso.

Salsa di Prugna Fresca

Fresh Plum Sauce
Makes 1¾ cups

Plums, or *prugne,* are served both fresh and dried in Italy. Dried plums are often poached in wine. When I want a quick, but fancy dessert I make Panna Cotta (page 298) and serve fresh plum sauce over the top. It is also good served over lemon sherbet or a plain tea cake.

Make this refreshing sauce with fresh, ripe, but not mushy plums. The skin of the plums should yield to gentle pressure when pressed with your finger.

3½ cups peeled, pitted,
and sliced Santa Rosa
or other large red or
purple plums

½ cup sugar

1 tablespoon fresh
lemon juice

1 tablespoon vanilla
sugar (page 7)

⅛ teaspoon ground
cloves

Place the plums and sugar in a saucepan. Cook over medium heat, stirring with a wooden spoon, until the mixture starts to boil. Add the lemon juice and continue to cook, stirring, for about 5 to 8 minutes, or until the fruit is glazed and a bit softened but not dissolved.

Pour the mixture into a bowl and add the vanilla sugar and cloves. Cover and let the sauce come to room temperature.

Note: You can double the recipe and keep the mixture in a jar in the refrigerature for up to 3 days.

Vanilla sugar is sold in grocery and gourmet food stores. It is also available mail-order. Vanilla sugar is made from vanilla beans and sugar. If not available, omit or make your own.

Salsa di Mortelle di Palude con Pere e Prugne

Cranberry, Pear, and Prune Sauce
Makes 3 cups

This sauce, made with *mortelle di palude,* or cranberries, is good for any fowl. I first had cranberries in northern Italy in the Trentino, served with venison. For this recipe, I have added dried prunes and pears. I like this sauce so much that I use it as the filling for a fall or winter tart.

2 large, ripe Bosc pears, peeled, cored, and cut into small chunks

1 12-ounce bag (2 cups) fresh cranberries

⅓ cup water

⅔ cup sugar

2 cinnamon sticks

3 whole cloves

½ teaspoon ground allspice

¼ teaspoon freshly grated nutmeg

½ cup dried prunes, pitted and cut into small pieces

Place the pears, cranberries, water, sugar, cinnamon sticks, cloves, allspice, and nutmeg in a saucepan. Stir and bring it to a boil. Add the prunes and stir with a wooden spoon until mixture thickens. Continue stirring for about 5 minutes, or until the cranberries are soft and the mixture coats the back of the spoon.

Cool the sauce. Remove the cinnamon sticks and discard. Serve the sauce warm or cold.

I Dolci

Desserts

In Italy on any day of the week, you can see trays and towers of jewellike sweets being delivered to customers from the local *pasticerria*. The first time I ventured into an Italian bakery, I was struck not only by the variety of sweets—from pastel-colored *meringhe* ("meringues") and *baci di dama* ("ladies' kisses") to rich liqueur-laced cakes and elegant clam-shell puff pastries filled with ricotta and citron—but also by the way orders were wrapped. All purchases are neatly arranged in a box, wrapped in bright colored paper, tied with gold ribbon, and given a seal from the bakery!

If you are lucky enough to be invited to dinner at someone's home as I was the first time I went to Italy, bring a tart or cake from a bakery. An American woman who had spent a lot of time in Italy told me: "Remember to bring three things: candy, flowers, and a cake." Italians love to receive sweets.

At home, baking was my mother's domain, but her knowledge and tricks for baking were learned from my grandmothers. Lard and chicken fat were essential ingredients in pastry and some cookies. Chicken fat was scraped from the tops of stews and soups and stored in jars in the refrigerator. Chicken fat was essential in Ma's Cookies (page 256), and fresh lard made her Pasta Frolla dough very flaky.

While these desserts are not elaborate, their success does depend on a few basic rules.

- Use unbleached all-purpose flour unless otherwise indicated.
- Preheat your oven as directed, and do not bake in a soiled oven; the heat will cause smoke to rise from the residue on the oven floor and impart an insipid taste to your cake or pie.
- Use the correct pan size. If a recipe calls for a jelly-roll pan, do not use a cookie sheet and expect to get the same results.
- Invest in parchment paper for lining cookie sheets, nonstick molds, cake testers, and a good electric mixer.
- A scale is very useful for measuring ingredients when baking. A case in point is flour. A cup of flour weighs approximately 4 ounces; flour packed too tightly into a measuring cup weighs about 5 ounces, and too much flour can significantly alter the texture and taste, and in some cases, the height of cakes.
- If stiffly beaten egg whites are to be used, they should be at room temperature before beating. Beat them in a copper or glass bowl; do not use plastic, as any residue of grease will cause the egg whites to remain flat. Also, take care when folding egg whites into batter. Bring your spatula down and over, folding until no streaks remain.
- Let cakes cool completely before removing them from pans, or the cake will break and you will ruin your hard work.
- Frozen desserts and puddings should be well wrapped and have sufficient chilling time in the freezer or refrigerator before un-molding.
- If you bake frequently, buy ingredients such as flour, sugar, and yeast in bulk; it is more economical.
- If a recipe calls for butter, do not substitute margarine.

Budino di Mele

Apple Bread Pudding
Serves 6 to 8

While this bread pudding calls for stale bread, I have also made it with stale Ciambella ("ring cake") and panettone with excellent results. If you don't want to make the caramel lining for the mold, then omit it and grease the mold with butter. The pudding is baked in a *bagnomaria,* or water bath.

½ cup raisins

⅓ cup brandy

12 slices stale bread, broken into pieces

1½ cups milk

1⅓ cups sugar

3 large eggs

3 tablespoons butter, melted

4 Golden Delicious apples, cored, peeled, and thinly sliced

½ teaspoon salt

⅓ cup water

Place the raisins in a small bowl, cover with the brandy, and marinate for 30 minutes.

Place the bread in a rectangular dish and pour the milk over it. Set aside.

In a large bowl, with a whisk, beat ½ cup of the sugar with the eggs, salt, and butter until well blended. Drain the raisins and add to the sugar mixture along with 2 tablespoons of the brandy. Add the apple slices and soaked bread and blend all the ingredients. Set aside.

Preheat the oven to 350°F.

In a saucepan set over medium-high heat, combine the remaining sugar and the water. Let the sugar dissolve completely, then boil until it darkens to a caramel color. Immediately and carefully pour the caramel into an 8-inch deep ring mold and swirl to coat the bottom of the mold. Be sure not to hold the mold by the bottom; otherwise you may burn your hands.

Pour the apple-bread mixture into the mold, spreading and packing it evenly. Place the mold in a baking pan and fill the pan with enough boiling water to come 1½ inches up the sides of the mold. Carefully place the pan with the ring mold in the oven and bake for 45 minutes, or until a cake tester inserted in the center comes out clean.

Remove the mold from the baking pan. Let it stand only for a few seconds, then carefully place a serving dish over the top of the mold and invert it. Shake the mold to release the pudding and the sauce. Cut the apple pudding into wedges and serve warm.

Buccellato Palermitano

Palermo Sweet Fig and Nut Cake
Makes four 6-inch cakes

The *buccellato* is a round, sweet cake that has many regional variations. This one is adapted from an old Palermo recipe, with butter substituted for lard. It reminds me of Cucciddatu, a sweet dough encased around a fig or date filling, which appears in my first cookbook. This recipe yields about 3¼ pounds of dough, or enough for four small *buccellati*. I make and freeze them ahead for Christmas. For gift-giving I wrap each one in colorful cellophane.

Filling

1 pound (3 cups) Mission figs

²⁄₃ cup raisins

1½ cups diced candied orange rind

½ cup chopped hazelnuts

½ cup chopped unblanched almonds

1 cup chopped walnuts

1½ teaspoons ground cloves

1¾ cups apricot jam

Dough

5½ to 5¾ cups unbleached all-purpose flour

1½ teaspoons baking powder

1 cup sugar

12 tablespoons (1½ sticks) butter or lard, at room temperature

1½ tablespoons grated lemon zest

1 cup milk

4 large eggs, slightly beaten

1 large egg beaten with 1 tablespoon water

In a food processor or by hand, chop the figs into small pieces. Place them in a bowl and add the remaining filling ingredients. Mix well, cover, and set aside.

In a large bowl, sift 5½ cups of the flour with the baking powder. Add the sugar and blend with a spoon. Add the butter or lard and lemon zest, and mix with your hands until the mixture is crumbly. Add the milk and eggs, and mix until a smooth ball of dough is formed; add more flour if necessary.

Turn the dough out onto a floured surface and knead until smooth and soft. Wrap the dough in waxed paper and chill for 2 to 3 hours.

Preheat the oven to 375°F. Grease 4 cookie sheets.

Divide the dough into 4 equal pieces. Work with 1 piece at a time on a floured surface, and roll into a 16-inch circle. Spread one fourth of the filling to within ½ inch of the edge. Roll up like a jelly roll, being sure to tuck in the sides as you go. Pinch the bottom edge closed. Bring the 2 ends together to form a ring. Place on a cookie sheet.

Repeat for remaining pieces of dough. Brush each ring with some of the egg and water mixture. Bake for 45 minutes or until nicely browned. Cool on racks.

Crema all'Amaretto

Amaretto Cream Pudding
Serves 6 to 8

Cocoa beans were one of the New World's offerings to Europe in the sixteenth century. Southern Italians embraced this new ingredient more than their northern neighbors, using it in sweet confections as well as in some vegetables dishes such as Caponata (page 13).

The combination of semisweet chocolate, amaretti cookies, and Amaretto liqueur in this chocolate cream dessert makes for a sublime ending to a dinner party. Be sure to use good-quality chocolate such as Lindt or Ghiradelli. I serve this in individual goblets, or use it as a filling to make chocolate pie.

4 large egg yolks	**1 tablespoon vanilla extract**
½ cup sugar	
4 cups plus 2 tablespoons cold milk	**2 tablespoons (¼ stick) butter**
	3 teaspoons Amaretto liqueur
½ cup lightly packed unbleached all-purpose flour	
	¾ cup coarsely chopped amaretti cookies
1 cup (7 ounces) finely grated semisweet chocolate	**½ cup sliced almonds**

Place the egg yolks and sugar in a saucepan and mix well with a wire whisk. Add 2 tablespoons of the milk and whisk until smooth. Sift in the flour a little at a time and continue whisking. Add the remaining milk and whisk to blend.

Place the saucepan over medium-low heat and cook the mixture, whisking constantly, until it starts to thicken slightly. Add the chocolate and continue whisking until the mixture reaches the boiling point. Whisk for a minute, taking care not to let the mixture burn, then remove the pan from the heat.

Add the vanilla, butter, and liqueur and blend carefully with a rubber spatula. Cover the mixture with a sheet of buttered waxed paper and let cool about 5 minutes.

Blend in the cookies, and pour the mixture into individual serving dishes or into a decorative serving dish. Cover with buttered waxed paper and refrigerate at least 4 to 6 hours or until set.

Just before serving, sprinkle the sliced almonds over the top.

Grand Torta della Nonna

Grandma's Great Pie
Makes a large rectangular pie

The pastry shop windows in any Italian town or city display works of edible art. Usually I try something new each time. At Il Forno in Florence, a popular local spot, I got in line with everyone else giving orders. I chose the *torta della nonna*, or grandma's pie, and I was not disappointed. This two-crusted flat pie, made in a long rectangular pan and cut in squares, was filled with ricotta and orange flavoring and topped with almonds and confectioner's sugar. I wanted to know exactly how it was made, and when I asked, the answer was "*Un po' di farina, zucchero, uove, e mandorle.*" What follows is my re-creation of this delicious pie. When I made it the first time, I was surprised how close it came in appearance and taste to the original.

Dough

4 cups unbleached all-purpose flour

1 cup granulated sugar

½ teaspoon salt

2 teaspoons baking powder

1 cup solid vegetable shortening or lard

½ cup milk

2 teaspoons vanilla extract

1 large egg

Filling

2 cups milk

½ cup semolina flour

2 cups well-drained ricotta cheese

2 large eggs

½ cup granulated sugar

2 tablespoons grated orange zest

2 tablespoons fresh orange juice

¼ cup apricot jam, warmed

¾ cup toasted slivered almonds

⅓ cup confectioner's sugar

In a large bowl, mix the flour, sugar, salt, and baking powder. With a fork or your hands, cut in the shortening or lard until the mixture is coarse.

In a separate bowl, lightly whisk the milk, vanilla, and egg together and add to the flour mixture. Combine with your hands until a soft ball of dough is formed. Cover the dough with plastic wrap and let rest at room temperature for 30 minutes.

In a medium saucepan, bring the milk for the filling just to a boil. With a wooden spoon, stir in the semolina flour in a thin stream and continue to stir until the mixture thickens and leaves the sides of the pan. Remove from the heat and let cool to lukewarm.

In a large bowl, mix the ricotta, eggs, sugar, orange zest, and juice. Add the semolina mixture and beat with an electric mixer just until blended. Set the filling aside.

Preheat the oven to 375°F.

Divide the dough in half and roll 1 piece on a floured surface into a 15- x 11½-inch rectangle. Place the dough on a greased cookie sheet of the same size and pat gently to fit. Fill any small holes by stretching and patting the dough into place. Spread the filling evenly over the dough to the edges. Set aside.

Roll the remaining dough into another 15- x 11½-inch sheet. Using your rolling pin, carefully lift the dough and place it over the filling. Use a fork to pinch the edges closed. If a tear occurs, patch it with some of the dough.

Bake the pie for 30 to 35 minutes, or until the crust is nicely browned. You may have to move the pie from the bottom rack to the middle rack for even browning.

Remove the pie from the oven and immediately brush with the warmed apricot jam. Sprinkle the almonds evenly over the top, gently pressing them to adhere, and let the pie cool completely.

Before cutting and serving the pie, sprinkle the top evenly and generously with confectioner's sugar. Cut into squares.

Variation: Add ½ cup each raisins and diced citron to the filling.

Pasta Ciotti

Custard Tarts
Makes a dozen 3-inch tarts

The recipe for these sweet, custard-filled tarts was given to me by Marie Rogers, a friend whose Italian women's group makes them for church fairs and at Eastertime. Originally, the dough was made with lard, but I have substituted vegetable shortening. The tarts can be made any size, from miniature to the 3-inch shells used here.

Dough

2 cups unbleached all-purpose flour

½ cup sugar

⅛ teaspoon salt

¾ teaspoon baking powder

½ cup solid vegetable shortening

¼ cup milk

¾ teaspoon vanilla extract

1 jumbo egg, well beaten

Filling

3 tablespoons cornstarch

⅔ cup sugar

1½ cups plus 2 tablespoons milk

1½ tablespoons butter

1 large egg yolk, slightly beaten

1 teaspoon almond extract

In a large bowl, sift together the flour, sugar, salt, and baking powder. Cut in the shortening with a pastry blender until the mixture is coarse. Add the milk, vanilla, and half the beaten egg. Use your hands to mix the ingredients quickly, forming a smooth ball of dough. Wrap the dough in plastic wrap and set aside.

In a medium saucepan, mix the cornstarch and sugar, smoothing out any lumps. Place the saucepan over medium heat and gradually add 1½ cups of milk and the butter. Cook the mixture, stirring constantly with a wooden spoon, until thickened. Remove the saucepan from the heat, add the egg yolk and almond flavoring, and stir. Set the custard aside.

Divide the dough in half. On a lightly floured surface, roll 1 piece to an 11-inch circle about ¼ inch thick. Do not roll the dough thinner. Using a 3-inch fluted biscuit cutter, cut out circles and press them into 3-inch tart shells, so that the dough completely lines the shell. Re-roll the scraps and cut additional circles. You should be able to fill 12 tart shells.

Place the tart shells on a cookie sheet. Spoon about 2 tablespoons of filling into each.

Roll out the second piece of dough like the first. Cut out twelve 3-inch circles and place a circle over each tart, pinching the edges closed.

Add the remaining 2 tablespoons milk to the reserved half beaten egg and mix well. With a pastry brush, paint the top of each tart. Refrigerate the tarts for 30 minutes.

Preheat the oven to 425°F.

Bake the tarts on the middle rack for 12 to 15 minutes or until the tops are golden brown. Remove the tarts to a rack and let cool completely. Carefully remove the tarts from the shells and serve.

Note: If you make miniature tarts, bake them for 8 to 10 minutes.

Panna Cotta

Cooked Cream
Serves 4

My friends Barbara and Antonio Masullo took me to a seafood restaurant in Perugia, the beautiful capital of Umbria. Ristorante Renato Sommella, on Via Baldeschi, 5, was run by Neapolitans, not Perugians. Everything was first-rate, but the best thing on the menu was *panna cotta,* or cooked cream. I was so busy eating this sublime dessert that I hurriedly scribbled notes on how it was made. Just cook sugar, cream, and gelatin, I was told. Here is my version. It is wonderful served as is, but I sometimes gild the dish with Fresh Plum Sauce (page 284) or a rich chocolate sauce. Make this the day before you plan to serve it.

½ cup half-and-half	1 2-inch piece vanilla bean
1 envelope unflavored gelatin	
2 cups heavy cream	Grated zest of 1 small lemon
¼ cup plus 2 tablespoons sugar	

Grease 4 ½-cup ramekins lightly with butter and set aside.

Pour the half-and-half in a small bowl and sprinkle on the gelatin, then stir to dissolve. Set aside.

In a medium saucepan, mix the cream, sugar, vanilla bean, and half-and-half mixture. Cook over medium heat, stirring constantly with a wooden spoon, until the mixture begins to boil. Take care not to let the mixture bubble up over the sides of the pan. Cook until the mixture begins to thicken slightly, then remove the pan and discard the vanilla bean.

Stir the lemon zest into the cream, then carefully pour the mixture into the ramekins. Place them on a tray and cover with plastic wrap. Refrigerate until set, about 5 hours or overnight.

To serve, run a butter knife around the sides of the ramekins. Place a serving plate on top and invert the plate. Shake the ramekins to release, or dip each mold quickly in hot water and then invert onto serving dishes. Serve at once.

Pasta Frolla

Pastry Dough
Makes two 10-inch pastry shells

This is a pastry dough that I use for the Easter pie in my first book, *Ciao Italia,* and in filled tarts. It is very versatile and easy to work with. Do not overmix the dough or it will be tough.

2 cups unbleached all-
purpose flour

1 cup pastry flour

1½ teaspoons salt

2 tablespoons sugar

8 tablespoons (1 stick)
butter, at room
temperature, cut into
small pieces

1 large egg, beaten

5 to 6 tablespoons cold
water

In a bowl, mix the flours, salt, and sugar. Add the butter and work it in until the mixture is the texture of coarse cornmeal. Add the beaten egg and just enough water to make a pliable dough. Do not overmix.

Form the dough into a ball, wrap it tightly in plastic wrap, and refrigerate for 1 hour or overnight before using.

Torta di Pesche Secche e Limone

Dried Peach and Lemon Tart
Makes one 9-inch tart

This fruit tart is an adaptation of ones I have sampled all over Italy. Since peach season is so short I developed this one, which uses dried peaches instead of fresh. The combination of dried peaches and a tart lemon filling make this tart refreshing all year long. The filling can be made the day before the tart is served.

Dough

1 cup (4 ounces) unbleached all-purpose flour

2 tablespoons granulated sugar

6 tablespoons (¾ stick) butter, chilled

1 large egg yolk

1 tablespoon cold water

1 tablespoon apricot jam

Filling

Juice and grated zest of 4 lemons

4 tablespoons (½ stick) butter, cut into pieces

1½ cups plus 1 tablespoon granulated sugar

4 large eggs, slightly beaten

2 cups (1 10-ounce package) dried peaches

½ cup water

1 teaspoon almond extract

Topping

1 cup heavy cream

⅓ cup confectioner's sugar

1 large tangerine, peeled and segmented

Fresh mint sprig, for garnish

Place the flour, sugar, and salt in a food processor or medium bowl. Add the butter and pulse to obtain a coarse mixture, or use a pastry blender to incorporate the butter. Add the egg yolk and water and pulse for 5 to

10 seconds, or mix with a fork. Do not overwork the dough. Form the dough into a ball, wrap in plastic, and chill it for 30 minutes.

Preheat the oven to 425°F.

On a lightly floured surface, roll the dough out to fit a 9-inch removable-bottom tart pan, or use a 9-inch round cake pan. With a fork, prick the dough all over and bake for 12 to 15 minutes. (If you wish, weigh the dough down with dried beans or rice.) Remove the tart shell from the oven and let cool completely.

In a double boiler over simmering water, combine the lemon juice and zest, butter, and 1¼ cups sugar. Stir with a wooden spoon until the butter melts. Stir in the eggs, and cook over medium-low heat until the filling thickens enough to coat the back of the spoon. Be careful not to let the mixture curdle. Remove from heat and let cool.

In a saucepan, boil the dried peaches in the water with the remaining sugar until they begin to soften. Stir the mixture occasionally as it cooks. The peaches should absorb all the water. Puree the peaches in a food processor or blender until smooth. Mix in the almond extract and set aside.

Heat the apricot jam in a small saucepan and brush it over the tart shell. Let the shell dry for about 10 minutes.

Spread the lemon filling in the shell all the way to the edges. Carefully spread the pureed peaches over the lemon filling. Refrigerate the tart until serving time.

In a chilled bowl, with an electric beater, whip the cream with the confectioner's sugar until stiff. Spread the cream over the tart or use a pastry bag to make a decorative pattern. Arrange the tangerine segments attractively on top and add a mint sprig in the center.

To serve, cut in wedges as a pie.

🌿

Torta di Agnello

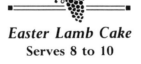

Easter Lamb Cake
Serves 8 to 10

In the baking section of my kitchen are two lamb-shaped cake molds that my mother used at Easter. On Holy Saturday, she would make enough rich batter to make a dozen cakes. The baked cakes, looking like a just sheared herd, were lined up on the kitchen table. Each was painstakingly decorated with pure white icing and colored confetti almonds running along the back. Purple bows were tied around their necks, then they were nestled on beds of paper Easter grass. They were wrapped in pastel sheets of cellophane and given to relatives, friends, and the parish priest. I continue this tradition at Easter, except that I've cut the herd to a pair.

2 cups cake flour

¾ teaspoon baking
powder

¼ teaspoon salt

⅛ teaspoon freshly grated
nutmeg

1 cup (2 sticks) butter
or margarine

1 cup granulated sugar

2 teaspoons grated
lemon zest

1 teaspoon grated
orange zest

1 tablespoon vanilla
extract

1 teaspoon almond extract

4 large eggs

½ cup finely ground
hazelnuts

Frosting

½ cup solid vegetable
shortening

½ cup (1 stick) butter

6 cups confectioner's
sugar

1 tablespoon almond
extract

Dried currants

Candied almonds

Preheat the oven to 350°F. Generously butter a 10- x 4-inch 2-piece lamb cake mold well and dust with flour.

In a bowl, sift the cake four, baking powder, salt, and nutmeg together.

In another bowl, with an electric mixer, beat the butter with the sugar until pale yellow. Add the zests and extracts. Beat in the eggs one a time, alternating with the flour mixture. Fold in the nuts.

Spread the batter in the bottom half of the lamb mold, filling the cavity well. Place the top of the mold over the bottom, making sure the fit is even. Bake for 40 to 45 minutes. Carefully lift the top half of the mold off and test the cake for doneness. If still soft in the middle, bake until firm, about 10 to 15 minutes longer, but do not replace the top.

Transfer the mold to a rack to cool completely. Run a knife around the edges and carefully remove the cake. Let the cake cool on a rack.

In a bowl, whip the shortening and butter until smooth. Add the confectioner's sugar. Stir in the extract. The frosting should be firm enough to put through a pastry bag. If not, add more confectioner's sugar.

Stand the cake upright on a cake stand or decorative platter. You may need to glue the base of the cake to the serving dish by spreading some frosting on it before placing the cake in upright position.

Fill a pastry bag fitted with a medium star tip with frosting, and squiggle the frosting over the cake to simulate wool. Use currants for the eyes and place some candied almonds along the lamb's back and at the base of the cake for a festive look. Tie a ribbon carefully around the neck.

To serve, cut the cake into thin slices.

Torta al Cioccolato

Chocolate Cake
Makes one 9-inch cake

I make this dense chocolate cake dotted with chopped hazelnuts frequently because it is a good keeper . . . but it rarely lasts long. Cut it in small wedges and serve it with espresso. For best results, lightly spoon the flour into your measuring cup; do not pack it in.

1½ cups hazelnuts	1½ cups unbleached all-purpose flour
1 cup (2 sticks) plus 1 tablespoon butter	½ cup baking cocoa
1 cup granulated sugar	1 teaspoon baking powder
5 eggs, separated and at room temperature	⅛ teaspoon salt
1 tablespoon vanilla extract	3 tablespoons confectioner's sugar

Preheat the oven to 350°F.

Place the nuts on a cookie sheet and toast in the oven for about 5 minutes. Watch carefully so they do not burn. Cool the nuts, then coarsely chop them and set aside.

In a large bowl with an electric mixer, cream 1 cup butter with the sugar until lemon colored. Add the egg yolks one at a time, beating each in completely. Add the vanilla and continue to beat a few seconds more.

Sift the flour, cocoa, and baking powder together. Using an electric mixer, gradually add the flour mixture to the egg mixture. Fold in the nuts and set aside.

In a separate bowl, beat the egg whites with the salt until very stiff. With a rubber spatula, fold the egg whites a little at a time into the egg mixture until no streaks of white remain.

With the remaining tablespoon of butter, grease a deep 9½-inch springform pan, then dust the pan with flour, shaking out the excess. Spread the batter in the pan and bake for 50 to 60 minutes, or until a cake tester inserted in the middle comes out clean.

Let the cake cool in the pan for 20 minutes. Carefully release the sides of the pan, remove the bottom, and let cake cool on a rack.

When ready to serve, dust the cake with confectioner's sugar.

Torta Fantasia di Cioccolato

Chocolate Fantasy Cake
Serves 8

Wondering what to do with some leftover mascarpone cheese (a sweet dessert cheese from northern Italy), a few dried out oranges, and some cold espresso coffee, I decided to make a cake. To me, it is the perfect cake—dense, yet moist—and needs no fancy embellishment. If wrapped well, it will remain moist for a week. It also freezes beautifully for up to 3 months. Ricotta cheese can be substituted for the mascarpone.

2 cups unbleached all-purpose flour	**½ cup orange juice**
2 cups sugar	**¼ cup plus 1 tablespoon baking cocoa**
1 teaspoon baking soda	**½ cup mascarpone cheese, at room temperature**
½ teaspoon salt	
8 ounces (1 stick) butter	**2 eggs, slightly beaten**
½ cup brewed espresso or other strong coffee	**2 teaspoons almond extract**

Preheat the oven to 350°F. Grease an 8- x 2-inch round pan and set aside.

In the bowl of an electric mixer, sift together the flour, sugar, baking soda, and salt. Set aside.

In a saucepan, melt the butter. Remove the pan from the heat and add the coffee, orange juice, and cocoa, stirring well to combine. Pour the butter mixture over the flour mixture. Add the cheese, eggs, and almond extract, and beat the ingredients until the batter is smooth.

Pour the batter into the pan and bake it for 35 to 45 minutes, or until a cake tester inserted into the middle comes out clean.

Let the cake cool in the pan, then carefully unmold it onto a serving plate. Serve the cake as is, or sprinkled with confectioner's sugar.

Il Bar

The Bar

My first trip to Italy gave me a gigantic headache, all because I tried to absorb centuries of history and culture in three weeks. I was so afraid of missing something important that I almost missed it all. For example, when visiting the Uffizi Art Gallery in Florence, I literally raced through the maze of connecting exhibit rooms, trying my best to see the artwork out of the front, back, and sides of my head. The words of a wise concierge at my hotel brought me to my senses. "Signora," he announced one day when I tried to rush him into helping me, "you may be of Italian extraction, but you do not think like an Italian."

On my second trip to Italy, I heeded these words and tried my best to be Italian in every sense of the word. Piano, or slowly, became my password. I soon learned to take advantage of it. To do this one must get in the habit of frequenting il bar, a refined standup or sit-down espresso, dolci, and gelato snack bar.

Throughout Italy, the bar is a gathering place for locals, who drink strong espresso or cappuccino from morning until night. For many Italians, the bar is their first stop on the way to work and the last stop on the way home. They pick up a cornetto ("croissant") or biscotti ("biscuits"), some caffè latte ("coffee with milk") or succo d'arancia ("orange juice"). They partake of these delicacies in due time, standing at the bar. For an added cost (un servizio), one can sit down outside at tables, watch the world go by, and catch up on world events with il giornale ("newspaper").

It took me a while, but I soon got the hang of bar stopping. One afternoon in Perugia, the wonderful capital city of Umbria,

I ordered an aqua minerale, took a seat outside, and did just what the Perugians do: Observe and stare. They stroll arm in arm. They kiss unabashedly. They push baby carriages. They argue most theatrically. They strut their fashion statements elegantly. They eat gelato.

Suddenly, my staring stupor was interrupted by a heralding of trumpets and drums. "Che succede?" "What's going on?" I asked in my halting Italian. "Oggi c'è una festa" came the excited reply. That day there was a festival and I had a ringside seat. From the top of the Corso Vannucci, the main street, a parade of horses, musicians, ladies-in-waiting, and officials of the city began. I jumped out of my chair and ran with my camera to the front of the street where people had gathered.

It was like something out of the Renaissance. In fact, it was the Renaissance. Period costumes of brocade, lace, and jewels glittered in the sun. The mayor, dressed in black velvet with a royal purple cape, plumed hat, and huge silver crest upon his chest, gestured with regal nods to the crowd gathered on either side of the street. His lady, splendid in a crimson gown with jeweled neckline and fur-trimmed train, walked reverently by his side, her swanlike neck stretching elegantly upward, her hand held high in his.

Men of high position, women of wealth and beauty, all dazzling in antique finery continued to come down the corso. I clicked away like a fashion photographer, following them all the way to the Palazzo dei Priori, or city hall, where the once powerful rulers of Perugia formulated laws. After a speech by the mayor and a host of proclamations, the elegant group disbanded into the waiting crowd of friends and relatives near the Piazza Grande to celebrate with good food and local wine.

For me it was an exhilarating and totally unexpected thing to have happened—and to think that I would have missed it all, had I not remembered piano, piano, *and* il bar.

Torta di Natale

Christmas Cake
Serves 10

There was never just one dessert for Christmas, but several, including cakes of different sizes and fillings. Christmas Cake filled with chocolate, mascarpone cheese, and pistachio nuts, was one of my favorites. If you cannot find mascarpone, substitute 8 ounces well-drained ricotta and 6 ounces cream cheese, beaten together.

Filling
- 2 cups mascarpone cheese, at room temperature
- 6 tablespoons sugar
- ⅔ cup chopped pistachio nuts
- ⅔ cup chopped semisweet chocolate

Cake
- 5 large eggs, separated and at room temperature
- 1 cup sugar
- 2 tablespoons fresh lemon juice
- 1 tablespoon almond extract
- ½ teaspoon salt
- 1 cup sifted unbleached all-purpose flour

Frosting
- 2 cups heavy cream
- ¼ cup plus 2 tablespoons sugar
- 1 tablespoon finely grated lemon zest
- 2 to 3 tablespoons baking cocoa

Place the mascarpone cheese in a bowl. Add the sugar, nuts, and chocolate and mix well. Cover and refrigerate filling while you make the cake.

Preheat the oven to 350°F.

Beat the egg yolks in a large bowl with an electric mixer. Gradually add ½ cup sugar, beating continually. Add the lemon juice and almond extract, and continue beating until the yolks are very pale, almost lemon colored. Set the mixture aside.

In a large bowl, beat the egg whites with the salt until foamy. Gradually add the remaining sugar a little at a time and continue beating until the whites are stiff and glossy.

Fold the egg yolk mixture into the beaten whites, a little at a time, alternating with spoonfuls of flour. Continue adding the egg yolk mixture and flour, gently folding into the whites.

Pour the batter into an ungreased 10-inch tube pan. Spread evenly. Bake the cake for 25 to 30 minutes, or until nicely browned and the center springs back to the touch. Remove the cake from the oven and invert the tube pan over the neck of a bottle and let cool.

When the cake is completely cool, carefully remove it from the pan. Cut the cake into 3 layers. Place 1 layer on a decorative plate. Spread half the filling over the layer. Place the second layer on top and spread the remaining filling over it. Place the third layer on top. Cover the cake carefully with plastic wrap and refrigerate several hours.

Just before serving, whip the cream with the sugar until stiff. Gently fold in the lemon zest. Spread some of the frosting evenly to cover the cake. With the remaining cream, fill a pastry bag with a star tip and outline the top and bottom of the cake. Dust the top of the cake with sieved cocoa and serve immediately.

Torta di Mascarpone

Mascarpone Cheesecake
Makes one 7-inch cake

Even though Italian cheesecake is traditionally made with ricotta cheese, this one uses mascarpone. It is just the right size for a small family. If you can't find amaretti cookies, substitute stale cookie crumbs. If desired, serve the cake with fresh strawberries or kiwi fruit.

¾ cup crushed amaretti cookies

1 tablespoon butter, melted

1 cup mascarpone cheese, at room temperature

1 tablespoon fresh lemon juice

1 teaspoon grated lemon zest

½ cup sugar

2 eggs, separated and at room temperature

½ cup unbleached all-purpose flour, sifted

⅛ teaspoon salt

Preheat the oven to 350°F. Grease a deep 7-inch springform pan and set aside.

In a small bowl, mix the cookie crumbs with the melted butter and pat into the bottom of the pan. Set aside.

In a bowl, use a wooden spoon to combine the cheese, lemon juice, zest, sugar, and egg yolks. Sprinkle the flour over the top of the batter and fold in with a rubber spatula.

In a separate bowl, beat the whites with the salt until the whites are stiff. With a rubber spatula, fold the whites into the cheese mixture until no streaks of white remain.

Spread the mixture in the pan. Smoothing the top. Tap the pan on the table to release any air pockets, then bake for 35 minutes, or until a knife inserted in the middle comes out clean.

Let the cake cool in the pan. It will fall some as it cools. Remove the sides of the pan. Place the cake on a serving dish and cut it into small wedges to serve.

Torta di Riso

Rice Cake
Serves 8

A dessert made for special occasions like Easter was this Torta di Riso, or Rice Cake. There are many versions of this cake in Italy, but this remains my favorite. If you cannot find citron, substitute candied fruit peel.

5 tablespoons butter	Grated zest of 1 lemon
¼ cup fine bread crumbs, toasted	⅛ teaspoon salt
¼ cup raisins	1 cup arborio rice
2 tablespoons sweet Marsala wine	2 large eggs, separated
2 cups milk	1 tablespoon vanilla extract
2 cups water	¼ cup diced candied citron
½ cup sugar	

Grease a 6-cup glass or ceramic mold with 1 tablespoon of the butter. Coat the mold with the bread crumbs, shaking out the excess. Refrigerate until ready to fill.

In a small bowl, soak the raisins in the Marsala for 30 minutes.

In a 1½-quart saucepan, combine the milk, water, sugar, lemon zest, and salt. Bring the mixture to a boil, add the rice, and cook slowly until all the liquid is absorbed, about 12 to 15 minutes.

Preheat the oven to 350°F.

Transfer the rice to a bowl and cool to warm, then mix in the egg yolks, vanilla, remaining butter, citron, and raisins with Marsala.

In a separate bowl, with an electric beater, beat the egg whites until stiff. Fold the egg whites into the rice mixture. Spread the rice evenly in the prepared mold and bake for 35 to 40 minutes, or until a knife inserted in the middle comes out clean.

Let the mold cool completely. Place a serving plate larger than the mold on top, invert, and release onto the plate. Cut into wedges to serve.

Torta di Ricotta

Ricotta Cake
Makes two 9-inch cakes

A very good keeper, this *torta,* or cake, is made with grappa, an Italian eau-de-vie made from the skins and seeds of grapes. It is a good company cake, especially for *l'ora della merenda* ("tea time"). I always make two because one is never enough. Be sure to use a good-quality chocolate such as Callebaut and Amaretti di Saronno cookies in the batter; they add just the right hint of bittersweet flavor.

1 cup golden raisins

4 tablespoons grappa or brandy

½ cup pine nuts

6 large eggs

2¼ cups granulated sugar

1 15-ounce container ricotta cheese

2 tablespoons milk or cream

1½ tablespoons grated orange or tangerine zest

3 cups plus 2 tablespoons unbleached all-purpose flour

2 tablespoons baking powder

⅓ cup coarsely chopped walnuts or hazelnuts

6 amaretti cookies, finely chopped

1 cup coarsely chopped semisweet chocolate

Confectioner's sugar

In a small bowl, soak the raisins in the grappa or brandy for at least 1 hour.

Preheat the oven to 375°F. Grease 2 deep 9½- x 1½-inch cake pans and fit a circle of parchment paper on the bottom of each. Grease the parchment paper and dust each pan with flour. Shake out the excess and set the pans aside.

Place the pine nuts on a cookie sheet and toast for 3 to 4 minutes. Watch carefully because they burn easily. Set aside to cool.

In a large bowl with an electric mixer, beat the eggs until pale and lemon colored. Gradually add the sugar and continue beating until the mixture is thick. Add the ricotta and milk or cream, and continue beating until the mixture is smooth. Sprinkle on the orange zest and fold in with a spatula.

Sift the 3 cups flour with the baking powder. Add the flour mixture gradually to the egg mixture, beating on low speed until the mixture is smooth.

Drain and dry the raisins and reserve the grappa. Toss raisins with the remaining 2 tablespoons of flour and add to the batter. Gently fold in the reserved grappa, pine nuts, walnuts or hazelnuts, and chocolate.

Divide the batter between the 2 cake pans. Smooth the tops and bake on the middle rack of the oven for 40 to 50 minutes, or until a skewer inserted in the center comes out clean. If the cakes brown too quickly on the top, place a loose piece of aluminum foil over the top. Cool the cakes on wire racks.

Remove the cakes from the pans and discard the parchment paper. Place each cake on a serving dish and sprinkle with a heavy layer of confectioner's sugar. Or freeze one cake for later use.

Note: This cake can be frozen for up to 3 months.

Torta di Ricotta
alla Bolognese

Ricotta Tart, Bolognese Style
**Makes 1 filled 11-inch tart and 1 rectangular
tart shell**

Golden-rich ricotta tarts are a specialty of the arcaded city of Bologna. Some are filled with hazelnuts and chocolate; others have sweet almond paste; and there are even some filled with tagliatelle! This one has an easy-to-make custard and ricotta filling.

The amount of pastry dough here is enough for 2 small tart shells. I make one large round tart and one long and narrow rectangular shell, which I freeze for future use.

Filling	*Dough*
2 large eggs plus 1 large yolk	1½ cups unbleached all-purpose flour
1¼ cups sugar	⅓ cup cornstarch
¼ cup unbleached all-purpose flour	½ cup sugar
2 cups milk, scalded and cooled slightly	8 tablespoons (1 stick) butter, cut into pieces
1½ cups ricotta cheese, well drained	1 large egg
Grated zest of 1 large lemon	1 tablespoon vanilla extract

In a medium stainless-steel saucepan, beat the whole eggs and ¾ cup sugar with a wire whisk until well blended. Add the ¼ cup flour a little at a time and blend well. Gradually add the milk and whisk well. Place the saucepan over medium heat and whisk the mixture constantly for about 6 minutes, or until it thickens enough to coat the back of a wooden spoon. Place the filling in a bowl and cover with a sheet of buttered waxed paper. Set aside.

In another bowl, with a hand-held mixer, beat the ricotta, remaining sugar, and egg yolk until very smooth. Fold in the lemon zest. Add the cooled filling, blend well, and set aside.

Preheat the oven to 375°F. Lightly grease an 11-inch round tart pan and a 14- x 4-inch rectangular pan with removable bottoms.

With a food processor or by hand, combine the flour and cornstarch in a bowl; add the remaining dough ingredients and mix until a soft ball begins to form. Knead the dough for just a few minutes on a floured surface, then divide it in half. Pat each half into a tart pan to cover the bottom and sides. Freeze the rectangular shell for future use.

Pour the filling into the round tart pan and smooth the top. Bake for 45 to 50 minutes, or until a knife inserted in the middle comes out clean. Remove the tart to a rack to cool completely. Remove the sides from the pan, place the tart on a serving dish, and cut into wedges to serve.

Variation: Cut thin slices of fresh strawberries or kiwi fruit to layer over the top. Glaze with warmed apricot or apple jelly.

As an alternative, make one thicker-crusted tart in a 16-inch tart pan.

Zeppole di San Giuseppe

St. Joseph's Day Cream Puffs
Makes about 48 puffs

On March 19, the feast of San Giuseppe (Saint Joseph), every Italian household makes its version of *zeppole*, or cream puffs. The shells can be made ahead and frozen, and the filling can be made a day before serving. The lard is what makes the recipe authentic, but you may use all butter.

2¾ cups unbleached all-purpose flour	**Cream Filling**
⅛ teaspoon salt	¼ cup potato starch or cornstarch
½ teaspoon baking soda	2 cups milk
2 cups water	2 tablespoons (¼ stick) butter
6 tablespoons (¾ stick) butter	¾ cup granulated sugar
3½ tablespoons lard	2 large egg yolks
6 large eggs	1½ teaspoons almond extract
	Confectioner's sugar

Preheat the oven to 425°F. Grease and flour a cookie sheet or line with parchment paper.

Sift the flour, salt, and baking soda together and set aside.

In a heavy saucepan, heat the water, add the butter and lard, and when melted, remove pan from the stove and add the flour mixture all at once. Beat with a wooden spoon, then return the pan to medium-high heat, beating the mixture until it comes away from the sides of the pan. Remove the pan from the heat and add the eggs one at a time, beating with a wooden spoon or hand mixer to blend each in well before adding the next egg.

Fill a pastry bag fitted with a ½-inch plain nozzle with some of the cream puff mixture. Squeeze out 1¼-inch puffs about ½ inch apart on cookie sheets. Bake the cream puffs about 20 minutes or until golden brown.

When done, carefully slit the side of each cream puff with a knife to allow steam to escape and prevent the puffs from becoming soggy inside. Transfer the cream puffs to cooling racks.

In a small bowl, mix the starch and sugar for the filling. Set aside.

In a medium saucepan, heat the milk and butter over medium-high heat until the butter melts. Add the starch mixture and cook over medium heat until it starts to thicken, about 2 minutes.

Remove the mixture from the heat and slowly add the eggs, beating well. Return the mixture to the heat for just a few seconds to cook the mixture, being careful not to scramble the eggs. Pour the filling into a bowl, add the almond extract, and blend. Cover with buttered waxed paper and refrigerate until ready to use.

To serve, use a small knife to cut off the top third of each cream puff. Add about 2 teaspoons filling (more if the puffs are larger), replace the tops, and put puffs on a decorative platter. Dust with confectioner's sugar and serve immediately.

Variation: Fill cream puffs with jam, chocolate cream filling, or ice cream. Drizzle chocolate sauce over the top instead of confectioner's sugar.

Semifreddo di Torrone

Frozen Torrone
Serves 8 to 10

Torrone is a nougat confection made from egg whites, sugar, and nuts found throughout Italy. Little blue boxes of the sweet could always be found in our shoes on December 6, the feast of San Nicola ("St. Nicholas"). Originally made in Cremona, in Lombardy, legend has it that, in 1441 at the wedding feast of Francesco Sforza to Bianca Maria Visconti, a sweet was made and fashioned into the shape of the famous and grand Cremona Torrione ("Tower of Cremona"), from which torrone derives its name.

Though torrone is usually eaten like candy, this recipe transforms the chewy nougat into festive frozen dessert, a perfect ending to an elegant summer meal. For best results, chill the bowl and beaters for whipping the cream. Amarena cherries are available in Italian specialty stores. Make this a day ahead of serving.

7 ounces torrone, chopped into small uniform pieces	2 cups heavy cream, well chilled
4 large egg yolks	3 tablespoons cognac
½ cup superfine sugar	½ cup Amarena cherries from a 21-ounce jar, with liquid

Line the bottom and sides of a 9- x 5-inch loaf pan with plastic wrap, leaving about a 2-inch overhang. Place half the torrone in the base of the pan and set aside.

In a bowl, using an electric mixer, beat the yolks with the sugar until light colored and doubled in volume.

In a separate chilled bowl, beat the cream until stiff. Add the cream to the egg mixture, folding it in gently along with the cognac.

Place half the mixture in the prepared pan and smooth the top. Sprinkle on the remaining torrone and add the remaining cream mixture, smoothing the top. Cover tightly with another piece of plastic wrap, then foil. Place the mold in the freezer overnight.

An hour before serving, place a serving dish in the refrigerator to chill.

When ready to serve, remove the foil and plastic wrap from the top of the pan. Loosen the semifreddo slightly by pulling carefully on the extended ends of the overhanging plastic wrap. Turn the pan upside down onto the cold serving dish and carefully unmold. Remove the remaining plastic wrap. Let the semifreddo stand 5 minutes before cutting.

To serve, cut the semifreddo into slices using a knife dipped in warm water. Spoon some of the cherries and their liquid over the top of each slice and serve immediately.

Note: You can also spoon the mixture into a bowl instead of a mold before freezing. Scoop it out like ice cream to serve.

Variation: Try strawberries in syrup as a topping instead of the cherries.

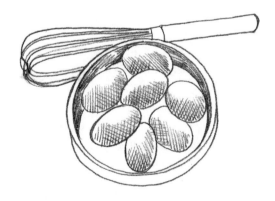

Eating Well in Italy

For me, eating out in Italy is one of the highlights of each day. Sometimes I am very organized about this, dining at a trattoria or ristorante that I have heard about or has been recommended to me. Sometimes, especially for lunch, I wander into an alimentari, a small grocery store, to pick up crusty bread, locally made cheese, marinated olives, and some fruit. Then I head for a spot in the piazza, usually the steps of the duomo, where I eat as I watch the daily street life.

For the first-time traveler to Italy, eating out can be a little intimidating and confusing, but some suggestions will help:

- Eating establishments go by many names: trattoria means a small, family-run restaurant. When there is a menu, it will be limited, always a good sign to me. The waitperson (usually a relative) will tell you what the day's specials are, and the prices. Prices tend to be cheaper in a trattoria than in a ristorante. A ristorante posts its menu and prices outside. If you don't see a posted menu, go somewhere else. Menu turistico means a tourist menu with a fixed price, usually including two courses, a dessert, a house wine, and service charge. I tend to avoid these, preferring to choose from the regular menu. A tavola calda is a restaurant serving a selection of hot dishes, usually cafeteria style. A pizzeria is a rustic place where constantly stoked stone ovens turn out an infinite variety of thin-crusted pizzas and foccacia; this is a good choice when you want an inexpensive supper.

- Familiarize yourself with the terms on an Italian menu. You will see antipasti, primi piatti, secondi, insalate, and dolci listed as well as vini ("wines") and aqua minerale ("mineral water") with or without gas. Appetizers are numerous and can include anything from melon and prosciutto and roasted peppers to toasted garlic bread and marinated seafood. Primi piatti are first-course choices such as pasta, rice, soup, or polenta. Secondi are main courses—meat, fish, game, or fowl. Contorni are the vegetables that accompany your meal. Insalate are salads. Dolci, or dessert offerings, can include local cheeses, fresh fruits, or elegant cakes like pan di spagna and tiramisù, as well as smooth puddings and unusual flavors of ice creams.

- There is a separate charge ("coperto") for bread, which does not come with butter since Italians don't butter their bread. A service charge is automatically added to your bill. This means that the tip is included, but if you wish to show your appreciation for good service, you can leave a few thousand lire at the table.
- Eat where the locals eat. Ask shop owners, the concierge at your hotel, and people on the street for recommendations, or go on the advice of others who have traveled in the same area.
- In big cities, avoid restaurants near the central piazza. I have always found better prices and better food off the beaten track.
- Give your Italian a try. A small phrase book is always a wise thing to keep in your pocket. Italians are delighted when you attempt to speak their language. Carry a small notebook to write down the name and location of favorite restaurants and what you ate. Save this useful information for the next time you travel or share it with others.
- When arranging your itinerary, keep in mind many restaurants are closed on Mondays in case you have a favorite place that you must try. Main meals are usually served between noon and 3 P.m., and 8 P.M. to 11 P.M.
- Go to a bar for espresso, pastries, cookies, and gelato. Tell the cashier what you want, pay for it first, and then take your receipt to the waitperson who fills your order.
- Sample the specialties in regions you are visiting. In Florence, have bistecca, or steak; in Bologna, try tortellini; in Rome, lamb is the choice or, if they are in season, fried artichokes. Eat fish and liver in Venice, and go out of your way to taste mozzarella made from buffalo milk from the Naples area, as well as pizza. Each region, every town, has its local specialties, and this is what makes eating out in Italy such an adventure and a pleasure.

Mail-Order Sources

The following companies have mail-order services or catalogs, or can offer information about the availability of their products in your area.

A & J Distributors
236 Hanover Street
Boston, Massachusetts 02113
617-523-8490
Italian equipment, cannoli forms, pasta machines, bakery equipment

Auricchio Cheese, Inc.
5810 Highway NN
Denmark, Wisconsin 54208
414-863-2123
Domestic Italian cheeses

Balducci's
Mail-Order Division
424 Sixth Avenue
New York, New York 10011
800-247-2450
General line of dried pasta, sun-dried tomatoes, olives, olive oil, cookbooks

Crate and Barrel
140 Faneuil Hall Marketplace
Boston, Massachusetts 02109
617-742-6025
Italian cooking gadgets, dishes

Dairy Fresh Candies
P.O. Box 7456
57 Salem Street
Boston, Massachusetts 02113
800-640-0654
Citron, almonds, pine nuts, baking chocolate, dried fruits

Dean & DeLuca
560 Broadway
New York, New York 10012
212-431-1691
Porcini, olives, olive oil, pasta, rice

G & B Ratto & Company, Inc.
821 Washington Street
Oakland, California 94607
800-325-3483
Complete catalog of international foods, spices, baking supplies

Joe Pace and Sons
42 Cross Street
Boston, Massachusetts 02113
617-227-9673
Prosciutto, salame, cheese, olive oil, biscotti, Italian groceries

King Arthur Flour
Box 1010
Norwich, Vermont 05055
802-649-3881
Baking supplies, malt extract, honey

Le Marché Seeds International
P.O. Box 566
Dixon, California 95620
Italian seeds

Manganaro's Foods
488 Ninth Avenue
New York, New York 10018
212-563-5331
Pasta, flour, vinegars, biscotti

**Providence Cheese and
    Provisions Company**
Atwells Avenue
Federal Hill
Providence, Rhode Island 02902
401-421-5653
Italian cheeses

Shepard's Garden Seeds
30 Irene Street
Torrington, Connecticut 06790
203-482-3638
Italian seeds

Tosi Trading Company
30 Willow Street
Chelsea, Massachusetts 02150
617-884-9333
Dried pasta, olive oil

Williams-Sonoma
P.O. Box 7456
San Francisco, California 94120
415-421-4242
Olive oil, cooking utensils, im-
    ported pasta

Bibliography

Apicius. *Cookery and Dining in Imperial Rome,* edited and translated by Joseph Dommers Vehling. New York: Dover Publications, 1977.

Barzini, Luigi. *The Italians: A Full-Length Portrait Featuring Their Manners and Morals.* New York: Atheneum, 1964.

Del Conte, Anna. *Gastronomy of Italy.* New York: Prentice Hall, 1987.

Frati, Ludovico. *Libro di Cucina del Secolo XIV.* Livorno: Arnaldo Forni Editore, 1899.

Gossetti della Scalda. *Le Ricette Regionali Italiane.* Milan: Casa Editrice Solares, 1987.

Grant, Michael. *History of Rome.* New York: Charles Scribner's Sons, 1987.

McConnell, Carol and Malcom. *The Mediterranean Diet.* New York: W.W. Norton and Company, 1987.

McGee, Harold. *On Food and Cooking.* New York: Charles Scribner's Sons, 1984.

Prezzolini, Giuseppe. *Spaghetti Dinner.* New York: Abelard Schuman, 1955.

Root, Waverly. *Food by Waverly Root.* New York: Simon & Schuster, 1980.

————. *The Food of Italy.* New York: Vintage Books, 1977.

Ross, Janet. *Leaves from a Tuscan Kitchen.* New York: Penguin Books, 1973.

Russo, Baldo. *Sapore di Sicilia.* Italy: La Nuova Ed. RI.SI., 1988.

Tannahill, Reay. *Food in History.* New York: Crown Publishers, 1988.

Tedeschi, Antonia Monti. *Il Cucchiaio d'Argento.* Milan: Editoriale Domus, 1987.

Index

Acciugata:
    pizza napoletana, 219
    salsa di pomodori e, alla Maria, 90
Aceto, cipolline sott', 21
Aglio, patate e zucchini al forno con, 172
Agnello, ragù d', 96
Almond(s):
    Amaretto cream pudding, 292–293
    bones of the dead, 264–265
    chocolate-glazed little cookies, 270–271
    cookies, 262
    filled chocolate cookies, 258–259
    Grandma's great pie, 294–295
    Palermo sweet fig and nut cake, 290–291
    paste bread, 242–243
Amaretti, 262
Amaretto:
    cream pudding, 292–293
    strawberry sauce, 281
Amaretto:
    crema all', 292–293
    salsa di fragole con, 281

Anatra:
    alla griglia, 135
    con pesche, 136–137
Anchovy(ies):
    Neapolitan pizza, 219
    and tomato sauce, Maria's, 90
Anice, biscotti d', 254–255
Anise biscuits, 254–255
Antipasti, 11–28
    bigne con formaggio e prosciutto, 28
    caponata, 13–14
    caponata del marinaio, 14–15
    cipolline sott'aceto, 21
    cocktail di gamberi, 24–25
    funghi ripieni al forno, 22–23
    panini arrostiti, 25
    un po' di tutto, 16–17
    rotolo al prosciutto, 26–27
    zucca gialla all'agrodolce, 20
Appetizers, 11–28
    broiled sandwiches, 25
    eggplant salad, 13–14
    a little bit of everything, 16–17

Appetizers (cont.)
    little puffs of cheese and ham, 28
    onions in vinegar, 21
    prosciutto roll, 26–27
    sailor-style salad, 14–15
    shrimp cocktail, 24–25
    stuffed baked mushrooms, 22–23
    sweet and sour yellow pumpkin, 20
Apple(s):
    bread pudding, 288–289
    slices, fried, 279
Aragosta, insalata di pere e, 196
Artichoke(s):
    braised, 159
    leek, fennel, and sausage tart, 181–183
    stuffed, 160–161
Arucola:
    insalata di avocado, fichi secchi e, 190
    petti di pollo con, 128–129
    salsa di limone, capperi e, 99
Arugula:
    avocado, and dried fig salad, 190
    chicken breasts with, 128–129
    lemon, and caper sauce, 99
Asparagi, zuppa di, 46–47
Asparagus soup, 46–47
Avocado:
    arugula, and dried fig salad, 190
    mixed raw salad, 188–189
Avocado:
    insalata di arucola, fichi secchi e, 190
    insalata di varie crudità, 188–189

Banana cream pudding, 277
Banane, bavarese alle, 277
Barbabietola, insalata di, 193
Basil, 7
    pizza Margherita, 215–216
    and tomato sauce, fresh, 85
    see also Pesto
Basilico:
    pizza Margherita, 215–216
    salsa fresca di pomodori e, 85
    see also Pesto
Bavarese alle banane, 277
Bean(s):
    broccoli and borlotti salad, 194–195
    minestrone, Genoa style, 36–37
    pasta and, 38–39
    soup, 40–41
Bean(s), green:
    homestyle ragù, 94–95
    and lettuce soup, 48–49
    and potatoes with pesto, 163
    in tomato sauce, 167

Beef:
    broth, 6, 32
    fillet of, with speck, 120
    homestyle ragù, 94–95
    molded macaroni casserole, 72–73
    stew, Lombardy style, 116–117
    stew in dark beer, 117
Beet(s), 6
    salad, 193
Besciamella, salsa di, 102
Biete:
    frocia d'ova ca pastetta, 108–110
    pizza casalinga, 206–207
    verdure miste, 162
Biscotti, 249–274
    amaretti, 262
    d'anice, 254–255
    biscottini glassati al cioccolato, 270–271
    di ciliegie, 260–261
    al cioccolato, 253
    dolci con melassa, 266–267
    dolci ripieni, 263
    di Mamma, 256–257
    di noci, 257
    ossi dei morti, 264–265
    papadelle, 271
    ripieni al cioccolato, 258–259
    savoiardi, 268–269
    sfinci di Lucia, 267
    stelline d'oro, 273–274
    di Vincenza, 255
Biscuits, sweet, 246
Bones of the dead, 264–265
Borage omelet, 107
Borragine, frittata di, 107
Bread, 7, 221–247
    almond paste, 242–243
    Aunt Baratta's fritters, 247
    cherry rolls, 240–241
    crescia, 226–227
    Easter dove, 244–245
    gnocco, 228
    Grandma Tavino's little buns, 224–225
    grape harvest, 234–236
    Helen's taralli, 227
    honey, 229–231
    raisin, 236–237
    sweet biscuits, 246
    sweet flatbread, 238–239
    whole wheat, 222–223
Bread pudding, apple, 288–289
Broccoli:
    and borlotti salad, 194–195
    Mom's spaghetti and, 59

Broccoli:
    insalata di borlotti e, 194–195
    e spaghetti alla Mamma, 59
Brodo:
    di manzo, 32
    di pollo, 31
Broth:
    beef, 6, 32
    chicken, 6, 31
Bucatini:
    with sardines, 60–61
    in the style of Amatrice, 61
Bucatini:
    all'amatriciana, 61
    con le sarde, 60–61
Buccellato palermitano, 290–291
Budino di mele, 288–289
Buns, Grandma Tavino's little, 224–225

Caffè italiano, 272
Cakes, 288
    chocolate, 304
    chocolate fantasy, 305
    Christmas, 308–309
    Easter lamb, 302–303
    Palermo sweet fig and nut, 290–291
    rice, 311
    ricotta, 312–313
Calamari e cappesante al forno, 154–155
Cannelloni ai funghi, 68–70
Cannelloni with mushrooms, 68–70
Caper, lemon, and arugula sauce, 99
Caponata, 13–14
    del marinaio, 14–15
Capperi, salsa di limone, arucola e, 99
Cappesante:
    e calamari al forno, 154–155
    con pesto, 153
Carciofi:
    ripieni, 160–161
    in tegame, 159
    torta di porri, finocchio, salsicce e, 181–183
Carne, 111–125
    brodo di manzo, 32
    coniglio alla moda mia, 134
    costolette di maiale con salsa di porcini, 122
    granatini, 113
    involtini della Nonna, 114–115
    ossobuchi in vino, 118–119
    pizza chena, 212–214
    pizza con salsicce e cipolle, 211
    portafogli di lonza, 121
    ragù casalinga, 94–95
    rotolo al prosciutto, 26–27
    salsiccia fresca, 124–125

    spezzatino alla birra scura, 117
    stracotto alla lombarda, 116–117
    timballo di maccarun, 72–73
    torta di porri, carciofi, finocchio, e, salsicce,
      181–183
    tournedos allo speck, 120
Carote, coroncine di, agli spinaci, 164–165
Carrot and spinach crowns, little, 164–165
Cassateddi ca ricotta, 104–105
Castagne, pasta di, 58
Cauliflower, 6
    sauce, Mrs. Vallone's, 97
Cavolfiore, salsa di, alla Signora Vallone, 97
Cheese(s), 6
    broiled sandwiches, 25
    cannelloni with mushrooms, 68–70
    chocolate fantasy cake, 305
    Christmas cake, 308–309
    five, penne with, 63
    fried egg sandwiches, 108–110
    Grandma's eggplant, 170–171
    homestyle pizza, 206–207
    little puffs of ham and, 28
    mascarpone cheesecake, 310
    molded macaroni casserole, 72–73
    onion soup, 45
    pizza chena, 212–214
    pizza with pesto, 220
    potato and spinach pie, 176–177
    potato gnocchi with Gorgonzola sauce,
      74–75
    ricotta dumplings, 76–77
    square pizza with olives, 216–217
    tomato and herb tart, 183–184
    see also Mozzarella cheese; Ricotta cheese
Cheesecake, 10
    mascarpone, 310
Cherry(ies):
    cookies, 260–261
    frozen torrone, 318–319
    rolls, 240–241
Chestnut pasta, 58
Chicken:
    breasts with arugula, 128–129
    broth, 6, 31
    and potatoes with wine, 130–131
    roasted in salt, 126–127
    rustic, 132
    tuna cups, 197
Chicken livers and onions, 133
Chocolate, 7
    Amaretto cream pudding, 292–293
    bones of the dead, 264–265
    cake, 304
    Christmas cake, 308–309

Chocolate (*cont.*)
    cookies, 253
    fantasy cake, 305
    filled cookies, 258–259
    –glazed little cookies, 270–271
    ricotta cake, 312–313
Ciliege:
    panini di, 240–241
    semifreddo di torrone, 318–319
Ciliegie, biscotti di, 260–261
Cioccolato:
    biscotti al, 253
    biscottini glassati al, 270–271
    biscotti ripieni al, 258–259
    crema all'Amaretto, 292–293
    ossi dei morti, 264–265
    torta al, 304
    torta di Natale, 308–309
    torta di ricotta, 312–313
    torta fantasia di, 305
Cipolla(e):
    fegatini di pollo con, 133
    pizza con salsicce e, 211
    zuppa di, 45
Cipolline sott'aceto, 21
Cod:
    baked, 141
    cakes, 148–149
Coffee, 7, 272
Colomba di Pasqua, 244–245
Coniglio alla moda mia, 134
Cookie pyramid cake, 251
Cookies, 10, 249–274
    almond, 262
    anise biscuits, 254–255
    bones of the dead, 264–265
    cherry, 260–261
    chocolate, 253
    chocolate-glazed little, 270–271
    filled chocolate, 258–259
    filled sweets, 263
    little stars of gold, 273–274
    Lucy's fried puffs, 267
    Ma's, 256–257
    molasses, 266–267
    nut, 257
    peanut, 271
    Savoy biscuits, or Italian ladyfingers,
        268–269
    Vincenza's, 255
Cranberry, pear, and prune sauce, 286
Cream, 7
    cooked, 298
    fennel sauce, 98–99
Cream puffs, St. Joseph's Day, 316–317

Crema all'Amaretto, 292–293
Crescia, 226–227
Custard tarts, 296–297

Desserts, 287–319
    Amaretto cream pudding, 292–293
    apple bread pudding, 288–289
    chocolate cake, 304
    chocolate fantasy cake, 305
    Christmas cake, 308–309
    cooked cream, 298
    custard tarts, 296–297
    dried peach and lemon tart, 300–301
    Easter lamb cake, 302–303
    frozen torrone, 318–319
    Grandma's great pie, 294–295
    mascarpone cheesecake, 310
    Palermo sweet fig and nut cake, 290–
        291
    pastry dough for, 299
    rice cake, 311
    ricotta cake, 312–313
    ricotta tart, Bolognese style, 314–315
    St. Joseph's Day cream puffs, 316–317
    see also Cookies; Fruit; Fruit sauces
Dolci, 287–319
    buccellato palermitano, 290–291
    budino di mele, 288–289
    crema all'Amaretto, 292–293
    grand torta della Nonna, 294–295
    panna cotta, 298
    pasta ciotti, 296–297
    pasta frolla, 299
    semifreddo di torrone, 318–319
    torta al cioccolato, 304
    torta di agnello, 302–303
    torta di mascarpone, 310
    torta di Natale, 308–309
    torta di pesche secche e limone, 300–301
    torta di ricotta, 312–313
    torta di ricotta alla bolognese, 314–315
    torta di riso, 311
    torta fantasia di cioccolato, 305
    zeppole di San Giuseppe, 316–317
    see also Biscotti; Frutte; Salse di frutte
Duck:
    grilled, 135
    with peaches, 136–137
Dumplings, *see* Gnocchi

Egg(s), 7, 103–110
    borage omelet, 107
    fried, sandwiches, 108–110
    omelet soup, 33
    pizza chena, 212–213

prosciutto roll, 26–27
ricotta cheese omelet, 106
ricotta cheese pancakes, 104–105
scrambled, with herbs, 110
whites, 288
Eggplant, 6
bundles, 168–169
Grandma's, 170–171
lasagne, Mary Ann's, 66–67
a little bit of everything, 16–17
minestrone, Genoa style, 36–37
salad, 13–14
vermicelli, Syracusan style, 62
Endive salad, 187
Erbe, 198–199
Escarole, Camille's stuffed, 180

Fagioli:
insalata di broccoli e borlotti, 194–195
minestrone alla moda genovese, 36–37
pasta e, 38–39
zuppa di, 40–41
Fagiolini:
e patate con pesto, 163
ragù casalinga, 94–95
in salsa di pomodori, 167
zuppa di lattuga e, 48–49
Fegatini di pollo con cipolle, 133
Fennel:
cream sauce, 98–99
leek, artichoke, and sausage tart, 181–
183
Fichi:
buccellato palermitano, 290–291
secchi, insalata di arucola, avocado e, 190
secchi, in vino, 278
Fig(s), 7
dried, arugula and avocado salad, 190
dried, in wine, 278
and nut cake, Palermo sweet, 290–291
Filled chocolate cookies, 258–259
Filled sweets, 263
Finocchio:
salsa di panna e, 98–99
torta di porri, carciofi, salsicce e, 181–183
Fiori di zucchini fritti, 175
Fish, 6, 139–155
baked cod, 141
baked squid and scallops, 154–155
baked swordfish, 144
cakes, 148–149
fried, 147
grilled swordfish, 142–143
lobster and pear salad, 196
Maria's anchovy and tomato sauce, 90
Neapolitan pizza, 219
scallops with pesto, 153
shrimp cocktail, 24–25
shrimp with linguine and lemon, 152

shrimp with spicy tomato sauce, 150–
151
spaghetti with sardines, 60–61
tomatoes stuffed with tuna, 200
tuna cups, 197
tuna steak with herbs, 145
Venetian marinated, 146
Flatbread, sweet, 238–239
Flour, 7, 288
Fontina cheese:
broiled sandwiches, 25
little puffs of cheese and ham, 28
pizza with pesto, 220
Formaggi(o):
bigne con prosciutto e, 28
cannelloni ai funghi, 68–70
cinque, penne con, 63
frocia d'ova ca pastetta, 108–110
gnocchi di patate con salsa di gorgonzola,
74–75
gnocchi di ricotta, 76–77
melanzane della Nonna, 170–171
panini arrostiti, 25
pizza casalinga, 206–207
pizza chena, 212–214
pizza con pesto, 220
scacciata con olive, 216–217
timballo di maccarun, 72–73
torta di mascarpone, 310
torta di Natale, 308–309
torta di patate e spinaci, 176–177
torta di pomodori ed erbe, 183–184
torta fantasia di cioccolato, 305
zuppa di cipolla, 45
see also Mozzarella; Ricotta
Fragole:
bavarese alle banane, 277
e pesche in Marsala, 280–281
salsa di, con Amaretto, 281
Frittata:
di borragine, 107
con ricotta, 106
zuppe di, 33
Fritters, Aunt Baratta's, 247
Frocia d'ova ca pastetta, 108–110
Frozen desserts, 288
torrone, 318–319
Fruit, 275–281
banana cream pudding, 277
dried figs in wine, 278
fried apple slices, 279
peaches and strawberries in Marsala,
280–281
Fruit sauces, 281–286
cranberry, pear, and prune, 286
fresh plum, 284–285
strawberry Amaretto, 281
Frutte, 275–281
bavarese alle banane, 277
fichi secchi in vino, 278
mele fritte, 279

Frutte (cont.)
  pesche e fragole in Marsala, 280–281
  see also Salse di frutte
Funghi:
  cannelloni ai, 68–70
  insalata di varie crudità, 188–189
  pizza con porcini, 210
  see also Porcini

Gallette dolci, 246
Gamberi:
  cocktail di, 24–25
  con salsa di pomodori saporiti, 150–151
  scampi con linguine e limone, 152
Garlic, 7, 178–179
  oven-roasted potatoes and zucchini
    with, 172
Gnocchi:
  potato, with Gorgonzola sauce,
    74–75
  pumpkin, my way, 80–81
  ricotta, 76–77
  saffron, 78–79
Gnocchi:
  di patate con salsa di gorgonzola,
    74–75
  di ricotta, 76–77
  al zafferano, 78–79
  di zucca alla moda mia, 80–81
Gnocco, 228
Gorgonzola, salsa di, gnocchi di patate con,
    74–75
Gorgonzola sauce, potato gnocchi with,
    74–75
Granatini, 113
Grape harvest bread, 234–236
Green beans, *see* Bean, green
Greens, 6
  and potatoes, 166–167

Ham:
  little puffs of cheese and, 28
  prosciutto roll, 26–27
  stuffed pork chops, 121
Hazelnuts:
  chocolate cake, 304
  chocolate-glazed little cookies,
    270–271
  molasses cookies, 266–267
  Palermo sweet fig and nut cake, 290–
    291
  ricotta cake, 312–313
  Vincenza's cookies, 255
Herb(s), 7, 198–199
Honey bread, 229–231

Indivia, insalata d', 187
Insalate, 185–200
  d'aragosta e pere, 196
  di arucola, avocado, e fichi secchi, 190
  di barbabietola, 193
  di broccoli e borlotti, 194–195
  caponata, 13–14
  caponata del marinaio, 14–15
  coppette tonnate, 197
  d'indivia, 187
  di mozzarella e peperoni, 192
  pomodori ripieni di tonno, 200
  di spinaci e patate, 191
  di varie crudità, 188–189

Ladyfingers, Italian, 268–269
Lamb sauce, 96
Lasagne, Mary Ann's eggplant, 66–67
Lasagne con melanzane alla Marianna, 66–67
Lattuga, zuppa di fagiolini e, 48–49
Leek, artichoke, fennel, and sausage tart,
    181–183
Lemon:
  arugula, and caper sauce, 99
  and dried peach tart, 300–301
  shrimp with linguine and, 152
Lenticchie, zuppa di, 35
Lentil soup, 35
Lettuce and green bean soup, 48–49
Limone:
  salsa d'arucola, capperi e, 99
  scampi con linguine e, 152
  torta di pesche secche e, 300–301
Linguine, scampi con limone e, 152
Linguine, shrimp with lemon and, 152
Livers, chicken, and onions, 133
Lobster and pear salad, 196

Macaroni:
  casserole, molded, 72–73
  on the guitar, 56–57
Maccarun, timballo di, 72–73
Maccheroni alla chitarra, 56–57
Maiale:
  costolette di, con salsa di porcini, 122–123
  granatini, 113
  involtini della Nonna, 114–115
  portafogli di lonza, 121
  salsiccia fresca, 124–125
Manaste patano, 166–167
Mandorle:
  amaretti, 262
  biscottini glassati al cioccolato, 270–271
  biscotti ripieni al cioccolato, 258–259
  buccellato palermitano, 290–291
  crema all'Amaretto, 292–293
  grand torta della Nonna, 294–295
  ossi dei morti, 264–265
  pane di pasta reale, 242–243
Manzo:
  brodo di, 32
  ragù casalinga, 94–95
  spezzatino alla birra scura, 117
  stracotto alla lombarda, 116–117

timballo di maccarun, 72–73
tournedos allo speck, 120
Marinade, Guy's, 93
Marinata di Gaetano, 93
Marsala, peaches and strawberries in, 280–281
Marsala, pesche e fragole in, 280–281
Mascarpone:
    torta di, 310
    torta di Natale, 308–309
    torta fantasia di cioccolato, 305
Mascarpone cheese:
    cheesecake, 310
    chocolate fantasy cake, 305
    Christmas cake, 308–309
Meat, 111–125
    beef broth, 6, 32
    beef stew, Lombardy style, 116–117
    beef stew in dark beer, 117
    bundles, Grandma's, 114–115
    bundles, little, 113
    fillet of beef with speck, 120
    fresh sausage, 124–125
    homestyle ragù, 94–95
    leek, artichoke, fennel, and sausage tart, 181–183
    molded macaroni casserole, 72–73
    pizza chena, 212–214
    pizza with sausage and onions, 211
    pork chops with porcini mushroom sauce, 122–123
    prosciutto roll, 26–27
    rabbit, my way, 134
    stuffed pork chops, 121
    veal shanks in red wine, 118–119
Melanzane:
    caponata, 13–14
    involtini di, 168–169
    lasagne con, alla Marianna, 66–67
    minestrone alla moda genovese, 36–37
    della Nonna, 170–171
    un po' di tutto, 16–17
    vermicelli alla siracusana, 62
Melassa:
    dolci con, 266–267
    papadelle, 271
Mele:
    budino di, 288–289
    fritte, 279
Merluzzo:
    gratinato, 141
    polpette di, 148–149
Miele, pane di, 229–231
Minestra di riso e zucchini, 42–43
Minestrone, Genoa style, 36–37
Minestrone alla moda genovese, 36–37
Molasses:
    cookies, 266–267
    peanut cookies, 271
Mortelle di palude, salsa di, con pere e prugne, 286

Mozzarella:
    fagiolini in salsa di pomodori, 167
    insalata di peperoni e, 192
    insalata di varie crudità, 188–189
    involtini di melanzane, 168–169
    lasagne con melanzane alla Marianna, 66–67
    melanzane della Nonna, 170–171
    panini arrostiti, 25
    penne con cinque formaggi, 63
    pizza chena, 212–214
    pizza con salsicce e cipolle, 211
    pizza Margherita, 215–216
    pizza napoletana, 219
    un po' di tutto, 16–17
    portafogli di lonza, 121
    timballo di maccarun, 72–73
    torta di patate e spinaci, 176–177
Mozzarella cheese:
    broiled sandwiches, 25
    eggplant bundles, 168–169
    Grandma's eggplant, 170–171
    green beans in tomato sauce, 167
    a little bit of everything, 16–17
    Mary Ann's eggplant lasagne, 66–67
    mixed raw salad, 188–189
    molded macaroni casserole, 72–73
    Neapolitan pizza, 219
    penne with five cheeses, 63
    and pepper salad, 192
    pizza chena, 212–214
    pizza Margherita, 215–216
    pizza with sausage and onions, 211
    potato and spinach pie, 176–177
    stuffed pork chops, 121
Mushroom(s), porcini:
    cannelloni with button mushrooms and, 68–69
    pizza with, 210
    sauce, 100, 101
    sauce, pork chops with, 122–123
    stuffed baked, 22–23
Mushrooms:
    cannelloni with, 68–70
    mixed raw salad, 188–189
    pizza with, 210

Noci:
    biscotti di, 257
    biscotti di Vincenza, 255
    biscottini glassati al cioccolato, 270–271
    buccellato palermitano, 290–291
    dolci con melassa, 266–267
    torta al cioccolato, 304
    torta di Natale, 308–309
    torta di riccota, 312–313
    see also Mandorle
Nut(s):
    chocolate cake, 304
    chocolate-glazed little cookies, 270–271
    Christmas cake, 308–309

Nut(s) (*cont.*)
 cookies, 257
 and fig cake, Palermo sweet, 290–291
 molasses cookies, 266–267
 peanut cookies, 271
 ricotta cake, 312–313
 Vincenza's cookies, 255
 see also Almond

Olive:
 nera, salsa di, 91
 salsa di acciugata e pomodori alla Maria, 90
 scacciata con, 216–217
Olive(s):
 black, sauce, 91
 Maria's anchovy and tomato sauce, 90
 square pizza with, 216–217
Olive oil, 5–6
Omelet:
 borage, 107
 egg, soup, 33
 ricotta cheese, 106
Onion(s), 6, 7
 chicken livers and, 133
 pizza with sausage and, 211
 soup, 45
 in vinegar, 21
Ossi dei morti, 264–265
Ossobuchi in vino, 118–119

Pancakes, ricotta cheese, 104–105
Pancetta, 6
Pane, 221–247
 colomba di Pasqua, 244–245
 crescia, 226–227
 gallette dolci, 246
 gnocco, 228
 integrale, 222–223
 di miele, 229–231
 panetti di Nonna Tavino, 224–225
 panini di ciliege, 240–241
 di pasta reale, 242–243
 schiacciata di vendemmia, 234–236
 schiacciata dolce, 238–239
 taralli di Elena Julian, 227
 all'uvetta, 236–237
 zaples di Zia Baratta, 247
Panini:
 arrostiti, 25
 di ciliege, 240–241
Panna:
 cotta, 298
 salsa di finocchio e, 98–99
Papadelle, 271
Parmigiano-Reggiano, 6
Parsley, 7
Pasta, 6, 7, 51–81
 basic egg, 53–54
 and beans, 38–39
 cannelloni with mushrooms, 68–70

 chestnut, 58
 fried penne, 64–65
 macaroni on the guitar, 56–57
 Mary Ann's eggplant lasagne, 66–67
 molded macaroni casserole, 72–73
 Mom's broccoli and spaghetti, 59
 Mrs. Vallone's cauliflower sauce, 97
 patches and peas, 54–55
 penne with five cheeses, 63
 shrimp with linguine and lemon, 152
 shrimp with spicy tomato sauce, 150–
  151
 spaghetti with sardines, 60–61
 squash and spinach soup, 44–45
 in the style of Amatrice, 61
 vermicelli, Syracusan style, 62
 see also Gnocchi
Pasta, 51–81
 basic recipe for, 53–54
 broccoli e spaghetti alla Mamma, 59
 bucatini all'amatriciana, 61
 bucatini con le sarde, 60–61
 cannelloni ai funghi, 68–70
 di castagne, 58
 e fagioli, 38–39
 gamberi con salsa di pomodori saporiti,
  150–151
 lasagne con melanzane alla Marianna, 66–67
 maccheroni alla chitarra, 56–57
 penne con cinque formaggi, 63
 pennette in padella, 64–65
 pezze e piselli, 54–55
 salsa di cavolfiore alla Signora Vallone, 97
 scampi con linguine e limone, 152
 timballo di maccarun, 72–73
 vermicelli alla siracusana, 62
 zuppa di zucca e spinaci, 44–45
 see also Gnocchi
Pasta ciotti, 296–297
Pasta dough, 7
Pasta frolla, 7, 299
Pasta per pizza, 203
Pastry dough, 7, 299
Patate:
 e fagiolini con pesto, 163
 gnocchi di, con salsa di gorgonzola, 74–75
 insalata di spinaci e, 191
 manaste patano, 166–167
 in padella, 171
 pollo e, con vino, 130–131
 torta di spinaci e, 176–177
 e zucchini al forno con aglio, 172
Peach(es):
 dried, and lemon tart, 300–301
 duck with, 136–137
 and strawberries in Marsala, 280–281
Peanut cookies, 271
Pear:
 cranberry, and prune sauce, 286
 and lobster salad, 196

Peas:
    little meat bundles, 113
    Mom's broccoli and spaghetti, 59
    patches and, 54–55
Pecorino Romano, 6
Penne:
    with five cheeses, 63
    fried, 64–65
Penne con cinque formaggi, 63
Pennette in padella, 64–65
Peperoni:
    casalinghi, 173
    insalata di mozzarella e, 192
    rossi ripieni, 174–175
Pepper, 9
Pepper(s), bell:
    homestyle, 173
    and mozzarella salad, 192
    stuffed red, 174–175
Pere:
    insalata d'aragosta e, 196
    salsa di mortelle di palude con prugne e,
        286
Pesce, 139–155
    bucatini con le sarde, 60–61
    calamari e cappesante al forno, 154–155
    cappesante con pesto, 153
    cocktail di gamberi, 24–25
    coppette tonnate, 197
    fritto, 147
    gamberi con salsa di pomodori saporiti,
        150–151
    insalata d'aragosta e pere, 196
    merluzzo gratinato, 141
    pizza napoletana, 219
    polpette di, 148–149
    pomodori ripieni di tonno, 200
    salsa di acciugata e pomodori alla Maria,
        90
    saor alla venezia, 146
    scampi con linguine e limone, 152
    spada, grigliata di, 142–143
    spada al forno, 144
    tonno alle erbe, 145
Pesche:
    anatra con, 136–137
    e fragole in Marsala, 280–281
    secche, torta di limone e, 300–301
Pesto, 92–93
    green beans and potatoes with, 163
    Guy's marinade, 93
    pizza with, 220
    scallops with, 153
Pesto, 92–93
    cappesante con, 153
    fagiolini e patate con, 163
    marinata di Gaetano, 93
    pizza con, 220
Pies:
    Grandma's great, 294–295

    pastry dough for, 299
    potato and spinach, 176–177
Piselli:
    broccoli e spaghetti alla Mamma, 59
    granatini, 113
    pezze e, 54–55
Pizza, 201–220
    chena, 212–214
    with cresciuta, 204–205
    dough, 203
    Grandma Saporita's, 218
    homestyle, 206–207
    Margherita, 215–216
    Neapolitan, 219
    with pesto, 220
    with porcini, 210
    with sausage and onions, 211
    square, with olives, 216–217
Pizza, 201–220
    casalinga, 206–207
    chena, 212–214
    with cresciuta, 204–205
    Margherita, 215–216
    napoletana, 219
    di Nonna Saporito, 218
    pasta per, 203
    con pesto, 220
    con porcini, 210
    con salsicce e cipolle, 211
    scacciata con olive, 216–217
Plum, fresh, sauce, 284–285
Pollame, 126–137
    anatra alla griglia, 135
    anatra con pesche, 136–137
    see also Pollo
Pollo:
    brodo di, 31
    coppette tonnate, 197
    fegatini di, con cipolle, 133
    e patate con vino, 130–131
    petti di, con arucola, 128–129
    rustico, 132
    al sale, 126–127
Pomodori:
    broccoli e spaghetti alla Mamma, 59
    bucatini all'amatriciana, 61
    bucatini con le sarde, 60–61
    coniglio alla moda mia, 134
    gnocchi al zafferano, 78–79
    granatini, 113
    lasagne con melanzane alla Marianna,
        66–67
    melanzane della Nonna, 170–171
    panini arrostiti, 25
    pizza Margherita, 215–216
    pizza napoletana, 219
    un po' di tutto, 16–17
    ragù casalinga, 94–95
    ragù d'agnello, 96
    ripieni di tonno, 200

Pomodori (*cont.*)
  salsa di, crudi, 86–87
  salsa di, fagiolini in, 167
  salsa di, saporiti, gamberi con, 150–151
  salsa di acciugata e, alla Maria, 90
  salsa di cavolfiore alla Signora Vallone, 97
  salsa fresca di basilico e, 85
  salsa pompeiana, 89
  scacciata con olive, 216–217
  secchi, salsa di, 88
  timballo di maccarun, 72–73
  torta di, ed erbe, 183–184
  verdure miste, 162
  vermicelli alla siracusana, 62
  zuppa povera, 34–35
Porcini:
  cannelloni ai funghi, 68–70
  pizza con, 210
  ripieni al forno, 22–23
  salsa di, 100, 101
  salsa di, costolette di maiale con, 122–123
Porcini mushroom, *see* Mushroom, porcini
Pork:
  chops, stuffed, 121
  chops with porcini mushroom sauce, 122–123
  fresh sausage, 124–125
  Grandma's meat bundles, 114–115
  little meat bundles, 113
Porri, torta di carciofi, finocchio, salsicce e, 181–183
Portafogli di lonza, 121
Potato(es):
  chicken and, with wine, 130–131
  gnocchi with Gorgonzola sauce, 74–75
  and green beans with pesto, 163
  greens and, 166–167
  oven-roasted zucchini and, with garlic, 172
  in a skillet, 171
  and spinach pie, 176–177
  and spinach salad, 191
Poultry, 126–133, 135–137
  duck with peaches, 136–137
  grilled duck, 135
  see also Chicken
Prosciutto, 6
  little puffs of cheese and, 28
  roll, 26–27
Prosciutto:
  bigne con formaggio e, 28
  rotolo al, 26–27
Prugne:
  fresca, salsa di, 284–285
  salsa di mortelle di palude con pere e, 286
Prune, cranberry, and pear sauce, 286
Puddings, 288
  Amaretto cream, 292–293
  apple bread, 288–289
  banana cream, 277

Pumpkin:
  gnocchi, my way, 80–81
  sweet and sour yellow, 20

Rabbit, my way, 134
Ragù:
  homestyle, 94–95
  lamb sauce, 96
Ragù:
  d'agnello, 96
  casalinga, 94–95
Raisin bread, 236–237
Rice:
  cake, 311
  poor soup, 34–35
  and zucchini soup, 42–43
Ricotta:
  cannelloni ai funghi, 68–70
  cassateddi ca, 104–105
  frittata con, 106
  frocia d'ova ca pastetta, 108–110
  gnocchi di, 76–77
  grand torta della Nonna, 294–295
  pizza casalinga, 206–207
  sfinci di Lucia, 267
  torta di, 312–313
  torta di, alla bolognese, 314–315
  torta fantasia di cioccolato, 305
Ricotta cheese, 6
  cake, 312–313
  cannelloni with mushrooms, 68–70
  chocolate fantasy cake, 305
  dumplings, 76–77
  fried egg sandwiches, 108–110
  Grandma's great pie, 294–295
  homestyle pizza, 206–207
  Lucy's fried puffs, 267
  omelet, 106
  pancakes, 104–105
  tart, Bolognese style, 314–315
Riso:
  minestra di zucchini e, 42–43
  torta di, 311
  zuppa povera, 34–35
Rolls, cherry, 240–241

Saffron gnocchi, 78–79
Salads, 6, 185–200
  arugula, avocado, and dried fig, 190
  beet, 193
  broccoli and borlotti, 194–195
  eggplant, 13–14
  endive, 187
  lobster and pear, 196
  mixed raw, 188–189
  mozzarella and pepper, 192
  sailor-style, 14–15
  spinach and potato, 191
  tomatoes stuffed with tuna, 200
  tuna cups, 197
Sale, pollo al, 126–127

Salse, 83–102
   di acciugata e pomodori alla Maria, 90
   di besciamella, 102
   di cavolfiore alla Signora Vallone, 97
   di finocchio e panna, 98–99
   fresca di pomodori e basilico, 85
   di limone, arucola e capperi, 99
   marinata di Gaetano, 93
   di oliva nera, 91
   pesto, 92–93
   di pomodori crudi, 86–87
   di pomodori secchi, 88
   pompeiana, 89
   di porcini, 100, 101
   ragù casalinga, 94–95
   ragù d'agnello, 96
Salse di frutte, 281–286
   di fragole con Amaretto, 281
   di mortelle di palude con pere e prugne,
     286
   di prugna fresca, 284–285
Salsicce:
   granatini, 113
   pizza con cipolle e, 211
   torta di porri, carciofi, finocchio e, 181–
     183
Salsiccia fresca, 124–125
Salt, 8–9
   chicken roasted in, 126–127
Sandwiches:
   broiled, 25
   fried egg, 108–110
   a little bit of everything, 16–17
Saor alla venezia, 146
Sarde, bucatini con le, 60–61
Sardines, spaghetti with, 60–61
Sauces, 5, 83–102
   black olive, 91
   fennel cream, 98–99
   fresh tomato and basil, 85
   Guy's marinade, 93
   homestyle ragù, 94–95
   lamb, 96
   lemon, arugula, and caper, 99
   Maria's anchovy and tomato, 90
   Mrs. Vallone's cauliflower, 97
   pesto, 92–93
   Pompeii, 89
   porcini mushroom, 100, 101
   sun-dried tomato, 88
   uncooked tomato, 86–87
   white, 102
   see also Fruit sauces
Sausage:
   fresh, 124–125
   leek, artichoke, and fennel tart, 181–
     183
   little meat bundles, 113
   pizza with onions and, 211
Savoiardi, 268–269
Savoy biscuits, 268–269

Scacciata con olive, 216–217
Scallops:
   baked squid and, 154–155
   with pesto, 153
Scampi con linguine e limone, 152
Scarola ripiena alla Camille, 180
Semifreddo di torrone, 318–319
Sfinci di Lucia, 267
Shrimp:
   cocktail, 24–25
   with linguine and lemon, 152
   with spicy tomato sauce, 150–151
Soups, 6, 29–49
   asparagus, 46–47
   bean, 40–41
   beef broth, 6, 32
   chicken broth, 6, 31
   egg omelet, 33
   lentil, 35
   lettuce and green bean, 48–49
   minestrone, Genoa style, 36–37
   onion, 45
   pasta and beans, 38–39
   poor, 34–35
   rice and zucchini, 42–43
   squash and spinach, 44–45
Spada, pesce:
   al forno, 144
   grigliata di, 142–143
   polpette di, 148–149
Spaghetti:
   Mom's broccoli and, 59
   Mrs. Vallone's cauliflower sauce, 97
   with sardines, 60–61
   shrimp with spicy tomato sauce, 150–
     151
   in the style of Amatrice, 61
Spaghetti:
   all'amatriciana, 61
   broccoli e, alla Mamma, 59
   gamberi con salsa di pomodori saporiti,
     150–151
   salsa di cavolfiore alla Signora Vallone, 97
   con le sarde, 60–61
Speck, tournedos allo, 120
Spezzatino alla birra scura, 117
Spinach:
   and carrot crowns, little, 164–165
   minestrone, Genoa style, 36–37
   mixed vegetables, 162
   poor soup, 34–35
   and potato pie, 176–177
   and potato salad, 191
   ricotta dumplings, 76–77
   and squash soup, 44–45
Spinaci:
   coroncine di carote agli, 164–165
   gnocchi di ricotta, 76–77
   insalata di patate e, 191
   minestrone alla moda genovese, 36–37
   torta di patate e, 176–177

Spinaci (cont.)
    verdure miste, 162
    zuppa di zucca e, 44–45
    zuppa povera, 34–35
Squash:
    gnocchi, my way, 80–81
    homestyle pizza, 206–207
    mixed vegetables, 162
    pizza with pesto, 220
    and spinach soup, 44–45
    sweet and sour, 20
    see also Zucchini
Squid, baked scallops and, 154–155
Stelline d'oro, 273–274
Stracotto alla lombarda, 116–117
Strawberry(ies), 7
    Amaretto sauce, 281
    banana cream pudding, 277
    and peaches in Marsala, 280–281
Sugar, vanilla, 10
Sweet biscuits, 246
Sweet flatbread, 238–239
Sweets, filled, 263
Swiss chard:
    fried egg sandwiches, 108–110
    homestyle pizza, 206–207
    mixed vegetables, 162
Swordfish:
    baked, 144
    cakes, 148–149
    grilled, 142–143

Taralli, Helen's, 227
Taralli di Elena Julian, 227
Tart(s):
    custard, 296–297
    dried peach and lemon, 300–301
    leek, artichoke, fennel, and sausage,
        181–183
    pastry dough for, 299
    ricotta, Bolognese style, 314–315
    tomato and herb, 183–184
Timballo di maccarun, 72–73
Tomato(es):
    broiled sandwiches, 25
    and herb tart, 183–184
    a little bit of everything, 16–17
    Mary Ann's eggplant lasagne, 66–67
    mixed vegetables, 162
    Mom's broccoli and spaghetti, 59
    Neapolitan pizza, 219
    pasta in the style of Amatrice, 61
    pizza Margherita, 215–216
    poor soup, 34–35
    rabbit, my way, 134
    spaghetti with sardines, 60–61
    stuffed with tuna, 200
    vermicelli, Syracusan style, 62
Tomato sauce:
    fresh basil and, 85
    green beans in, 167

    homestyle ragù, 94–95
    lamb, 96
    Maria's anchovy and, 90
    Mrs. Vallone's cauliflower, 97
    Pompeii, 89
    spicy, shrimp with, 150–151
    sun-dried, 88
    uncooked, 86–87
Tomato sauce, prepared:
    Grandma's eggplant, 170–171
    little meat bundles, 113
    molded macaroni casserole, 72–73
    saffron gnocchi, 78–79
    square pizza with olives, 216–217
Tonnate, coppette, 197
Tonno:
    alle erbe, 145
    pomodori ripieni di, 200
Torrone, frozen, 318–319
Torrone, semifreddo di, 318–319
Torta:
    di patate e spinaci, 176–177
    di pomodori ed erbe, 183–184
    di porri, carciofi, finocchio, e salsicce,
        181–183
Torta (dolci):
    di agnello, 302–303
    al cioccolato, 304
    fantasia di cioccolato, 305
    grand, della Nonna, 294–295
    di mascarpone, 310
    di Natale, 308–309
    di pesche secche e limone, 300–301
    di ricotta, 312–313
    di ricotta alla bolognese, 314–315
    di riso, 311
Tuna:
    cups, 197
    steak with herbs, 145
    tomatoes stuffed with, 200

Uova, 103–110
    cassateddi ca ricotta, 104–105
    frittata con ricotta, 106
    frittata di borragine, 107
    frocia d'ova ca pastetta, 108–110
    pizza chena, 212–214
    rotolo al prosciutto, 26–27
    strapazzate alle erbe, 110
    zuppa di frittata, 33
Uvetta, pane all', 236–237

Vanilla, 7, 10
Veal:
    little meat bundles, 113
    molded macaroni casserole, 72–73
    shanks in red wine, 118–119
Vegetables, 6, 157–184
    braised artichokes, 159
    Camille's stuffed escarole, 180
    eggplant bundles, 168–169

fried zucchini flowers, 175
Grandma's eggplant, 170–171
green beans and potatoes with pesto,
  163
green beans in tomato sauce, 167
greens and potatoes, 166–167
homestyle peppers, 173
leek, artichoke, fennel, and sausage
  tart, 181–183
a little bit of everything, 16–17
little carrot and spinach crowns,
  164–165
mixed, 162
oven-roasted potatoes and zucchini
  with garlic, 172
potato and spinach pie, 176–177
potatoes in a skillet, 171
stuffed artichokes, 160–161
stuffed red peppers, 174–175
tomato and herb tart, 183–184
Verdure, 157–184
  carciofi in tegame, 159
  carciofi ripieni, 160–161
  coroncine di carote agli spinaci, 164–165
  fagiolini e patate con pesto, 163
  fagiolini in salsa di pomodori, 167
  fiori di zucchini fritti, 175
  involtini di melanzane, 168–169
  manaste patano, 166–167
  melanzane della Nonna, 170–171
  miste, 162
  patate e zucchini al forno con aglio, 172
  patate in padella, 171
  peperoni casalinghi, 173
  peperoni rossi ripieni, 174–175
  un po' di tutto, 16–17
  scarola ripiena alla Camille, 180
  torta di patate e spinaci, 176–177
  torta di pomodori ed erbe, 183–184
  torta di porri, carciofi, finocchio, e salsicce,
    181–183
Vermicelli, Syracusan style, 62
Vermicelli alla siracusana, 62
Vinegar:
  garlic-flavored, 179
  onions in, 21
Vino:
  fichi secchi in, 278
  ossòbuchi in, 118–119
  pesche e fragole in Marsala, 280–281
  pollo e patate con, 130–131
Vitello:
  granatini, 113
  ossobuchi in vino, 118–119
  timballo di maccarun, 72–73

Walnut(s):
  cookies, 257
  Palermo sweet fig and nut cake, 290–
    291
  ricotta cake, 312–313
  Vincenza's cookies, 255
Wine:
  chicken and potatoes with, 130–131
  dried figs in, 278
  peaches and strawberries in Marsala,
    280–281
  red, veal shanks in, 118–119

Zafferano, gnocchi al, 78–79
Zaples di Zia Baratta, 247
Zeppole di San Giuseppe, 316–317
Zucce:
  gialla all'agrodolce, 20
  gnocchi di, alla moda mia, 80–81
  pizza casalinga, 206–207
  pizza con pesto, 220
  verdure miste, 162
  zuppa di spinaci e, 44–45
  see also Zucchini
Zucchini, 6
  broiled sandwiches, 25
  flowers, fried, 175
  a little bit of everything, 16–17
  minestrone, Genoa style, 36–37
  mixed vegetables, 162
  oven-roasted potatoes and, with garlic,
    172
  and rice soup, 42–43
Zucchini:
  fiori di, fritti, 175
  minestra di riso e, 42–43
  minestrone alla moda genovese, 36–37
  panini arrostiti, 25
  e patate al forno con aglio, 172
  un po' di tutto, 16–17
  verdure miste, 162
Zuppe, 29–49
  di asparagi, 46–47
  brodo di manzo, 32
  brodo di pollo, 31
  di cipolla, 45
  di fagioli, 40–41
  di frittata, 33
  di lattuga e fagiolini, 48–49
  di lenticchie, 35
  minestra di riso e zucchini, 42–43
  minestrone alla moda genovese, 36–37
  pasta e fagioli, 38–39
  povera, 34–35
  di zucca e spinaci, 44–45